Victorian Heritage

Lectures to celebrate the 150th anniversary of European settlement in Victoria

EDITED BY A. G. L. SHAW

Arranged by the Australian Academy of the Humanities and the Academy of the Social Sciences in Australia

ALLEN & UNWIN
Sydney   London   Boston

© Australian Academy of the Humanities and
The Academy of the Social Sciences in Australia 1986
This book is copyright under the Berne Convention.
No reproduction without permission. All rights reserved.

First published in 1986
Allen & Unwin Australia Pty Ltd
8 Napier Street, North Sydney, NSW 2060 Australia

Allen & Unwin New Zealand Limited
60 Cambridge Terrace, Wellington, New Zealand

George Allen & Unwin (Publishers) Ltd
18 Park Lane, Hemel Hempstead, Herts HP2 4TE England

Allen & Unwin Inc.
8 Winchester Place, Winchester, Mass 01890 USA

National Library of Australia
Cataloguing-in-Publication

Victoria's heritage.

ISBN 0 04 909026 7 (pbk.).

1. Victoria—History—Addresses, essays, lectures.
I. Shaw, A.G.L. (Alan George Lewers), 1916–

994.5

Set in 10/11 pt Plantin by Graphicraft Typesetters Ltd., Hong Kong
Printed by Colorcraft Ltd., Hong Kong

Contents

Figures		*vi*
Illustrations		*vii*
Contributors		*ix*
Preface		*x*
1	The background to Victorian life A. G. L. Shaw	1
2	The picture of Melbourne 1835–1985 Graeme Davison	12
3	Melbourne economists in the public arena: *from Copland to the Institute* Marjorie Harper	37
4	The cabbage garden and the fair blank sheet: *an historical review of environment and planning* J. M. Powell	56
5	Literature in Victoria: *from the wild white man to the carnival of language* Chris Wallace-Crabbe	84
6	Popular entertainment in Victoria Frank van Straten	98
7	Visual Victoria: *waterfalls, tents and meat pies* Margaret Plant	109
8	Against the mainstream: *the inclusive tendency in Victoria's architective, 1890–1984* Conrad Hamann	144
9	Drama and music in colonial Melbourne Harold Love	179
	Index	201

Figures

Chapter 4

4.1 Excursion venues, Field Naturalists' Club of Victoria, 1884–1916
4.2 Selected regional planning structures
4.3 National parks and related reserves in post-war Victoria
4.4 Selected metropolitan plans
4.5 Distribution of Victorian membership, Australian Conservation Foundation, 1983

Illustrations

Chapter 2

S. T. Gill, 'Queen's Wharf, Melbourne, West End', 1857, lithograph
Ludwig Becker, 'Old Princes Bridge and St Paul's by Moonlight', 1857 oil, La Trobe Library
A. C. Cooke, 'Melbourne and Suburbs', lithograph from *Illustrated Australian News* July 1873, La Trobe Library
George Rowe, 'A Panoramic View of Melbourne from the Flagstaff Gardens', 1859, coloured lithograph, La Trobe Library
(Julian Ashton and A. C. Cooke?) 'Collins Street, looking east', from *The Picturesque Atlas of Australasia*
Arthur Boyd, 'Melbourne Burning', 1946–7, oil and tempera, private collection
'The New Rialto', 1984, photo courtesy Bond Miles Coulter and St Martin's Properties

Chapter 7

Louis Buvelot, *Wannon Falls*, 1868, Queensland Art Gallery
Eugene von Guérard, *Waterfall, Strath Creek*, 1862, oil on canvas, Art Gallery of New South Wales
John Perceval, *Merric Boyd*, 1946, private collection
Tom Roberts, *The Artist's Camp*, 1888, National Gallery of Victoria
Albert Tucker, *Portrait of John and Sunday Reed*, 1982, private collection (Tolarno Gallery)
Arthur Boyd, *Nude Black Dog and Tent by a Black Pool*, 1961, private collection

viii *Victoria's Heritage*

Jan Senbergs, *Liardet's Beach*, 1980, private collection
Dale Hickey, *Pie*, 1974, private collection

Chapter 8

Beverley Ussher and Henry Kemp, *Travancore*, John Cupples' house, Riversdale Road, Camberwell, 1899–1900
Harold Desbrowe–Annear, House, The Eyrie, Eaglemont, c. 1900
Philip Hudson and J. H. Wardrop, Shrine of Remembrance, St Kilda Road, Melbourne, 1922–34
Walter Burley Griffin, Auditorium, Capitol Cinema, Swanston Street, Melbourne 1921–4 (altered)
Frederick Romberg, *Stanhill Flats*, Queen's Road, South Melbourne. 1943–51
Gregory Burgess, *Hackford House*, Traralgon, 1981–2
House, Marshall Street, Ivanhoe, c. 1956
Maggie Edmond and Peter Corrigan, Chapel of St Joseph, Strabane Avenue, Box Hill, 1976–8
Maggie Edmond and Peter Corrigan, Primary School, Resurrection Parish Centre, Keysborough, 1974–9

Contributors

Professor Graeme Davison, FASSA, Professor of History, Monash University
Dr Conrad Hamann, Lecturer in Visual Arts, Monash University
Ms Marjorie Harper, Senior Lecturer in Economic History, University of Melbourne
Dr Harold Love, Reader in English, Monash University
Professor Margaret Plant, FAHA, Professor of Visual Arts, Monash University
Dr J.M. Powell, FASSA, Reader in Geography, Monash University
Emeritus Professor A.G.L. Shaw, FAHA, FASSA, Monash University
Mr Frank van Straten, Director, Museum of Performing Arts, Melbourne
Mr Chris Wallace-Crabbe, FAHA, Reader in English, University of Melbourne

Preface

As their contribution to the commemoration of the 150th anniversary of European settlement in Victoria, the Australian Academy of the Humanities and the Academy of the Social Sciences in Australia decided to sponsor a series of lectures on some of the aspects of Victorian history that were particularly relevant to their concerns, and subsequently to publish them in book form. They are here presented with an introductory chapter (Chapter 1) which gives a brief historical background to the special subjects with which they deal.

The Academies are most grateful to the contributors for agreeing to join this venture, to Deakin, La Trobe and Monash Universities for grants towards the costs of publication, and to the University of Melbourne for a similar grant and for hosting the lecture series.

A. G. L. Shaw, FAHA FASSA
Editor

1

The background to Victorian life

A. G. L. SHAW

'I beheld a second Rome rising from the coalition of banditti. I beheld it giving laws to the world, and superlative in arms and in arts, looking down with proud superiority upon the barbarous nations of the northern hemisphere'. These were the words of James Tuckey, a lieutenant in *HMS Calcutta* which brought convicts to Port Phillip in 1803, more than 30 years before the first permanent Anglo-Celtic settlers took up their residence in the area. Melbourne has not become a second Rome, but it and the state of Victoria have made great strides since 1834–35 when the first squatters crossed Bass Strait to occupy, without permission from any Australian or British authority, parts of the territory still included within the boundaries of New South Wales.

Victoria has a mild and beneficent climate, despite the assertions of many Australians, whether they live there or not, and this helped to lessen some of the difficulties of the district's pioneers; however the bitter struggle for existence, which is a necessary element in the first stage of any settlement, could not be avoided, even though it was a little alleviated by the presence of neighbouring colonies. Squalor, suffering, wretchedness, hardship, and the conditions of a cultural semi-desert were part of the price paid by Victoria's first pastoralists, as it was for the first gold diggers and later for wheat and dairy farmers (and their families, when they had them).[1] These people took little heed of the local Aboriginal culture which had existed for some 40 000 years. They battled for survival in their own way, with a rather materialistic outlook, thinking mainly of short-term profits. It would be some time before they would have more wealth and leisure to devote to the advancement of art and science and the elegances of prosperous cities. Patronage, whether by the state or by a well-to-do class with leisure time, is essential for the development of any type of 'luxury' or non-subsistence living. Since Victoria had neither an ancient aristocracy, nor a wealthy established church nor a prosperous government, any development of the arts was bound to be slow.

However, in 1851 separation from New South Wales (which brought local independence) and the discovery of gold (which brought people and wealth) transformed the district. Its population of 100 000 quadrupled in five years, making it larger than the total population of Australia had been in 1850, and despite a sprinkling of riffraff among the diggers, this influx undoubtedly improved the quality of Victoria's population. The convict 'taint', which was never very pronounced in Victoria, was virtually obliterated by 'respectable' migrants. Certainly they were seeking their fortune, but, as Dr Serle has written, they were a group of people from the 'middle stratum' of society that 'was magnificent economic material, with educational qualifications and professional and industrial skills superior to any other group of migrants to Australia, at least in the nineteenth century'.[2] These people would soon change the character of the colony from a squatter-dominated pastoral estate into a highly diversified modern society, with a bustling capital and a number of provincial towns.

Of course there were difficulties. There was a huge government deficit. On the goldfields, many diggers earned no more than an ordinary labourer. Others lost everything. Problems of law and order, intensified by maladministration, culminated in the Eureka rebellion in December 1854. Excessive imports became unsaleable. There was a severe commercial crisis, and unemployment was widespread. But the financial difficulties passed and most of the political unrest was calmed by the adoption of a new democratic constitution, which by 1860 had given the colony universal male franchise and voting by secret ballot. On the industrial front, in 1856 all craftsmen in the building trade and many other artisans won their eight-hour day—'a landmark in working class history', says Serle.[3] Artists like Strutt, Gill, Chevalier, von Guérard and many others, all of whose work is still most highly prized (and priced), began to paint in the colony, just as in Melbourne the Philharmonic Society began to sing and the theatre and even opera began to flourish. In 1853 began the construction of the Yan Yean water supply and the first railways—to Port Melbourne and Geelong. The University, the public library, the Treasury building, the Mint, the Customs House, the new Melbourne Club house, Victoria Barracks and the first church spire at Wesley Church quickly followed; Collins Street came to be compared with Regent Street in London, as public and private authorities alike gave work to architects and builders.[4]

For twenty years after the great loan exhibition of 1869, when 2489 items were on show, the construction of 'Marvellous Melbourne' brought more display and sometimes ostentation. In the public sphere came Parliament House, the Law Courts, a Government House larger than those of the Viceroy of India or the Lord Lieutenant of Ireland, with a bigger ballroom than that of Buckingham Palace, a 'hybrid

Florentine-French' Exhibition Building and a spate of grandiloquent town halls. Outside the public domain, St Patrick's Cathedral, Scots Church and St Paul's Cathedral were accompanied by an 'orgy of decoration and display in business palaces and suburban mansions'. Hotels, coffee-palaces, banks and commercial firms put up their seven-storey 'sky-scrapers' equipped with the new Waygood lifts; one of twelve stories, in Elizabeth Street, was higher than New York's highest. All this helped to create the city 'which untravelled colonists deemed the finest in the world'.[5]

The 'eighties marked the heyday of this development, when the new cable tramways and the growing suburban railway network enlarged the area of the city and encouraged the land speculation that was a major cause of the financial crash that followed. But before disaster struck, amid the 'blowing' already deplored by Anthony Trollope on his visit in 1872, occurred a great extravaganza of light and shade—the Great Exhibitions, sweatshops, huge retail stores, Sabbatarianism, new churches, sectarian rancour, insanitary conditions, baroque towered mansions, suburban villas, notorious brothels, the National Gallery School of painting, artists at Heidelberg, larrikins, drunkards, new parks, the International Exhibitions of 1880 and 1888, Carbine's Melbourne Cup (1890), the J. C. Williamson 'triumvirate', Nellie Stewart and the new Princess Theatre.[6]

This florescence had naturally followed economic and population growth. Though immigration declined after the lure of gold had gone and the government stopped giving assisted passages, the population still doubled between 1861 and the turn of the century, passing the million mark in 1887. This was mainly due to natural increase, although there was a brief spurt of immigrants in the booming 'eighties, when the net figure of arrivals exceeded 100 000.

By that time the colonists were feeling less isolated. English mails, which were taking only six weeks, came and went regularly, the weekly 'mail-day' being a day of some importance. In July 1872 the completion of the overland telegraph had meant that important news could reach Melbourne in a couple of days at most, instead of a couple of months. But distance still affected the economy, adding to the cost of imports and exports and, with no refrigeration, making the transport of perishables impossible. Though gold was more easily transported than most commodities, the mining of it gradually declined in importance, and diggers drifted into the city or onto the land. The land acts of the 'sixties were intended to help small farmers to buy land on easy terms, but unintentionally they allowed many squatters to buy large properties as well. However, many wheat farmers were able to settle in the Wimmera and on the northern plains, where they began to agitate for railway communication with the capital and the ports. Railway construction, financed by borrowing overseas, stimulated the boom. The towns, cities and ports were the service and market centres, and led of course by Melbourne, their population surpassed that of the rural areas. Factories and workshops appeared; most were small but a few were quite large. Their development was helped by a cheap and efficient labour force, by the natural protection afforded by distance, by the government's preference for local products in its purchases and contracts, and after 1866 by steadily increasing duties on imports coming from both the other colonies and overseas—especially on boots, clothing, furniture and machinery.

Almost inevitably depression followed the boom, and then came the great bank crash of 1893. Over-borrowing, the collapse of the land market, the curtailment of overseas credit, and falling wool and wheat prices all led to unemployment and financial stress. Falling demand ruined many apparently prosperous concerns; paper fortunes disappeared, and when numerous banks were forced to close, thousands lost their genuine savings. The provident suffered with the improvident, and with 30 per cent of the workforce unemployed and no 'dole', many depended on charity for their subsistence—and this was often inadequate.

Recovery was slow. Thousands left the colony—many for the newly discovered goldfields of Western Australia. In 1892 the population of New South Wales became greater than that of Victoria, and soon afterwards Sydney surpassed Melbourne, both cities reaching the half-million mark around the turn of the century. However, prospects looked brighter on the agricultural scene, owing to better farm techniques following locally invented improvements in machinery and greater knowledge of fertilisers; the development of refrigeration permitted the export of butter and the creation in Victoria of the most efficient dairying industry in Australia. Unfortunately, the agricultural progress which increased the acreage under wheat two and a half times also created environmental problems that were not appreciated at the time. Clearing and overgrazing caused erosion of trees, weed growth destroyed good land, and timber cutters destroyed the forests, at a time when nature lovers, 'defenders of the bush' and conservationists were still few and not always well informed.[8]

But although environmental problems were being created for the future, the establishment of a federal government reduced the difficulties created by separate colonial jurisdictions and removed some other obstacles to economic and social progress. The economic depression was not confined to Victoria, and it revealed the need for some common action to deal with it. Intercolonial customs houses were becoming increasingly troublesome with the growth of intercolonial travel and trade, adding to the groundswell in favour of a federation of the colonies. Industrial disputes, banking problems, defence, foreign affairs and immigration all seemed to call for nationwide regulation. In the campaign for federation, Victoria undoubtedly led the way, and in the referenda on the question returned the most decisive figures in favour. Although it is impossible to prove that any single factor brought about Federation, probably the most influential was the growth of a feeling of neighbourhood that followed improvements in communications. One important result for Victoria was the opening of the markets of the other colonies to her factories, thanks to the interstate free trade which Federation brought about, and this, plus better steamship communication, was probably the reason why the number of factory workers roughly doubled between 1900 and the outbreak of war in 1914.

There were other improvements too. In 1892 the newly established Melbourne and Metropolitan Board of Works began to tackle the city's sewerage problem—halving the death rate from typhoid and allied diseases in ten years. City and town councils began to introduce an electricity supply. The telephone made its appearance and in Melbourne the number of subscribers increased from about 1000 in 1887 to 20 000 in 1910. In 1896 an effective and widely embracing factory act established Wages Boards and soon eliminated the worst abuses of sweatshops. Depression relief funds were used to convert the main roads from the city—at least for a couple of miles—into fine boulevards.

However, for some years part of the verve and intellectual and artistic distinction seemed to disappear from Melbourne. On the educational front, the University was hampered by the embezzlement of part of its funds and the refusal of the government to help it, though by 1910 it seemed to have recovered, in that year an act was passed providing for the establishment for the first time of a system of state secondary schools. The Victorian literary scene was rather dull, and most of the leading painters—Conder, Roberts, Streeton, Phillips Fox, and Bunny, for example—had gone overseas; but McCubbin and Withers remained and in 1904 the famous Felton Bequest provided funds for the National Gallery to acquire over the years a major collection of works of international standing. The compulsory Saturday half-holiday introduced in 1909 gave more time for sport and other leisure activities. In 1912 the level of activity in new building was back to that of 1888. The growth of population resumed, and by 1914 Melbourne had about 650 000 people and Victoria a total of about 1 400 000. This increase was helped by the revival of immigration, with 75 000 (43 000 assisted) arriving from Great Britain and Ireland between 1910 and 1914, though an unemployment rate between 6 and 9 per cent persisted to disillusion many newcomers.

The outbreak of war in 1914 brought out widespread enthusiasm for the Mother Country for, although four out of five Victorians were then Australian-born, nearly all their parents had come from the United Kingdom, and Australian national feeling was cheerfully subsumed in loyalty to the British Empire. In four years, 112 000 Victorians volunteered for active service—amounting to 8 per cent of the population, and 38.6 per cent of males aged between 18 and 44. They suffered roughly 56 000 casualties; 16 000 were killed. Throughout the war, loyalty remained high; unfortunately it was associated with much petty persecution of innocent aliens and former Germans who had long since been naturalised. There were spy witch-hunts and absurd criticisms of German literature, language and music. From 1916 on, the emotionally bitter struggle in the two referenda on conscription aroused both anti-Irish and anti-Catholic feelings as the Roman Catholic Archbishop Mannix emerged as the most outspoken leader of the 'no conscription' campaigns. In Victoria, the first referendum was narrowly won and the second narrowly lost, but both were defeated nationally since opponents included not only civil libertarians, Irish sympathisers and those who feared industrial conscription, but some employers and conservatives as well. War-weariness also began to appear, if only on a small scale, as the apparently profitless slaughter continued on the battlefields of France. In the industrial field there was some unrest as prices rose by about 70 per cent (all the more disturbing because price stability was then the norm), and wages increased by rather less than one-third. However, the war marked a great step in the emancipation of women as they took over work in offices and factories that had hitherto been performed only by men.

Culturally, the inter-war period was somewhat depressing. The artistic world was dominated by conservatives who raged against 'decadent' modern contemporary art. The reading and study of literature was stifled by a burst of censorship which stopped the works of James Joyce, Aldous Huxley, D. H. Lawrence, Hemingway and others from entering the country. The record of the commercial theatre was mediocre. Gregan McMahon's repertory theatre company had a constant struggle to keep alive, and so did the privately sponsored symphony orchestras until the Australian Broadcasting Commission revitalised the musical scene during the 'thirties.

For a time, pre-war economic prosperity re-appeared. Between 1918 and 1927, 2500 new factories were established and the factory work force increased by one-third to 162 000 (or one in ten of the population). A net figure of 100 000 immigrants arrived. Melbourne boomed again with suburban development and city re-building. By 1930 there were 180 000 motor vehicles in the state, and 230 000 licensed drivers—or roughly one in every second family. The use of electricity spread, as after 1924 the State Electricity Commission gradually extended its services and replaced small and rather inefficient rural generating plants. More than half the people owned (or were buying) their own homes, and participation in sporting activities increased.

Towards the end of the 'twenties, increasing costs and falling prices for agricultural commodities heralded the onset of the 'Great Depression'. This caused tremendous distress. On the land many settlers had to leave their farms. In 1932 about one-third of the work force was unemployed—half of them had been so for more than two years. They had to rely on 'susso' (sustenance payments), soup-kitchens or private charities, as in the 1890s. Many more could find only part-time work and were lucky to earn £3 per week. In the suburbs, some families were evicted from their homes, and in many places shanty towns appeared. Some people tried to hide their poverty, but eventually it would become unbearable. Much less beer was drunk, less tobacco smoked. Attendances at races and football matches thinned; those at cinemas fell by half. Neither Victoria nor Australia was any more the 'working man's paradise'.

Naturally there was much argument about the policies needed to bring about recovery—the 'battle of the plans'—and this resulted in a sort of compromise. An ideal of balanced budgets was proclaimed but not realised, the currency was depreciated, and though borrowing for public works and to meet deficits was controlled, more debt was incurred than strictly orthodox financiers thought desirable.

Slowly the economy recovered. Farmers were helped by debt adjustments and the depreciated currency, while a marketing scheme which set a minimum price for wheat was added to a similar scheme for butter which had existed since 1925. Manufacturers benefited from cheaper power, whether provided by electricity, brown briquettes or coal, from some reduction in wages, and from increased protection against imports; as a result, by 1935 factory employment was greater than it had been in 1927, and by 1939, it had increased by nearly 20 per cent more to over 200 000 people.

But the inter-war years saw what the United States' visiting scholar, C. Hartly Grattan, called a 'slump in alertness in social matters',[9] and successive Victorian administrations kept a tighter rein on social service expenditure than did those in other states. There were neither widows pensions nor child endowment, as in New South Wales, nor unemployment insurance, as in Queensland. The Victorian Year Book reports that in 1939 the state's schools were then the worst equipped in the Anglo-Saxon world.[10] Post-primary education facilities remained sketchy and lacked the upgrading provided in New South Wales. In health, the record was more progressive. In 1922 a milk pasteurisation scheme was introduced. There were improvements in maternity, child welfare and bush-nursing services. There was some hospital rebuilding, particularly in the intermediate and 'pay-wards' area, though the hospitals' problems were intensified by a growing demand for the increasingly beneficial but expensive services that were becoming available. Perhaps the most significant development in welfare services was the establishment of the Housing Commission in 1938, following an investigation which revealed the deplorable living conditions of many working men and their families, but it was able to do little before the second World War broke out in 1939.

At first this had comparatively little impact, but in time, especially after the entry of Japan into the war at the end of 1941, it affected Australia a great deal. Overall, 206 000 Victorians joined the army, about 70 000 joined the RAN or the RAAF and 20 000 women enlisted too. These people made up roughly 14 per cent of the population, compared with 8 per cent in the first AIF, but the number killed (nearly 9000) was less than half that in World War I: about 0.4 per cent of the population instead of 1.5 per cent.

But while military operations had less tragic consequences for Victorians, there was far more involvement than before on the home front. Apart from the voluntary activities of the Red Cross, the war comforts funds, war savings drives and suchlike, manpower regulations, direction of employment (including conscription for military service), rationing of food, clothing and petrol, air-raid precautions and the 'brown-out', restrictions on travel, and the requisitioning of schools and other buildings were some of the ways in which 'total war' affected the civilian population. Factory production greatly increased, especially in munitions of all kinds, optical instruments, machine tools, armoured fighting vehicles, ships and clothing. The 1947 census revealed that since 1939 the numbers employed in manufacturing had risen from 200 000 to 260 000, that the rural population had declined from about 36 to 30 per cent and that of Melbourne had risen from about 55 to 60 per cent of the two million odd then living in the state.

When fighting ceased, shortages and rationing continued for some time, but despite the inconvenience caused by the inability of public services—particularly those concerning power (coal and electricity)—to keep up with increasing demand, full employment enabled the community to improve its living standards, and the development of social services provided far greater security for the more impoverished than in the past. Industrialisation made further great strides in the 'fifties, particularly in engineering, clothing, motor vehicles and electrical goods. Melbourne alone then produced nearly 30 per cent of Australia's industrial output, although since then this proportion has declined a little and the city can no longer be unhesitatingly said to be the financial or industrial capital of Australia. Unemployment increased again after 1975, especially among the young. There were still many living in poverty. Manufacturers faced increasing overseas competition and many Victorians felt slightly bewildered by economic developments. However since 1950 there has been a great growth in the national income and improvement in the general standard of living. Even in the country districts, though rural manpower has declined and farmers constantly complained of their lot as droughts, fires and fluctuating markets and prices produced many ups and downs, agricultural output was greater than ever.[11]

Between 1947 and 1984 the state's population doubled, and 1.2 million overseas immigrants settled in Victoria (out of 1.9 million since 1836). As Richard Broome has commented,

Perhaps only Israel out does Victoria in the scale and diversity of the newcomers it has accepted in the post-war years. Victoria is now a multi-ethnic society. In 1981 about a hundred different birth places were listed in the census. Twenty-three per cent of Victorians in 1981 were overseas-born and together with their Australian-born children they formed thirty-eight per cent of the Victorian population.[12]

This influx helped to bring Melbourne's population to 2.5 million and to change its character considerably. Highrise office blocks of 50 storeys or more came to dominate the city's skyline, as its centre was almost completely rebuilt. Outside it, some large Housing Commission blocks were put up, but more commonly the population spread to the suburbs, with single-storey houses, each for one family, adding to the suburban sprawl, increasing the cost of such services as water supply, sewerage, roads, and gas. However Victorians have preferred to have their own homes and gardens than to live in apartments, and as a result suburban shopping and entertainment facilities have been expanded and improved; even so, such living has often meant that people had to make increasingly long journeys to work on either congested roads or overcrowed trains.

This journey to work somewhat reduced the increased leisure which economic growth produced, but enough leisure time remained—with increased mobility provided by the motor car—to widen greatly the scope of people's activities. Even if since the introduction of television in 1956, one of the most popular leisure pursuits is probably watching 'the box', more energetic pastimes have prospered too. Cricket and Australian rules football still hold their sway, though much is watched as well as played. In 1956 athletics received a great boost from the holding of the Olympic Games in Melbourne, and since then the appeal of running has greatly widened with the popularity of 'jogging'. Thanks to improved international transport, an increasing number of the world champion golfers, tennis players, bowlers, runners, surfers and many others now compete in and raise the standard of local tournaments, and the numbers actively engaged in these sports have greatly increased. Yatching and fishing are popular, as is evident from the ever increasing numbers of boats on the water (and those towed through the streets). Ski-runs and surfing beaches can now be easily reached by car and the appearance of the 'wet-suit' has provided perhaps a partial answer to those who have long decried Victoria as too cold for ocean swimming.

At the cultural level, the Melbourne arts complex, with its art gallery completed in 1968, and performing arts museum, concert hall and theatres completed in 1984, has been complemented by the development of sixteen regional art galleries, most of which have been opened since 1965. The Victorian Arts Council, established in 1969, has encouraged local community arts groups. The Melbourne Theatre Company, Ballet Victoria, the Victorian State Opera and Film Victoria have all, in recent years, been able to encourage various fields of the performing arts. The dominance of the art world by a reactionary 'Old Guard' ended and painting saw an exciting advance. Artists, both painters and sculptors, have been finding more outlets for their work. Both pop groups and concerts of classical music have increasingly contributed to the entertainment of Victorians, and the frequency and scale of performances of plays, opera and ballet now exceed the wildest dreams of those who battled for their survival in the inter-war years.

European migrants have made a considerable contribution to this development. The appearance and growth of different ethnic communities and the development of a stronger Australian national feeling has undoubtedly resulted in the disappearance of the idea of Great Britain as 'home' or 'the Mother Country'. But despite this, and the decreasing economic links with the United Kingdom (once the state's largest market and supplier), Victoria's institutions and culture still clearly reveal their Anglo-Celtic origins. One may hope that for many years to come the state will continue to build on the best features of this inheritance, and at the same time, that its people may be less tempted to misuse or damage as much of its natural resources as they have done in the past.

Notes

1. Tony Dingle *The Victorians: Settling*, Melbourne: Fairfax, Syme and Weldon Associates, 1984, Chapters 2–4
2. Geoffrey Serle *The Golden Age*, Melbourne: Melbourne University Press, 1963, p. 47
3. ibid. p. 214
4. James Grant and G. Serle (eds) *The Melbourne Scene, 1803–1956*, Melbourne: Melbourne University Press, 1957, pp. 114–5
5. G. Serle *The Rush to be Rich*, Melbourne: Melbourne University Press, 1971, pp. 272–7; cf. Serle *From Deserts the Prophets Come*, Melbourne: Melbourne University Press, 1973, p. 29
6. For a more strictly economic account of the boom in Melbourne, see Dingle *The Victorians: Settling* Chapter 8. The 'triumvirate' were Williamson, Garner and Musgrove.
7. Richard Broome *The Victorians: Arriving*, Melbourne: Fairfax, Syme and Weldon Associates, 1984, pp. 94ff
8. Dingle *The Victorians: Settling* Chapters 6 and 7; Geoffrey Bolton *Spoils and Spoilers*, Sydney: George Allen & Unwin, 1981; J. M. Powell *Environmental Management in Australia, 1788–1914*, Melbourne: Oxford University Press, 1976
9. Quoted by J. R. Robertson in F. K. Crowley (ed.) *A New History of Australia*, Melbourne, Heinemann, 1974, p. 442
10. *Victorian Year Book 1984*, no. 98, pp. 20 and 31
11. See Dingle *The Victorians: Settling* Chapter 11, and A. G. L. Shaw 'History and Development of Australian Agriculture', in D. B. Williams (ed.)

Agriculture in the Australian Economy 2nd edn, Sydney: Sydney University Press, 1982, pp. 18–28. See also Susan Priestley *The Victorians: Making their Mark*, Melbourne: Fairfax, Syme, and Weldon Associates, 1984, part 3, for the period after 1930; see also parts 1 and 2 for the preceding 100 years.

12 Broome *The Victorians: Arriving* pp. xii–xiii

The author wishes to thank Dr Richard Broome, Dr Tony Dingle and Ms Susan Priestley for the valuable comments they made on an earlier draft of this chapter.

2

The picture of Melbourne 1835–1985

GRAEME DAVISON

All city dwellers carry in their heads an image, or rather a cluster of images, of their surroundings. When they visit new cities they often buy picture postcards or souvenir picture books to send home to their envious friends and relations, or to keep as a reminder of their visit. Cities are big and complex places and touring can be a strenuous pastime, so publishers and tourist promoters help us to refine and fix our impressions by producing a set of ready-made images. A present-day visitor to Melbourne, for example, may buy a view of the city skyline from the Botanic Gardens, an aerial view of the city from the west, or a picture of Collins Street with its green and gold trams. Those who remember Melbourne for its night life may prefer a picture of the city lights. Those whose interests are more historical may take home a picture of 'Como' or 'Ripponlea'. Whatever view is selected, it will reflect the outlook of the visitor as well as the character of the city itself.

These conventional views of the city are important to citizens as well as visitors, for they help to crystallise a sense of belonging and to symbolise the city's special character or image. The 'imageability' of the city, as the planner Kevin Lynch calls it, is an important ingredient in the satisfaction of city dwellers with their environment.[1]

Views of the city have a history and the picture postcards of the 1980s are the successors of the scenic views, stereopticon slides and engravings of earlier generations. The most popular modern views of Melbourne—the aerial photograph, the city skyline, the city lights, the street scene—also have their nineteenth-century counterparts. Over the past 150 years the picture of Melbourne has been constantly evolving in ways that reflect the changing preoccupations of its people and the remarkable physical and social changes in their environment. Every picture tells its own story, and expresses its own sense of pride, regret, apprehension or nostalgia about the city and its history. The picture of

Picture of Melbourne 1835–1985 13

Melbourne is a mirror of the city's changing sense of identity.

The gap between popular, mass-produced city views and the work of more sophisticated urban artists is narrower than we often suppose. Celebrated Melbourne painters, such as Fred McCubbin, were often strongly influenced in their choice of subjects and the ways in which they tackled them by conventions of popular pictorial art, although the most talented artists nearly always transcended the merely conventional view by imparting some fresh nuance or perspective to their often familiar subjects.[2] What we see in their pictures is the outcome of a complex interaction between the personality of the individual artist, the conventions of artistic presentation, the medium in which the artist works and the market for which he produces it.[3]

Alone among the Australian capital cities, Melbourne was established by businessmen and erected on the foundations of free enterprise. The first settlers—Batman, Fawkner and their rival syndicates—were concerned above all with the search for land (land-dealing has remained the Melburnian's favourite hobby to this day) and they appraised the landscape mainly with an eye to its value as real estate. When Batman in 1834 marked out the site at the bottom of present-day William Street as 'the place for a village', he was responding to practical, business advantages—fresh water, safe moorings for small ships and a nearby wooded hill above the reach of floodwaters. Robert Hoddle and Robert Russell, the government surveyors who later arrived on the scene and laid out the township, were as concerned as the rest of the avaricious inhabitants with questions of ownership and commercial practicality. Robert Russell's 1837 map of Melbourne clearly shows the topographical advantages of the site—the slight widening of the river near the Yarra falls which became the city wharf, Batman's Hill, the rising wooded ground to the north-east, and, clearly marked upon the as yet unformed road plan, the properties and residences of the principal inhabitants.

The first views of Melbourne, drawn by surveyors like Russell, architects like Samuel Jackson, or amateur painters like John Adamson or Wilbraham Liardet, were little more than scenic versions of these maps. They carefully delineated each building and identified its owner; they sketched in the surrounding terrain and sometimes indicated the main economic activities. Their purpose was as much utilitarian as aesthetic. Often they were prepared with lithographic reproduction in mind, so that pictures of the new settlement could be circulated among prospective settlers or investors in Britain to demonstrate the strides which the colonists had already made in civilising the new land.[4] The engraving of Adamson's 1839 view of Melbourne prepared by Clark and Company, the colonial booksellers of Fenchurch Street, London, is accompanied by a key identifying such landmarks as the home of John Batman (symbolically, given the number one), the Emigration Office, the Customs House and the Melbourne Club. Liardet's view of

1842 was also praised for its fine detail. 'Nearly every house is visible, and may be separately recognised by those who have an intimate acquaintance with the Town', remarked the *Port Phillip Gazette*[5] Executed by an insolvent publican in the midst of an economic depression, Liardet's view seeks nonetheless to create an image of material and moral advance. The forces of order and civilisation, represented by the mounted figures of Superintendent La Trobe, Mayor Condell and Police Magistrate Lonsdale advance from the right of the picture towards a camp of unsuspecting Aborigines.

The topographical tradition dominated colonial landscape and townscape depiction until the 1850s. But the gold rushes not only transformed the town of Melbourne; they also brought important changes in the role of the artist and in his perception of the urban environment. Views of the Victorian goldfields and its upstart capital were now in demand from a much wider public and the new wealth of the goldrush generation also created a small, but growing, market for more finished works of art. The new artists of the gold rush, such as Henry Burn, Ludwig Becker, Eugene von Guérard, Nicholas Chevalier and S. T. Gill, were accomplished professionals rather than ambitious amateur draftsmen although, as their careers demonstrate, the financial position of the artist in colonial society could still be very precarious. Burn and Gill both died in poverty and obscurity.[6]

By the early 1850s the early colonial tradition of exact, topographical drawing had given way to more elaborate, self-consciously artistic views of Melbourne. The sense of measured progress and calm possession was supplanted by a mood of excitement and chaotic movement as the gold rush overtook the town. Views of the city still focussed mainly on the riverside wharves at the western end of town which were then jammed with shipping as goods were unloaded and migrants disembarked. Antoine Fauchery's photograph of 1857 captured the physical congestion and disorder of the down-river wharves, and other views of the Customs House and its surrounds by J. G. Boyd and Edmund Thomas also depicted the unimproved environs of the waterfront. The Yarra wharves remained the symbolic gateway to the city and contemporaries never tired of describing the human drama of immigration. After his passage up the river, the newcomer landed on a

> bustling wharf, piled up with merchandise, crowded with porters, clerks, dealers and hangers-on, and lined with drays, whose owners are receiving their loads.... On landing, the stranger is struck with the broad macadamised roads, and the busy crowds and ceaseless tide of traffic that rolls through them. So much bustle and activity, is indeed, rarely witnessed in the 'old country', except in London itself.[7]

The newcomer's impressions have their pictorial counterpart in S. T. Gill's brilliant engraving of the scene on Queen's Wharf in 1857. No other artist captured the social turmoil of the gold rush as vividly as

S. T. Gill, 'Queen's Wharf, Melbourne, West End', 1857

Gill.[8] His goldfields studies of diggers are well known, but his Melbourne streetscapes are also a remarkably inventive response to contemporary traditions of town depiction, particularly the drawings of his London contemporary George Cruickshank. Other Melbourne artists, such as Nicholas Chevalier and Henry Burn, focussed mainly on the physical transformation of the gold-rush city and introduced human figures only as a decorative element in their essentially architectural compositions. S. T. Gill's studies of Queen's Wharf, the Post Office or Collins Street are no less precisely drawn, but he treats the street or the building mainly as a backdrop for a more human encounter.

Most of Melbourne's gold-rush painters had learned their craft as town topographers in Britain and followed the methods popularised since the late eighteenth century by their British counterparts. The dominant pictorial convention was that of the pastoral landscape in which the city was viewed from a distance and framed within a picturesque and often idealised countryside. Usually little attempt was made to delineate the townscape in exact architectural or topographical detail—except, perhaps, for a distinctive landmark such as a church spire—and the mood of the picture was dictated by the character of the setting. By accentuating contrasts of tone and line, or by varying the proportion between the subject and its setting, the artist could suggest something of his own response to the experience of urban growth, and to the changing relationship between city and countryside. For example, popular views of Manchester in the 1840s emphasised the calamitous social and moral impact of industrialisation by accentuating the contrast between the dark, smoky and angular skyline of the city and the light, clarity and softness of the surrounding countryside. The rustic simplicity of the foreground figures underscored the artist's conviction of a social gulf between the old agrarian and the new industrial eras.

Sydney, with its magnificent harbour, was a subject ready-made for romantic landscape. In the 1840s Conrad Martens had used the city as the focal point in Turneresque landscapes that dramatised the opposition between the primeval Australian wilderness and the tiny outpost of civilisation huddled on the farther shores of a harbour. From Martens, through Arthur Streeton and down to Lloyd Rees, Sydney painters have continued to view their subject from a romantic distance, across a wide expanse of blue water and bathed, usually, in a rosy afternoon glow.[9] Whatever its commercial or cultural advantages, Melbourne could never hope to rival Sydney's glorious setting. Its only vistas were from the elevated eastern and southern suburbs back towards the city and the only expanse of water within view of the city was that overgrown creek, the Yarra. It was a pictorial handicap that Melbourne artists were to struggle against, with more ingenuity than success, for more than a century.

The 1850s saw the gradual emergence of what was to become the conventionally picturesque view of Melbourne. Early in the decade artists still frequently emphasised the pioneer setting of the town. In J. B. Henderson's drawing of 1853 a tree stump and an uncompleted fence marked the passage of settlers outward from the town, while in the middle ground a cluster of tents denoted an improvised canvas town. In Henry Burn's 1855 watercolour from the same vantage point on St Kilda Road, the contrast between city and country was emphasised by the rustic foreground of bullockies and waggons. Burn had learned his trade as a town topographer in provincial England and his Australian bushmen still sometimes wore the smocks of English rural labourers.[10] In Ludwig Becker's view of 1854 the vantage point swung further to the south-east to view the city across the newly constructed Princes Bridge. The gold-rush setting was deftly suggested by a ground of dark and rather sinister-looking Chinese in coolie hats.

By the end of the 1850s Melbourne had begun to overcome the chaos and improvisation of the gold-rush era and to present a more dignified and orderly face to the world. In Troedel's 1864 print of Queen's Wharf, the new Custom's House stood amidst substantial brick and stone warehouses and shipping offices. The town had cast off its air of adolescent gawkiness and had begun to assume one of commercial solidity and prosperity. Along the south bank of the Yarra, Baron von Mueller had planted his new Botanical Gardens and, in another of the Troedel prints, Melbourne was viewed, not from a primeval wilderness in the manner of Conrad Martens, nor even from an improving

Ludwig Becker, 'Old Princes Bridge and St Paul's by Moonlight', 1857

countryside, but from a neatly manicured parkland where ladies and gentlemen promenaded in Sunday dress. The bourgeois Melburnians of Henry Gritten's 1867 oil painting stood with their backs to the viewer, gazing admiringly at the well-ordered, domesticated landscape of the Yarra valley. Henry Burn, on the other hand, pictured a more informal park, complete with picnickers and grazing cows, as the foreground of his fine oil painting of Melbourne from the Domain. Making fewer concessions to peculiarities of Australian vegetation and climate, Burn contrived to depict places like Richmond Park—the area where the MCG now stands—in the same luscious greens and soft contours as contemporary English painters applied to Richmond-upon-Thames.

If there was a single measure of civic improvement that symbolised the disappearance of the frontier town and the arrival of the provincial metropolis, it was the lighting of Melbourne's streets by gas. Not only in Melbourne, but in cities all over the world, the introduction of gas lighting was welcomed as 'a criterion of a highly civilized society' and a deterrent to vice and crime. Once the streets were lit, the *Argus* predicted, the footpads and ruffians who had terrorised the streets throughout the 1850s would be put to flight.[11]

By making the city visible at night, gaslight also expanded the possibilities of urban picture-making and reinforced the traditional moral symbolism of darkness and light. In Ludwig Becker's eerie picture of 'Old Princes Bridge and St. Paul's by Moonlight', painted about a year after the opening of the gasworks, the still-feeble light of the newly installed street lamps was aided by a full moon peeping from behind a bank of black cloud. The prominence of the gas lamp and the appearance of two policemen in the foreground underlined its contemporary message. Three years later, when Henry Burn painted the same scene by daylight, its physical features were almost unaltered but the crisp lines and opalescent colouring of his picture conveyed an entirely different sense of place. Once again the figures peopling the landscape set the mood of the two pictures. The dark, plebian and largely male figures in Becker's night scene make a strong contrast with the jaunty, almost playful, bearing of Burn's fashionable townsfolk.

By the 1870s, then, pictures of Melbourne may be roughly grouped in four categories, each representing a different facet of the city's self image. The topographical view, which aimed at an exact, detailed and comprehensive depiction of the townscape and of its individual sites and landmarks, was the earliest tradition to emerge. Expressing ideas of pride, material progress and possession, the topographical artist was the natural ally of the land developer, the speculator and the city booster. The streetscape or wharfside view focussed upon the city's busy commercial and social life, and conveyed ideas of commercial vigour and enterprise. It was a favourite image of the merchant and the shopkeeper. The pastoral landscape presented a more distant view of the city and posed the problematical relationship between city and country, civilised and rustic values. Its underlying values were perhaps not strictly urban at all, but rather the nostalgic longings of a rural upper class. Nocturnal scenes of Melbourne, like Becker's 'Old Princes Bridge', drew upon a sense of the moral ambiguities and contrasts of urban life. This was the pictorial language of the slumming journalist and the moral reformer.

During the last quarter of the nineteenth century this repertoire of conventional city images was further extended and refined. The booming 1880s saw Melbourne's population almost doubled and the townscape changed almost out of recognition. When William Westgarth, a pioneer of the 1840s, visited Melbourne in 1888 he found 'the old Melbourne of my time, of a full generation past ... entirely swept away'.[12] Rapid growth generated pride in the city's material progress and in its commercial vigour and enterprise. But growth, especially the reckless growth of the landboom era, could also create an atmosphere of anxiety and insecurity. Apprehensive about their immediate future, Melburnians became nostalgic about their urban past. All these contradictory attitudes were registered in contemporary pictures of the city.

The 1880s marked a new era in the development of artistic activity in Melbourne. Since the 1850s there had been an immense growth in the market for pictorial art, not only in painting but also—perhaps more importantly—in photography and engraving. In 1891 the census-taker counted 196 painters, 164 engravers and 259 photographers in Melbourne. The development of the dry-plate camera enabled a new generation of photographers, like the German-trained J. W. Lindt, to rival the black and white engravers as recorders of urban life. Many of the city's young painters, including key members of the emerging 'Heidelberg School' such as Arthur Streeton and Tom Roberts, were to serve their artistic apprenticeships as photographers or lithographers. The most popular images of Melbourne were probably those created for the illustrated papers, such as the *Australasian Sketcher*, or coffee-table books of the day such as the *Picturesque Atlas of Australasia* and Alexander Sutherland's *Victoria and its Metropolis*. Landscape painters often borrowed their subjects, and even their pictorial techniques, from these popular illustrators.

Cheap lithographic reproduction for a mass reading public was the secret of the most popular of nineteenth-century city images—the bird's-eye view. Like the old topographical view, of which it was the more sophisticated descendant, the bird's-eye view was designed to reinforce a sense of urban progress and 'metropolitan vastness'. In the 1850s Henry Mayhew, the celebrated explorer of London low life, took a balloon view over the city and reported the elation he felt in being able to view the world's metropolis in a single glance. Just a few years later Melbourne witnessed its first balloon flight and by the 1880s many city buildings boasted towers, domes and lookouts designed to offer sweeping views of the metropolis.[13]

This new interest in aerial observation stimulated the development of new pictorial conventions designed to give the viewer a complete and accurate record of the urban landscape. The purchaser of a bird's-eye view of panorama—many such views were sold either by subscription or as special supplements to the illustrated newspapers—was able not only to take in an impressive vista, but to locate familiar landmarks, such as his own house or workplace, within the broader urban landscape. As Roland Barthes reminds us, a panorama was designed not only to be perceived, but to be deciphered; it revealed the city, not only in its sweeping grandeur, but in its intricate structure.[14] That structure was, in part, historical, for in picking out each house and building, the viewer was also recognising the contribution of its builder or owner to the growth of the city. Like the great biographical encyclopaedias such as Alexander Sutherland's *Victoria and its Metropolis* or the *Cyclopedia of Victoria*, bird's-eye views usually appeared on civic anniversaries or at moments of high celebration when sentiments of pride and progress were uppermost in people's minds.

Bird's-eye views were also popular because they gave city dwellers

20 *Victoria's Heritage*

A. C. Cooke, 'Melbourne and Suburbs'

the illusionist thrill of seeing their surroundings from a novel angle. Their creators, of course, did not actually sit in a balloon gondola to draw them but simply superimposed sketches of the facades and rooflines of the city's buildings onto an isometrical projection of its street plan. The fine bird's-eye view of Melbourne in 1854 published by the London engraver N. Whittock was based upon sketches supplied by a Melbourne businessman, G. Teale, and contemporary maps, probably including Kearney's survey. It views the city from an imaginary peak in South Melbourne and highlights the crowded waterfront of the goldrush port as well as such new symbols of urban progress as the Legislative Assembly building, the Sandridge railway line, the Williamstown telegraph line and the Exhibition Building.

As the city sprawled the balloonist or the imaginary bird had to fly higher to take in the growing number of suburbs. In their isometrical plan made in the year of Melbourne's second exhibition, 1866, the printers de Gruchy and Leigh included the nearer suburbs as well as the central business district, while the view published in the *Illustrated Australian News* of 1873 spanned almost the entire metropolis. The International Exhibition of 1880–81 brought businessmen from all over the world to view the young metropolis. The souvenir views published by the illustrated papers focussed on the city centre, offering only sketchy impressions of the suburbs which now extended far beyond a bird's eyesight. One looked down from the north as though from a balloon floating high above the dome of the Exhibition Buildings; one from the traditional vantage point south of the Yarra. Another view published in 1887 looked westwards across the city from the Fitzroy Gardens, while a series of finely detailed views published in a city guide book in the mid 1890s completed the tour of the compass by showing the four quarters of the central business district from the west.

A more sophisticated development of the bird's-eye view was the panoramic or cycloramic view. Since the end of the eighteenth century panoramas and cycloramas of London, often exhibited to paying customers in special cylindrical galleries, had been a favourite amusement in the Empire's capital. In 1823, while the dome of St Paul's Cathedral was undergoing repairs in London, the artist Thomas Hornor spent several dizzy, chilly weeks crouched on the scaffolding above the lantern painstakingly recording a 360-degree view of the city. His 2000 detailed sketches were later transformed by the entrepreneur Edmund Parris into a great cyclorama, covering some 4000 square feet of canvas and housed in a specially built gallery in Regent's Park.[15] Only a few years after Melbourne's foundation, in 1841, the architect Samuel Jackson made a 360-degree panoramic drawing from inside a revolving barrel on the walls of the partially completed Scots Church. A similar panoramic sketch of the city from the south side of the Yarra was made by Eugene von Guerard in 1855, and four years later the Dorset-born painter and engraver George Rowe executed a charming hand-coloured

22   *Victoria's Heritage*

George Rowe, *'A Panoramic View of Melbourne from the Flagstaff Gardens'*, 1859

lithograph of the city from the Flagstaff Gardens. Rowe not only depicted such important landmarks as the Exhibition Buildings, the gasworks, the Railways Works, the Police Barracks and the Houses of Parliament; he also peopled the landscape with such colourful representatives of gold-rush society as Chinese, Aboriginals, gold diggers, a detachment of police, a gold escort, and a Cobb and Co. coach.[16]

The development of photography simplified, and eventually superseded, the cycloramist's art. Standing atop a tall building and swinging his wide-angle camera through 360 degrees, a photographer in a few hours could take a series of panoramic views that would have taken a draughtsman several days or weeks. The panoramic engraving produced by the publishers de Gruchy and Leigh in 1863 was based upon a series of photographs taken from the top of Parliament House. In 1875 the Paterson brothers produced an excellent series of panoramic photographs taken from the top of the new Scots Church, and in the mid-1880s Charles Nettleton, who had photographed the city since the 1860s, took his third series of panoramic photographs.

The excitement of the land boom had once again focussed public attention on the old port and commercial district of the city—Queen's Wharf and its environs. The opening of the Coode Canal in the early 1880s and of Victoria Dock in the early 1890s drew a lot of shipping activity downriver and away from the city centre, and photographs of Queen's Wharf in the mid-1880s show a crowded, but not overly busy, scene. Yet contemporary engravings, such as those in *Victoria and its Metropolis* and the *Picturesque Atlas of Australia*, depict a waterfront pulsing with activity. Great steamers belch forth plumes of black smoke while busy tugboats guide them to their moorings. In 1888 Fred McCubbin, the most loyal Melburnian among the Heidelberg painters, completed a remarkable picture of 'The Yarra below Princes Bridge'. McCubbin had grown up in West Melbourne working first of all as a baker's apprentice and later as a clerk not far from the section of the city shown in this picture. Yet his vision of Melbourne was not a cosily familiar one. When the picture was first exhibited a reviewer complained that it was 'rather lacking in picturesqueness'.[17] But it was not picturesqueness so much as a sense of power which McCubbin aimed to achieve. His was a portrait of a city dominated by steam-driven commerce. The pastoral landscape artists viewed the city distantly from an idealised countryside; McCubbin accentuated the height and massing of the city's spires and towers by foreshortening his perspective and reflecting the skyline in the river. 'Melbourne in the Eighties', as the picture is now known, was a deliberate essay in commercial pride. McCubbin had painted similar riverside scenes in the manner of contemporary London painters and other Melbourne artists, such as Walter Withers, would also paint the waterfront. But no other picture of the late 1880s so succeeded in capturing the inflated self-esteem that lay behind the smoke-screen of the land boom.

[Julian Ashton and A. C. Cooke?] 'Collins Street, looking east'

Melbourne is a city of two great streets. Since the 1850s Collins Street has been the street of quality and style, the centre of the most powerful boardrooms, the most exclusive clubs, the most fashionable shops. Bourke Street, on the other hand, has been the street of the people, the centre of theatres and restaurants, of paddy's markets and bargain basements. At the peak of the gold rush, as spendthrift diggers thronged the Theatre Royal and crowded its chophouses and shooting galleries, Bourke Street became the city's leading street. Thirty years later, as mushroom companies raised their stucco skyscrapers, and Toorak matrons strove to outdo each other in extravagant apparel, Collins Street again recaptured the spotlight.

Like photographic studies of the waterfront, early photographs of Melbourne streets somehow fail to capture the pace and vigour of the boom metropolis. It was difficult for wet-plate photographers to freeze moving figures and many street photographs have the forlorn appearance of having been taken at 9 o'clock on a Sunday morning. J. W. Lindt, a pioneer of the new dry-plate technique, was the first photographer to catch some of the 'bustle and life' of Melbourne's most fashionable street. Even more vivid, however, are the contrived street scenes in contemporary black and white engravings. Freed from the frozen literalism of photography, the black-and-white artist was able to emphasise the height and grandeur of the new skyscrapers, dress the crowds of pedestrians in the latest fashions and underline the sense of urban progress symbolised by the cable tram, the telephone pole and the plumes of dark industrial smoke.

The most famous picture of Melbourne in the boom years, Tom Robert's 'Bourke Street' (1886), makes a striking contrast to this boosting tradition. Roberts has not focussed on the city's most fashionable street or directed his gaze towards the gentlefolk of Eastern Hill. His subject is unfashionable Bourke Street looking towards the saddlers' shops and horse auction markets of its grubby western end. The black-and-white engravers typically view the street from the pavement looking up towards the towering office buildings with their assertive flags; but Roberts stands above the street looking down on the broad expanse of sunlit carriageway. The boosters crowd the scene with trams, carriages and telephone poles; 'Bourke Street', painted only months before the arrival of a cable tram, is a tribute to the passing of the horse-drawn cabs. The engravers show us a grand boulevard in the international style; Roberts portrays a dusty, sunny and unmistakably Australian street. The brown earth still shows through the veneer of civilisation; the metropolis, he seems to say, has still to throw off the roughness of the frontier town.[18]

As the city grew larger and the momentum of change accelerated, signs of unease began to appear among artists and social critics. The sprawling anonymity of the metropolis made people long for a reassertion of a more human scale. They looked back nostalgically to the tiny encampment from which the city had so recently sprung. Again and again, they reminded themselves of the startling contrast between Melbourne's present grandeur and John Batman's simple village.[19] One of the most popular exhibits at the Centennial Exhibition of 1888 was a scale model of Melbourne in 1838 commissioned by the Melbourne City Council and executed by Justin Drouhet, a French-born engineer employed by the Victorian Railways. After the Exhibition closed it was installed in the Melbourne Town Hall where it was expected to become 'one of the most interesting objects for many years to come as instancing the marvellous development of Melbourne'.[20] An illustrator, Clarence Woodhouse, conjured up the same vision of material progress when he juxtaposed a coloured lithograph based on Drouhet's model, a bird's-eye view of the city in 1887 and a plan from an early Melbourne land sale. In 1892 John Hennings, a German-born scenic artist, painted an enormous panoramic view of Melbourne in 1841 based on Samuel Jackson's drawing which became the main attraction at the newly opened cyclorama in the Exhibition Buildings. After they had visited the great barrel-shaped gallery to view the infant city in replica, patrons were invited to climb the stairs to the observation platform under the dome of the Exhibition Building to view the sprawling metropolis it had become.

The more conscious they became of their civilised attainments, the more Melburnians romanticised their founding years. By 1888 the landfall of John Pascoe Fawkner's *Enterprise* on the Yarra was pictured amidst the gloom of a primeval forest. The city's few surviving pioneers gained new fame an annalists and raconteurs. The surveyor Robert Russell continued to sketch and paint the Yarra as it was, and as he remembered it, into his nineties. Captain W. F. E. Liardet, who had first depicted the city in 1843, returned to the same subject in his mid-seventies. The 40 watercolours of the city's early sites and landmarks which he completed in 1875 have an innocence and directness of expression in sharp contrast to the growing sophistication of the boom metropolis.[21]

Perhaps the most powerful way of expressing the sophistication and moral ambiguity of metropolitan life was through the view of the city by night. When slumming journalists sought to recreate Melbourne's low life, they instinctively reached for images of light and darkness. John Stanley James's *Vagabond Papers* were subtitled 'Studies of Melbourne Life in Light and Shade' and John Freeman's sketches of Melbourne's street folk were published under the title *Lights and Shadows of Melbourne Life*.[22] The gaslit streets were a favourite subject for black-and-white artists who relished the effects produced by the contrast of light and shadow and the glint of lamplight on wet pavement. Painters were also coming to appreciate the possibilities of nocturnal cityscapes. Girolamo Nerli, the Italian artist who strongly influenced some of the younger generation of Melbourne painters, made several striking impressions of Sydney's nightlife, and the British provincial painter Atkinson Grimshaw, who visited Melbourne briefly in the late 1880s, left behind an attractive gaslit view of Swanston Street.

Some of the Heidelberg painters had been influenced by Whistler's evocative studies of twilight on the lower Thames and later attempted their own impressions of twilight on the lower Yarra.[23] These pictures have never been among their most esteemed work. The streaky orange and violet sky of Arthur Streeton's 'Princes Bridge: Between the Lights' (1888) struck a contemporary critic as 'rather livid'.[24] But in trying to capture the half-light of evening on the Yarra, Streeton was perhaps not only making an 'impressionistic' experiment but also

Picture of Melbourne 1835–1985 27

hinting at the moral ambiguities of big-city life. The newly opened Princes Bridge, Melbourne's newest symbol of progress, divides a metropolitan backdrop of steamships and skyscrapers from a shabby foreground of rowing boats and riverside vagrants. Tom Robert's 'Evening Train to Hawthorn', also painted in 1888, is another twilight study. The composition of the picture, dominated by the silhouetted tower of the Independent Church, is reminiscent of the 'pastoral landscapes' of Burn and Becker. But the spiky outlines of telegraph poles, the clouds of steam and the bright headlamp of the advancing locomotive give the picture an unmistakably metropolitan aura. In this word-portrait 'The Metropolis', Melbourne's foremost contemporary historian, Alexander Sutherland, described the scene at sunset as the city's workers surged towards the Flinders Street railway terminus. The scene, he wrote,

> is picturesque. The tram-cars lit with fairy-gliding lights of many colours; the clock tower with its shining face; the wreathing smoke beyond, and the lines of tapering masts against the feeble glow of the western sky, all contribute to the striking effect of a most characteristically metropolitan prospect.[25]

Roberts's painting is a free adaptation, rather than a literal transcription, of Sutherland's vision but, like McCubbin's 'Melbourne in the Eighties', it symbolises a moment, unique in the city's history, when Melbourne was felt to be 'most distinctly a metropolis'.[26]

The depression of the 1890s marked a watershed in artistic, as well as literary, image-making in Melbourne. The fall of 'Marvellous Melbourne', just at the time when artists like Roberts and McCubbin were beginning to develop a more positive and sharply focussed image of their urban environment, goes a long way towards explaining both the rural preoccupations of artists throughout the 1890s and the dearth of townscape painting in Melbourne for the following two or three decades. 'I want to stay here [in Australia] but not in Melb.', wrote Arthur Streeton to Tom Roberts as they turned their minds to the creation of the mythic bush pictures with which we will always associate their names.[27] Fred McCubbin, who stayed on in the doomed metropolis, forsook his bold experiments with colour and composition, such as 'Melbourne in the Eighties', for the bland conventionality of the pastoral landscape. Ever responsive to popular taste, he retreated from the strident urbanism of the 1880s to the detachment of rural romanticism.

In the twentieth century popular visions of the city were revolutionised by a series of new developments in photography—the telephoto lens, the moving picture and aerial photography. The first enabled the photographer to achieve the foreshortened perspective of the city skyline which McCubbin had striven for in his 'Melbourne in the Eighties'. By the 1920s the architects of the Empire State and the

28 Victoria's Heritage

Chrysler buildings in New York had shown the world how to sculpt a city skyline.[28] Melbourne shuffled in tentative pursuit as the Manchester Unity and T & G buildings edged towards the City Council's 132-feet height limit. The moving picture enabled photographers at last to escape the technical limitations of the old wet-plate camera. Some early movie clips of Melbourne are little more than moving postcards, with only a stray pedestrian to enliven an otherwise static view of the Exhibition Building or the Houses of Parliament. But when he sat his camera on the dummy of a moving cable tram as it surged through the helter-skelter of pedestrians, carriages and motor cars, the cinematographer was able at last to capture the constant movement that was the essence of metropolitan life. The last of the new inventions —the aerial photograph—was the successor and destroyer of the old bird's-eye view. From 1919, when the Royal Australian Flying Corps took the first rather fuzzy pictures of Melbourne from the air, down to the present day there has been a gradual refinement in their clarity and detail.

New movements of urban art in Paris, Berlin and New York were also transforming the pictorial conventions which Melbourne's painters inherited from their nineteenth-century predecessors. Under the impact of war and depression, as well as the economic decline of the city itself, they fashioned new and starker images of the metropolis. In John Brack's 'Collins Street, 5 p.m.' the high Victorian facades of 'Marvellous Melbourne' become the backdrop for a procession of grim-faced, Akubra-hatted commuters. The eerie half-light of Streeton's 'Princes Bridge' turns blacker and more malignant in Albert Tucker's 'Night Images', and even the hubris of McCubbin's 'Melbourne in the Eighties' has its nemesis in the waterfront wasteland of Jan Senbergs' 'Port Liardet' paintings.

Yet despite the new pictorial possibilities opened up by modern art and technology, the standard picture of Melbourne, and the most accurate mirror of its moods, remained the pastoral landscape—the now-hackneyed view of the city viewed across the Yarra from the south-east. For more than 80 years this view of Melbourne—calm, distant and detached—has been reproduced again and again in oil paintings, postcards, tea towels, hearth rugs and mulga-wood souvenirs. It is the view which the tourist always takes home with him. For most of us it has become a familiar signature almost emptied of social meaning.

Yet over the years its treatment has also subtly changed in ways that reflect our moods of optimism or pessimism about the city's prospects. In buoyant times the focus sharpens and zooms in upon the city skyline; in hard times, as the pace of growth slackens, the focus widens and becomes fuzzier, emphasising the foreground of river and gardens and the slow organic growth of the city itself. Tourists in the 1930s were invited to enjoy, not the dynamism of a 'Marvellous Melbourne' but the

Arthur Boyd, 'Melbourne Burning', 1946–7

'patiently created loveliness' of a city in the economic doldrums. By the 1940s Melbourne's unchanging skyline had become almost a symbol of the city's economic and cultural stasis. The 'Antipodeans', John Perceval and Arthur Boyd, even used it in satirical vein as a backdrop for the symbolic flight of the Holy Family from Egypt and of the people of Sodom from their burning city—a fitting gesture, perhaps, for a generation of expatriates shaking the dust of philistine Melbourne from their feet as they boarded the P & O liners on their way to Europe and real civilisation.[29]

In the 1960s, as the economic development of Bolte's Victoria got underway, the distant, contemplative, proportionate picture of Melbourne gave way to the foreshortened and dynamic picture of a city on the move. The camera now focussed more directly upon the city's new buildings and engineering works rather than their garden setting. Aerial views, for example, highlighted the construction of the new King Street Bridge. In 1959 the erection of ICI House at last breached the 60-year-old height limit on Melbourne buildings and photographers, flushed with renewed civic pride, got out their telephoto lenses to burnish the city's 'New York' image. In the mid-1960s Henry Bolte roofed a section of the old railway yards and erected two slab-like Gas Company buildings along the southern side of Flinders Street, obliterating in one blow Melbourne's allegedly 'perfect skyline'. Once the 'glass house revolution' was under way there was no stopping it. With the rise of Nauru House, Collins Place and now the Rialto, Melbourne has acquired a skyline with all the charm of a half-felled forest.

The old aesthetic, which defined the picture of Melbourne in the nineteenth century, has been destroyed. But no new urban aesthetic has

'The New Rialto', 1984

evolved to take its place. In Sydney, the old tradition of romantic landscape begun by Conrad Martens and Arthur Streeton lives on in the work of Lloyd Rees and hundreds of weekend daubers. While 1930s Melbourne remained slumped in suburban torpor, Sydney modernists—Grace Cossington Smith and Roland Wakelin—began to fashion a new urban aesthetic around that great symbol of urban progress, the Sydney Harbour Bridge. The modernist image of Sydney continues to develop and thrive in the work of John Olsen and Brett Whiteley.[30] But Melbourne, it seems, has an image problem. Postcard makers and tourist promoters continue to crank out the old 'garden city' image, sometimes tying it to nostalgic images of Melbourne's genteel nineteenth-century past. Developers and politicians meanwhile seek a new modern image of the city, sometimes calling, as Sir Rupert Hamer vainly did, for a new city landmark that would act, like Sydney's Opera House or Bridge, as a magnet for growth.

But somehow we remain transfixed by our dilemma. Our predicament is nowhere better illustrated than in an advertisement for the recently completed Rialto building. 'For years', the promoters tell us, 'Melbourne has sought a landmark—a symbol of the Victorian Capital's importance as one of the great cities of the world ... Exciting in concept, sensitive in design, Rialto marries history with the future ...' But is Rialto's shot-gun marriage of history and development likely to prosper? Melbourne's landmark is a 60-storey skyscraper indistinguishable from those in any other middle-sized city in the world and its 'tall, graceful, handsome structure' dwarfs and mocks the puny monuments to Melbourne's former greatness crouched at its feet. As McCubbin's 'Melbourne in the Eighties' symbolised the towering optimism and confidence of 'Marvellous Melbourne', so the new Rialto reflects our present mood of doubt and anxiety.

Notes

1 Kevin Lynch *The Image of the City*, Cambridge Mass.: M.I.T. Press, 1960; see also Sam Bass Warner Jr 'The Management of Multiple Urban Images' in Derek Fraser and Anthony Sutcliffe (eds) *The Pursuit of Urban History*, London: Edward Arnold, 1983, pp. 383–394. I wish to acknowledge the helpful suggestions of two art historians, Leigh Astbury and Mary Eagle, and the stimulus of George Seddon's 'The View from King's Park: A Visual History of Perth', an unpublished preliminary paper on the topic of his forthcoming book, *A City and its Setting. Images of Perth, Western Australia*, to be published by Fremantle Arts Press in 1986. I confine my attention in this chapter to views of the central business district; another, perhaps longer and equally interesting, essay could be written about evolving views of the suburbs and the urban fringe. See, for example, Helen Topliss *The Artists' Camps: Plein Air Painting in Melbourne 1885–1898*, Melbourne: Monash University Gallery, 1984

2 Leigh Astbury 'Frederick McCubbin: the Spirit of the Pioneers', *Australia

32 Victoria's Heritage

1888 7, April 1981, pp. 26-58; Astbury 'The Heidelberg School and the Popular Image' *Art and Australia* 17, March 1980, pp. 263-5; Ann Galbally *Frederick McCubbin*, Melbourne: Hutchinson, 1981, pp. 36-40

3   R. L. Heathcote 'Early European Perceptions of the Australian Landscape: the first hundred years', in George Seddon and Mari Davis (eds) *Man and Landscape in Australia*, Canberra: AGPS, 1976, pp. 31-34
4   Bernard Smith, *Australian Painting 1788-1970*, Melbourne: Oxford University Press, 1971, p. 18
5   Weston Bate (ed.) *Liardet's Water-colours of Early Melbourne*, Melbourne: Melbourne University Press, 1972, p. 5
6   Marjorie Tipping 'Nicholas Chevalier', *Australian Dictionary of Biography*, 3, 1969, pp. 387-8; Tipping 'Ludwig Becker', *Australian Dictionary of Biography*, 3, pp. 127-8; E. J. R. Morgan 'Stanley Thomas Gill', *Australian Dictionary of Biography*, 1, 1966, pp. 444-5
7   G. H. Wather *The Gold Colony of Victoria in 1854*, London: Longman, 1855, pp. 20-1
8   *Victoria Illustrated 1857 and 1862*, Melbourne: Lansdowne Press, 1971
9   Sandra McGrath and Robert Walker *Sydney Harbour Paintings from 1794*, Sydney: Jacaranda Press, 1979
10 Patricia Reynolds 'A Note on Henry Burn 1807-1884' *La Trobe Library Journal* 3, 11, April 1973, pp. 49-59
11 Yi-Fu Tuan 'The City: its Distance from Nature' *Geographical Review* 68 1, January 1978, pp. 8-11; John Keating *The Lambent Flame* Melbourne: Melbourne University Press, 1974 pp. 48-54
12 William Westgarth *Half A Century of Australasian Progress: a Personal Retrospect*, London: Low, Marstin, Searle and Rivington, 1889, pp. 46-7
13 Asa Briggs *Victorian Cities*, London: Odhams, 1964, pp. 52-3; G. M. Hibbins *A History of the City of Springvale* Melbourne: Hargreen, 1984 p. 38
14 Roland Barthes *The Eiffel Tower and Other Mythologies*, New York: Hill and Wang, 1979, p. 9
15 Richard Altick *The Shows of London*, Cambridge Mass.: Harvard University Press, 1978, pp. 141-3
16 'George Rowe on the Bendigo Diggings' *La Trobe Library Journal* 3, 12 October 1973, p. 90
17 *Illustrated Australian News*, December 1888
18 Marian Vickery 'Bourke Street' *Victorian Arts Centre Magazine* September 1983, p. 16; Virginia Spate *Tom Roberts*, Melbourne: Lansdowne Press, 1974, pp. 24-5
19 Graeme Davison *The Rise and Fall of Marvellous Melbourne*, Melbourne: Melbourne University Press, 1978, pp. 242-6
20 *Table Talk* 5 October 1888, p. 2; compare 'A Melbourne Journalist' 'The Centennial Exhibition' *Centennial Magazine* 2, 1888, p. 62
21 Weston Bate (ed.) *Liardet's Water-colours of Early Melbourne*; Robert Russell 'Melbourne from the Falls' October 1838 (1882) in Michael Cannon (ed.) *Historical Records of Victoria* vol. 3, pp. 48-9
22 Graeme Davison and David Dunstan 'This Moral Pandemonium—Images of Low Life' in Graeme Davison, David Dunstan and Chris McConville (eds) *The Outcasts of Melbourne*, Sydney: Allen & Unwin, 1985
23 Ann Galbally *Arthur Streeton*, Melbourne: Lansdowne Press, 1969, p. 18

Picture of Melbourne 1835-1985   33

24 *Illustrated Australian News* 22 December 1888, p. 219
25 *Victoria and Its Metropolis*, Melbourne: McCarron Bird & Co, 1888, p. 547
26 Several other pictures with 'city' themes such as McCubbin's 'The City's Toil' and 'The Morning Train' were also exhibited in the late 1880s, but have since disappeared from view; see *Catalogue of the Australian Artists' Association Winter Exhibition 1887.*
27 R. H. Croll (ed.) *Smike to Bulldog*, Sydney: Ure Smith, 1946, p. 40
28 Alan Tractenburg 'Image and Ideology: New York in the Photographer's Eye' *Journal of Urban History* 10, 1894, pp. 453-64; Donald D. Cuspit 'Individual and Mass Identity in Urban Art: the New York Case' *Art in America* 5, October 1977, pp. 67-77
29 Richard Haese *Rebels and Precursors: The Revolutionary Years in Australian Art*, Melbourne: Allen Lane, 1981, p. 273; compare Franz Philipp *Arthur Boyd*, London: Thames & Hudson, 1967, p. 50
30 For a good selection of modernist pictures of Sydney see *City/Art*, Social Education Materials Project, Melbourne 1978; and for a parallel discussion of city imagery in Europe and America see *Cityscape 1910-1939 Urban Themes in America, German and British Art*, Arts Council of Great Britain, 1977
31 *Age* 11 October 1983

Pictures mentioned in the text

Robert Russell, Official Survey Map showing the site of Melbourne, 1837, in Weston Bate (ed.) *Liardet's Water-colours of Early Melbourne*, Melbourne: Melbourne University Press, 1972; *Melbourne in 1838* broadsheet published by M. L. Hutchinson based on Russell in Michael Cannon (ed.) *Historical Records of Victoria, Foundation Series*, vol. 3: *The Early Development of Melbourne*, Melbourne: Government Printer, 1984, pp. 48-9

Robert Russell, 'Melbourne from the Falls October 1838', watercolour, La Trobe Library in Cannon (ed.) *Historical Records of Victoria*, vol. 3, p. 57

John Adamson, 'Melbourne from the South Side of the Yarra', 1839, lithograph, La Trobe Library, in Cannon (ed.) *Historical Records of Victoria*, vol. 3, opp. p. 69

Wilbraham Liardet, 'View of Melbourne, Port Phillip', 1843, lithograph, Mitchell Library reproduced as endpapers to Weston Bate (ed.) *Liardet's Water-colours of Early Melbourne*

[Antoine Fauchery?] 'The Yarra below the Falls, Melbourne', photograph, in *Sun Pictures of Victoria The Fauchery—Daintree Collection 1858*, Melbourne: Currey O' Neil Ross, 1983, p. 45

J. G. Boyd, 'The Wharf, Melbourne, from the Customs House', watercolour, La Trobe Library c. 1854, in *National Bank Calendar 1977*

Edmund Thomas, 'River Yarra Yarra from south side of Princes Bridge,

34   Victoria's Heritage

Melbourne', c. 1853, lithograph in *National Bank Calendar 1977*

S. T. Gill, 'Queen's Wharf, Melbourne, West End', lithograph, Sands and Kenny Melbourne, 1857, in S. T. Gill and Nicholas Chevalier *Victoria Illustrated 1857 and 1862*, Melbourne: Lansdowne Press, 1971, p. 50

S. T. Gill, 'Post Office, Melbourne', lithograph, Sands and Kenny Melbourne, 1857, in Gill and Chevalier, *Victoria Illustrated 1851 and 1862*, p. 64

J. B. Henderson, 'Melbourne 1853 from St. Kilda Road', watercolour in *Joseph Brown Gallery Spring Exhibition October 1979*, p. 18

Henry Burn, 'Melbourne from the south, near the St. Kilda Road, June 1855', lithograph, Mitchell Library reproduced with added tinting in *National Bank Calendar 1967*

Ludwig Becker, 'Melbourne 1854', tempera and watercolour in *Nineteenth and Twentieth Century Australian Art*, Block Gallery and Deutscher Gallery exhibition catalogue 1979

F. Cogné, 'Queens Wharf (Yarra Yarra 1863)', lithograph in Charles Troedel *The Melbourne Album*, Melbourne, 1863, facsimile published by Troedel and Cooper 1961

F. Cogné, 'Botanical Gardens (1863)', lithograph in Troedel, *The Melbourne Album*

Henry Gritten, 'Melbourne from the Botanical Gardens', c. 1867, oil, La Trobe in Library Downer and Phipps (eds) *Victorian Vision: 1834 Onwards*, Melbourne: National Gallery of Victoria, 1985, p. 37

Henry Burn, 'Melbourne from the Domain 1871', oil, La Trobe Library

Henry Burn, 'Wellington Parade, Jolimont, looking towards the City', 1873, oil, *in Early Australian Paintings, Prints, Drawings and Maps*, Melbourne: Joshua McClelland Print Room, 1983

Henry Burn, 'South Yarra Hill (Vic.)', 1864, watercolour, La Trobe Library in *National Bank Calendar 1976*

Ludwig Becker, 'Old Princes Bridge and St Paul's by moonlight', 1857, oil, in Downer and Phipps (eds) *Victorian Vision*, p. 25

A. C. Cooke, 'Melbourne and Suburbs', lithograph, supplement to *Australasian Sketcher* 9 October 1880

Samuel Calvert, 'Melbourne 1880', lithograph, supplement to *Illustrated Australian News* October 1880, reproduced by Australian National Library
A. C. Cooke, 'Melbourne from the Fitzroy Gardens', 1887, lithograph, supplement to *Illustrated Australian News* June 1887 and *Leader* 4 August 1888

Picture of Melbourne 1835–1985

'The City of Melbourne, Australia drawn by N. Whittock, from official surveys and from sketches taken in 1854 by G. Teale Esqr. Melbourne'. La Trobe Library

Samuel Jackson, 'Panoramic Sketch of Melbourne Port Phillip from the walls of Scots Church on the Eastern Hill July 30th 1941', pencil drawing, reproduced in Cannon (ed.) *Historical Records of Victoria* vol. 3, opp. p. 472

Eugene von Guérard, 'Panoramic Sketch of Melbourne', 1855, pencil, La Trobe Library

George Rowe, 'A Panoramic View of Melbourne from the Flagstaff Gardens', 1859, coloured lithograph in Alan McCulloch *Artists of the Australian Gold Rush*, Melbourne: Lansdowne Press, 1977, p. 90

Bird's-eye views of city blocks in *The Melbourne Guide Book*, Melbourne: 1895, in Graeme Davison (ed.) *Melbourne on Foot*, Adelaide: Rigby, 1980, pp. 24–5

Frederick McCubbin, 'Melbourne in the Eighties', originally titled 'The Yarra below Princes Bridge', c. 1888, oil, National Gallery of Victoria in Downer and Phipps (eds) *Victorian Vision*, p. 145

'Collins Street—Looking East', *Australasian Sketcher* 21 September 1886, p. 152

Tom Roberts, 'Bourke Street, Melbourne', c. 1886, oil, National Library of Australia, in Bernard Smith *Australian Painting 1788–1970*, Melbourne: Oxford University Press, 1971, p. 88

Clarence Woodhouse, 'Melbourne in 1838 from the Yarra Yarra', 1888, coloured lithograph, La Trobe Library in *Melbourne 1840–1900 The Phenomenal City*, La Trobe Library exhibition catalogue 1984

John Hennings, 'Cyclorama of Melbourne in 1841', La Trobe Library; some panels in Michael Cannon (ed.) *Historical Records of Victoria*, vol. 3, opp. p. 256

Atkinson Grimshaw, 'Swanston Street, Melbourne, a Winter Evening', c. 1890, oil, private collection described in *Views in Victoria and New South Wales 1826–1927*, Joshua McClelland Print Room, December 1984

Arthur Streeton, 'Princes Bridge: Between the Lights', 1888, oil, private collection

Tom Roberts, 'The Evening Train to Hawthorn', 1888, oil, private collection, in Helen Topliss *Tom Roberts 1856–1931 A Catalogue Raisonné* vol. 2, plates, Oxford University Press, Melbourne: 1985

John Brack, 'Collins Street, 5 p.m.', 1955, oil, in Downer and Phipps *Victorian Vision*, p. 72

Albert Tucker, 'Images of Modern Evil no. 14', oil, in James Mollison and Nicholas Bonham *Albert Tucker*, Sydney: Macmillan, 1981, p. 93

Jan Senbergs, 'Port Liardet II', in Jenny Zimmer 'Jan Senbergs: history painter' *Art and Australia* 22, 2, 1984, pp. 206–11

John Perceval, 'Negroes at Night', 1944, oil, Australian National Gallery, Canberra, in Richard Haese *Rebels and Precursors The Revolutionary Years in Australian Art*, Melbourne: Allen Lane, 1981, p. 209

Arthur Boyd, 'Melbourne Burning', 1946–7, oil and tempera, Haese, *Rebels and Precursors*, p. 275

3

Melbourne economists in the public arena: *from Copland to the Institute*

MARJORIE HARPER

'What can a mere economist do?' This rhetorical question was often posed by Douglas Copland, one of Melbourne's most notable economists in the public arena.[1] Occasionally the question reflected frustration; more often it expressed irony. For Copland believed that in a country where so many political problems are economic, the economist has much to give, should be seen to be giving and should thus wield influence in the sphere of public policy.

Such an attitude requires great faith. Pure theorists must be convinced that their vision of the economic world is worth pursuing in an abstract way to the frontiers of knowledge; applied economists must believe, strongly, that the tools provided by theory and the data collected empirically are not too fragile for use in the real world.

For most of the nineteenth century Victorians did not place much faith in the skills of their few economists. Only from the 1920s did the work of economists begin to have impact. By 1985, however, even the schoolchildren of Victoria can be seen debating economic issues. This incredible change in public awareness has stemmed from the great expansion of education in economics, and from the fact that academic economists have been prepared to extend their role from university work to extensive public debate.

It is possible to tell a valid (even if partial and selective) story of this transformation by reference to the work of three Melbourne University economists—Douglas Berry Copland, Richard Ivan Downing and Ronald Frank Henderson. Each of these men was Cambridge orientated and/or Cambridge trained; each had the 'cool head and warm heart' of the 'ideal-type' Cambridge economist.[2] They thought in terms of the economy as a whole and the relationships between economic development, employment, welfare and social justice. They made sustained efforts to instruct the people in the essentials of public policy, and, as they did so, their work threaded together to form a coherent, continuous pattern.

In Victoria's sesqui-centenary year it is a pertinent preliminary to ask why academic economists had so little impact on policy in the nineteenth century, and why the profession developed so late. After all, economic problems were central to the colony of Victoria. From as early as 1855, the University of Melbourne offered courses in political economy, but they attracted relatively few students, and by the end of the century even the teachers had lost interest. Was it because political economy was a young discipline, bred in the Old World, and thought to be irrelevant or unpalatable in a new and developing country?

When James Cook was surveying the southern seas, Adam Smith, the Scottish philosopher, was finishing his *Wealth of Nations*.[3] That celebrated book laid the foundations for the disciplined study of political economy. Smith conceptualised an integrated economic system of mutually interdependent parts and he asked questions: How could such a system grow in opulence? What determines the growth and structure of its annual product? By what mechanisms would its product be naturally distributed to the members of society? Could government intervention improve the natural working of the system? He thus posed in a general way the set of fundamental and durable problems which form the core of economics to this day, and for which applied economists still seek concrete answers.

Smith believed that improved technology and widening markets constitute the dynamics of a growing economic system. When the economic functions of government are minimal, individuals, by following their own self-interest, are guided by the invisible hand of Providence to contribute to the social good. Deregulation was his appropriate policy prescription.

By the time Governor Phillip and the First Fleet sailed into Sydney Harbour, Smith's ideas were gaining wide currency in the intellectual and political circles of Britain, Europe and America. They were not, however, an appropriate blueprint for an authoritarian convict outpost of the Empire.

In the 50-odd years between the first arrivals at Sydney and the beginnings of settlement at Melbourne, English political economy flowered into its classical form. In an atmosphere of social hostility generated by the French Revolution, the post-Napoleonic-War depression and the dislocations of the Industrial Revolution, attention in this class-dominated society shifted to distributive shares. Political economists tried, deductively, to establish economic laws; their studies came later to be described as 'viciously abstract'.[4] Nevertheless the policy implications were clear—it was best to allow natural laws to work unfettered; it was counter-productive for governments to legislate for the amelioration of economic or social conditions. Monetary systems also should be devised which would work automatically and correctively. Against these conclusions a radical and Marxian dissent began to develop, and political economy generally became known as 'the dismal science'.

By 1851, when Victoria was proclaimed a separate colony, English interest in political economy was waning. There was a certain feeling among its adherents that it was largely a 'completed' science, for the major practical objectives, particularly free trade, had been achieved. Among advanced social thinkers classical political economy was considered as obstacle to government-sponsored social reform and therefore to be disdained. The discipline had reached a stage of arrested development which was to continue into the 1880s. 'If Political Economy be merely what a widely prevalent opinion supposes it to be, if the sum and outcome of its teachings be *laissez-faire*, the field for its activity, in this country at least, must henceforth be a narrow one. Under these circumstances, it is not strange if the interest felt in the study is of a languid sort', remarked a London professor of political economy.[5]

It was classical political economy which was brought to Melbourne University in 1855 by W. E. Hearn, the young foundation Professor of Modern History and Literature, Political Economy and Logic. He wrote a textbook for his students, in which he expounded the 'natural workings' of the economy as if the policy-prescription of *laissez-faire* automatically followed.[6] 'Whereas English work stressed scarcity, his work was highly optimistic in tone for he saw the Australian environment as blessed with an abundance of resources. In his optimism, he deplored the tendency of people to turn to government with their economic and social problems. As the alluvial gold supplies ran out in Victoria, men looked for work, especially in manufacturing, which they hoped would be protected by tariffs. Hearn was opposed to any forced pace of development, particularly by way of protection, or to government cossetting by way of social services. 'Men have no faith in the existence or in the operation of the natural laws that regulate society ... but ... have full reliance on their own powers [to regulate]', he wrote. 'This strange presumption arises from two defects, the one intellectual, the other moral ... which proceeds ... from ... a want of faith.'[7]

For Hearn, the forum of the University was too small, and he wished to implement his views by entering the Legislative Assembly. He tried twice, unsuccessfully, but was so active that the University legislated to prevent the participation of professors in politics. However, in 1873 Hearn resigned his chair, became Dean of the newly created Faculty of Law, and successfully entered the Legislative Council.[8] He was the first Melbourne academic economist in the public arena, but his economic ideas did not relate to the living ideas of Victorians.

When Hearn retired from teaching political economy at the University in 1878, he was succeeded by one of his own students, J. S. Elkington, who held the Chair of History and Political Economy for 34 years. The professor seems to have had little interest in political economy, except to declare himself for *laissez-faire* and free trade. He had few students, about half of whom were ladies. 'Ladies,' he said, 'seem very partial to political economy'; also that he 'treated ... theory ... very, very lightly indeed'.[9]

This was unfortunate, for the great depression of the 1890s brought complex economic problems which, for the people of Victoria, desperately needed understanding.

In England, the study of political economy, or economics, had been revivified by the work of two great economists—W. Stanley Jevons and, more conspicuously, Alfred Marshall, founders of the English neo-classical school. By a curious coincidence, these two men were directly influenced in their lives by the Victorian gold rushes. In 1854, at the age of eighteen, Jevons came to Sydney to work as an assayer at the Mint. A fall in the family fortunes had caused him to interrupt his life as a university science student at London. In Australia, Jevons observed economic conditions in a country where class distinctions were less important than in England, but the clash of interest groups over the best use of resources was very plain to see. Development policies were considered crucially important, for they affected growth and the distribution of wealth and income. Jevons watched the bargaining and became interested in political economy. He began to study it, and as a scientist was dismayed by its omnibus nature and the confusion of theory and policy prescription. In 1859 he decided to return to London, study political economy and reform it.[10] In the process, he clearly recognised that economics is a very subordinate science—in policy-making, subject to ethics.[11] So too, did Alfred Marshall, who was enabled to escape his apparent destiny as a clergyman only because of financial help from a rich uncle who made his fortune as a pastoralist in Victoria during the 1850s. He believed 'ethical instincts' and commonsense to be the 'ultimate arbiters' in practical issues, even of an economic nature.[12] Marshall's work was to shape the study of economics in English-speaking countries for nearly a century, but not in Melbourne until Copland's time.

The work of Jevons and Marshall could have contributed much to the economic education of Victorians before the 1920s, but it was comparatively neglected in Melbourne. Victoria achieved a reputation for social reform, but policy decisions with a strong socio/economic content tended to be debated piecemeal, without sufficient leadership from the academic community. With Elkington's retirement in 1912, the University Council approached the State government for provision for a Chair in Political Economy and Sociology. The Premier was reluctant. He indicated that only an Australian appointee with appropriate (interpreted as protectionist) views would be acceptable— an implied condition which the Univeristy would not accept. As a consequence, the study of political economy was even more downgraded. World War I, however, brought such acute economic problems in its trail, that in 1923 the idea was revived in a modified form, and the following year Douglas Berry Copland was appointed Professor in the newly created School of Commerce.[13]

Douglas Copland was a 30-year-old New Zealander, then Professor and Dean of Commerce at the University of Tasmania. He came from a Presbyterian family with a strong sense of community welfare, eager that their son should qualify for a 'worthwhile' profession. Choosing between teaching and the ministry, Copland had first qualified as a teacher of mathematics. An interest in economics, however, had led him to the deliberate choice of a career as an applied economist. He became a distinguished economics graduate of Canterbury College, Christchurch, of which J. M. Keynes was to say that the training in economics 'was as good as at any place in the world'.[14] Copland's specialisation was monetary economics, born out of his interest in the economics of depression, but he was always interested in the interrelations of the economy as a whole.

In Tasmania the professor was well known for his extremely outspoken comments on government policies, not all of which he approved. He had, for example, spoken and written against extensive soldier settlement, against heavy borrowing rather than taxation for wartime finance and for post-war hydro-electricity development,[15] against rises in tariff protection,[16] and against trade union pressure for wage rises which outstripped productivity increases.[17] Despite this outspokenness he was not unpopular—he knew how to be both conciliatory and aggressive, having learned these skills as the thirteenth child in a family of fifteen. He was generally constructive in approach, enormously energetic, ambitious and tough-minded. He had the gift of 'clothing dry-as-dust theories' with 'living vitality'.[18]

The question was: 'Would he bring peace or a sword to Melbourne?'[19] Although realising that his first concerns must be to build up the Commerce School by setting high standards of teaching and research, he did not intend to confine himself to academic life. The economic problems of the day were too pressing; and clearly governments, the public service and the general populace needed instruction. The level of economic literacy in Melbourne, seat of the Victorian and the Federal governments, was much too low.

Clearly Copland intended to be highly visible. Only the year before coming to Melbourne, he had provocatively declared that 'just at the moment it so happens that the economist is (or should be) king'.[20] Physically, he was not easily overlooked. His frame was tall and broad-shouldered, his figure lean and athletic until middle age, thick and bulky thereafter. His face was somewhat heavy, given mobility by a curious and attractive lightness in the eyes, and a genial expression of *bonhomie*. Without the geniality, its expression was pensive and aloof, sometimes bleak. He had an ebullient personality and an unusual booming, rasping voice which could be used to good effect. These attributes seemed to ensure distinct, though varied responses among those with whom he came in contact. People were rarely indifferent to Copland.

He quoted with approval a Cambridge view that 'in respect of the sciences of human society, be their appeal as bearers of light so high, it is through the promise of fruit, and not of light, that they chiefly merit one's regard'.[21] But he realised clearly that fruit could only be plucked at its best if the people had already seen the light.

From his strategic position as an academic, the professor created avenues through which to inform and advise. Apart from University courses—after 1925 there were never less than 400 annual student enrolments in Commerce until the wartime restrictions of 1942[22]—he organised study circles for graduates, gave public lectures and radio broadcasts and wrote syndicated columns in the leading newspapers. He was willing to speak, practically on demand, to the Chamber of Commerce, the Chamber of Manufacturers, the Commercial Travellers' Association, the Australasian Insurance and Bankers' Association, to farmers' and graziers' organisations, and to trade unions. Teachers invited him to their schools, the boy scouts to their camps. He was popular among women's gatherings and church groups.[23] To link town and gown he fostered the activities of the very energetic Economic Society of Australia and New Zealand, which he helped to establish in 1925.

Copland's enthusiasm was unquenchable and his efforts went far beyond the call of obligation. He was highly successful at establishing empathy with his listeners, 'being at home, no matter what the constitution of his audience' according to a leading trade unionist.[24] He himself attributed his 'at-home-ness' to experiences in working with different sections of the community. He had not lived in an ivory tower.

Coming from a farming background, to which he continually returned on vacation, Douglas Copland sympathised with the man on the land. He boasted that he could do most farming jobs, and was willing to work until the sweat ran freely. His doctoral thesis had been on the wheat industry,[25] and shortly after his arrival in Australia, he had established bonds with wheat growers and graziers. He often toured country areas speaking to dairy farmers, butter producers, sugar growers and fruit growers, showing interest in production techniques and in their problems of marketing.

There were links, too, with workers and trade union officials. While still a degree student in New Zealand, Copland became a lecturer with the Workers' Educational Association and in Tasmania was Director of Tutorial Classes (i.e. WEA classes). In that capacity, he greatly expanded the scope of WEA activities, particularly in mining areas. His economics and history courses for WEA classes examined the development and flaws of capitalism, the concepts of socialism and the origins of Bolshevism. Due attention was given to the aspirations of the trade union movement. Copland taught that the conditions of the workers would be bettered, and the evils of unemployment relieved, by policies of economic growth. Increased productivity was a prime economic necessity and productivity increases should be shared with labour. There should be worker participation in management, and redistribution of wealth through the fiscal system. A 'just society' was seen to be in the mould of advanced welfare capitalism, partly managed by workers, geared to technological change, the fruits of which were to be equitably distributed.[26] In Melbourne, he took care to preserve his links with the WEA and the trade unions.

More conspicuously, as Professor and Dean of Commerce at the University of Melbourne, Copland identified with the business community. His first residential addresses in Melbourne were within Canterbury's 'golden mile', and the luxury of his University offices astonished his academic colleagues. Melbourne's commercial and financial interests were represented on the Faculty, and the usual destination of commerce students was into the world of business. In Hobart he had come to the notice of Mr Herbert Gepp and his colleagues; in Melbourne he became a close and long-time associate and friend of the Collins House group. At times the newspapers speculated that the professor was perhaps a businessman, masquerading in academic garb.

These links with the different sections of the community gave Copland great confidence. It did not mean that he became their mouthpiece, or that his relationships were in harmony with group interests. He was above all an academic, and hoped always to achieve the objectivity which such an occupation should imply. He would stand above sectional interests as the informed and competent lofty leader. He would bare the basis of sectional conflict in an effort to confront it, minimise it, and promote consensus. He was no stranger to the ideas of accord, then being espoused so strongly by Secretary of Commerce Hoover in the USA. But consensus, he believed, must operate within constraints. Copland had a strong sense of history and a very good knowledge of the history of theoretical economics. He felt very clear about the distinction between economic science, with its core of fundamental truths which must be respected, and its collection of particular theoretical constructs which could be argued about and were certainly not sacrosanct. He was also acutely aware of the distinction between economic analysis and economic policy-making, which he considered to be an art, requiring judgment of a high order. By making these distinctions he was able to define his stand, to identify the limits of conflict and consensus, and to defend his advocacy of particular practical policies which were more often the result of compromise.

What was the burden of Copland's message to Victorians in the 1920s? He believed in strong economic development, but he was mindful that Australia was an open economy. He was wary of forcing the pace of economic development—of optimistic land development schemes designed to settle British migrants on the land, of the extension of transport facilities to service them, of schemes financed by heavy borrowing from London and of bringing funds to swell the banking reserves in a system which bankers had not yet learned to manage efficiently. Being basically a free trader, he was wary of the forced pace of manufacturing development behind tariffs granted without discrimination by the Tariff Board, of the consequent belief that industry could afford to pay higher wages out of line with those overseas, of the spread of protection to the rural industries. The Victorian economy, like that of the nation, was becoming increasingly vulnerable.

Copland was confirmed in these opinions as early as 1926 during an overseas tour. At the end of 1925 he had been appointed Australian representative of the Rockefeller Institute of New York, and under their auspices travelled extensively in Britain, Europe, Canada and the USA, meeting the foremost economists in academia, in government circles and in banking. He realised full well the problems of over-production in world agriculture, of monetary instability in the world economy and of the disagreement among leading authorities as to how best to cope with it. As a long-term student of the trade cycle, he visited centres of trade cycle research—The Brookings Institution, The National Bureau of Economic Research and Harvard—and feared that the next cyclical downturn would find the world unprepared to meet it.[27]

In his approach to the people of Victoria and Australia, Copland did not wish to sound like a Cassandra. His was an optimistic nature. Rather he stressed the need for information, particularly for National Income statistics. There was a great need for more and better statistics to be gathered; for their finer classification; for the promotion of quantitative studies in economics. More facts needed be known about the environment, both geographical and historical, so that the interdependence of economic relationships could be better understood. Indeed, he hoped to have a statistical laboratory at the Commerce School. He wanted to awaken the public's critical faculties.

It was against this background that Copland slipped easily into the role of economic adviser, and into the role of publicising his advice. In 1927 Prime Minister Bruce asked him to join in an enquiry into the effects of the Australian tariff; the Development and Migration Commission used him as a consultant on feasibility schemes of development and to write a report on growing unemployment; the Commonwealth Bank summoned him to discuss his 'heretical' views on banking. He helped in the creation of the Loan Council and in 1931 he chaired an expert committee to help solve the budgetary problems of the depression. For all this, and similar work, he received no payment.

A consideration of just two of these activities illustrates how Copland tried to combine economic expertise and commonsense judgment.

Work on the Tariff Report took much of his spare time over nearly two years, for it presented a number of dilemmas.[28] The committee of five consisted of C. H. Wickens and L. F. Giblin, Commonwealth and Tasmanian government statisticians respectively; J. B. Brigden, Professor of Economics at Hobart; E. C. Dyason, a Melbourne businessman, and Copland. It was asked to report on the effects of protection, not just in terms of general principles but quite specifically, and to bear in mind the immediate practicalities of any proposed change of tariff policy. The Report was difficult to write because Brigden began as sympathetic to protection but gradually moved towards a free trade position, Giblin was agnostic in general but opposed to rural protection, while the Melbourne people were basically free traders. Copland, however, felt that in view of the unemployment situation the time was not particularly appropriate for the reduction of tariffs and therefore leaned towards finding some justification for protection. Despite the heroic efforts of Wickens, Giblin and Dyason, the three who undertook the empirical research, all members were dissatisfied with the perceived inadequacies of the statistical measurements. To overcome these difficulties they drew up a list of 44 questions which they apportioned among themselves, and then circulated for comment and, if possible, for consensus. They realised that they were obliged to work on a 'best effort' basis, pasted and polished over the disjunctions as best they could, and at last, in 1929, presented a compromise status quo document which they considered to be of temporary importance. Just before it was completed, Copland wrote to Brigden: 'No doubt it is good tactics to concede as much to the protectionists as possible, and although we shall be severely criticised for our free trade leanings, I feel that the report has gone as far as possible in favouring a limited tariff and that any further revisions would be in the direction of lower tariffs.'[29]

In later years Copland was to look on the Report with more favour. It received critical acclaim both at home and abroad. He became interested in developing an improved theoretical case for protection, and after the Ottawa agreements of 1932 he also tended to give greater weight to tariffs as bargaining chips in the conduct of world trade.

The onset of the 1930s depression confirmed Copland's previous fears of a downturn in the world trade cycle, a downturn complicated by intense monetary difficulties. He tried to organise the professional economists of Australia so that they would be prepared to present a united front to any proposals put forward by the newly elected Federal government. Labor, he felt, had a natural suspicion of economists. In this task he was at first singularly unsuccessful. He had a 'best' plan for a package of a depreciated currency, a liberal money policy and pegged wages and salaries. This was rejected by his fellow-economists. He then evolved his 'second-best' plan: depreciation of the currency, stabilisation of prices and a cut in wages and salaries—a compromise between the first plan and severe deflation. Even for this plan, he was branded by many fellow economists as an inflationist and a 'dangerous tempter' to the 'easy road to ruin'.[30] They used his proposals to stimulate intense public debate.

By early 1931 the situation was absolutely critical. All Treasury finances were deteriorating rapidly, and Commonwealth and State governments faced the alarming prospect of default because the Commonwealth Bank refused to continue to accommodate them. Under the auspices of the Loan Council and under the chairmanship of Copland, a committee of economic experts was called in to give advice. They sat for an exhausting and frustrating ten days and finally devised the Premiers' Plan—a compromise plan to restore a degree of budgetary health based on hard-won consensus among the economists, governments, bankers and businessmen.[31]

When it was adopted, Copland, as man of the hour, was extravagantly praised and extravagantly blamed. He was called the 'Keynes of the Commonwealth'.[32] Since then, the Plan has been vested with an importance out of proportion to its original purpose and has been widely debated—professionally and non-professionally—in terms of its potential as a plan of recovery from the depression.

After 1931 Copland operated in a much wider public arena. Already established as a national figure, he became widely recognised internationally among the company of economists. He became economic adviser to the governments of Victoria, New South Wales, the Commonwealth and sometimes of New Zealand; he gave guest lectures at the universities of Cambridge, Oxford, Harvard, Columbia and Princeton, among others; he represented Australia at international economic conferences; he became wartime Prices Commissioner. At the conclusion of World War II, he resigned his Melbourne chair and became successively Australian Minister to China, founding Vice-Chancellor of the Australian National University, High Commissioner to Canada, President of the United Nations Economic and Social Committee (1953), and, briefly, Director of the Labour Institute of the International Labour Organisation. These and other activities kept him firmly in the public arena, but not necessarily in that of Melbourne.

For a great part of his professional life, Douglas Copland was sustained by a mutually supportive relationship with Lyndhurst Falkiner Giblin, a colleague 21 years his senior. Copland first met Giblin in Hobart, where the latter was Tasmanian Government Statistician, having earlier graduated in mathematics at Cambridge. In 1928, at Copland's urging, he became the first occupant of the newly established Ritchie Chair of Economics at Melbourne. This chair was devoted almost solely to research. Although ready and willing to enlighten the public and engage in popular debate, Giblin never usurped Copland's role as chief public spokesman for the Faculty.

After World War II when Copland and Giblin had both left

Melbourne, the task of public economist fell principally to the Ritchie Professor. (The teaching professors, notably Wilfred Prest, were too heavily involved in coping with the post-war boom in commerce students, and engaged in specific government assignments.) During the late 1940s and during his tenure of the Ritchie Chair (1954–75), Richard Downing filled the role of public educator with distinction and flair. He combined dark good looks, a beautiful voice and an unruffled manner with a warm and caring personality. According to a colleague 'he was *the* economist for his generation of Australians because Economics mattered to him in a way the public could understand'.[33]

As the twig is bent, so is the tree inclined. Richard Downing was a product of the University of Melbourne. Beginning his economics degree in 1932, at the age of seventeen, he was immediately accustomed to the notion that economists gave devoted and sustained public service. He was excited by the fact that staff members, particularly Copland and Giblin, were so heavily involved in policy-making.

While still a student, Downing was given part-time employment by Giblin as a research assistant in statistics, a position which was extended after his graduation. Giblin became 'strongly impressed' by Downing's 'general competence, his persistence and thoroughness and practical efficiency in investigation work and in his general sanity of judgement.'[34] From Copland, Downing learned to look to the world environment, for in the 1930s Copland made several visits abroad— absorbing, discussing and arguing theoretical developments in major academic centres. As always, Copland's (and Giblin's) closest ties were with Cambridge, England. Copland had spent time there in 1933 delivering (at Keynes's suggestion) a series of lectures on Australia's method of meeting the world crisis and also attending study circles discussing Keynes's theoretical solutions to unemployment. In 1936 Melbourne eagerly awaited the publication of Keynes's *General Theory of Employment, Interest and Money*.[35] The first copy of the book to reach Melbourne (in March 1936) was brought directly by Brian Reddaway, a Cambridge graduate coming to undertake research under Giblin.

Richard Downing's heart and mind had been well prepared to receive the Keynesian doctrines. He had observed depression unemployment and distress. His studies of monetary and trade cycle theories had been demanding. 'The depression-bred generation of students', said Downing later, 'took to the *General Theory* like ducks at last finding water'.[36] He thought the *General Theory* 'probably the greatest work written since Darwin's *Origin of the Species*'[37] because 'it brought people quickly to realise that they could control their own economic destiny through government action'.

Downing went to Cambridge in 1937 and returned to Melbourne in 1940, quickly becoming assistant to Copland as Prices Commissioner and Economic Adviser to the Prime Minister. During that time he became associated with Dr H. C. Coombs of the Department of

Post-War Reconstruction, and gradually became involved in the tortuous production of that Department's white paper on *Full Employment in Australia*.[38] In that milieu he was a calming influence among his colleagues and showed great skill in drafting and negotiating.

After the war he spent short periods in Montreal, Melbourne and Geneva considering the tools of full employment policy. For the International Labour Organization he investigated the economics of public investment and in particular of public housing;[39] and for Australian university and senior school students he produced a textbook explaining the presentation and use of the Australian national accounts.[40]

During this stage of his career Downing was an optimistic idealist sharing Coombs' faith in the possibilities of government control. According to Copland, who was less sanguine in his expectations, the younger economists belonged to '"the perfectionist school" with the motto enshrined on their banners—"more jobs than people to fill the jobs."'[41] Copland, who was concerned about wage discipline, believed they had 'an excess of confidence'.

That confidence was to be tested, and would rest to a large part on the perceived adequacy of information. In 1954 Downing, as Ritchie Professor, joined periodic group discussions of macro-economic policy which were convened by Coombs, by then Governor of the Commonwealth Bank. These meetings revealed an urgently felt need among economists for a programme of on-going surveys of the state of the economy to be used as the basis for public discussion. From 1956 the Treasury undertook to do this; at the same time Downing decided that alternative and independent surveys should be provided biennially through *The Economic Record* of which he was editor. The Treasury documents followed a coherent and consistent pattern over time, and were presented in a fairly conservative and moralising fashion, reflecting a continuity of creation.[42] Ronald Henderson, visiting Australia in 1959–60, was dismayed by their persistently deflationary bias. *The Economic Record* surveys, on the other hand, were the products of a succession of individual economists beginning with Downing. Obviously their individuality lessened their comparability and continuity. What was required was team effort, and, in the words of Ronald Henderson 'a lot of expensive drudgery'[43] which the Ritchie Chair could not support. They were continued, however, until 1967, after which time the Institute of Applied Economic Research undertook the task.

In the early years of the Keynesian era, policies to control inflation were seen as the obverse side of full employment policies. In his first economic survey of the Australian economy in 1956, Downing complained that it was difficult to get anyone to do anything about inflation and argued that the economist must persuade otherwise. This he tried to do, until his death in 1975.

He tried to resolve in his mind the relationship between growth and development, full employment, pressures for social change and the acceleration of inflation. The basic economic questions relating to the growth and structure of the economy, the distribution of the product and the role of government intervention were viewed by him within a social, political and moral framework. 'I see social welfare as the principal objective of all human effort and economic analysis as one of its servants.'[44] He believed there should be a natural progression from full employment and high growth to redistributive social justice via changes in social attitudes and an increasing role for the public sector.

Peaceful redistribution through the tax system should soften social struggles by providing for those people outside the work force—the aged, the sick and the unemployed—as well as for the needy within its ranks. It was in this area that much of his work lay. In 1940 he suggested the introduction of a national child endowment scheme financed by a payroll tax as a trade-off for the deferral of a rise in the basic wage. During the 'fifties and 'sixties he suggested various schemes of provision for the aged, both in the form of means-tested pensions and the introduction of national superannuation. He cooperated with Henderson to investigate poverty in Melbourne; he proposed methods of tax reform and he experimented with ideas of indexation as a means of moderating wage inflation.

Each of these issues was, Downing realised, of a controversial nature. He had absorbed Copland's views on conflict and consensus, but his methods were more emollient than those of his mentor. On the one hand he saw interest-group conflict as 'an important ingredient not only in economic and social progress, but also in bringing about a healthy harmonization of individual interests'. However, carried too far it was 'destructive of a society and its economy'. On the other hand, 'co-operation need not be pushed so far as to create a corporate state with its overtones of fascism, stagnation and rigidity. If society is to progress, it needs pushers. But the pushers need limits'.[45] He felt that the specialised knowledge and insights of the economist should be directed towards the task of helping to define the limits of conflict and consensus and of producing policies that would 'reduce rather than exacerbate' tension. 'Precisely what we are trained for [is] to identify what it is that we have to give up, and how much, in order to get a little more of something else we want; to present the facts to the people; and to leave them to choose what they want.'[46] 'The job of the economist is to throw up ideas, to test them, to assess their costs and benefits, and to talk about them widely, influentially and persuasively.'[47] This he certainly did.

After his death, Richard Downing's friends and admirers subscribed to a memorial fund. This has been used to endow Downing Fellowships, which regularly bring international scholars of high distinction in the field of social economics to share their wisdom and experience with the people of Melbourne. To date, there have been four Downing Fellows.

After 1962 Downing had drawn strength from the work of the Institute of Applied Economic Research. He had successfully promoted a suggestion made in 1960 by Ronald Henderson for the establishment of an independent research institute. Preferring for himself the role of solitary researcher, he had persuaded Henderson to come to Melbourne as its Director. The new Director had the active look of one who loves the outdoors. Silver-haired, with a fair, tanned complexion, he had the straight blue-eyed glance which inspires confidence. His energy, decisiveness and clear sense of direction brought an air of fresh vigour. A brisk start for the Institute was ensured.

Born in Dundee of a Scottish father and an Australian-born mother, Ronald Henderson had visited Australia since childhood. His wife was a Melbourne girl. Two years younger than Downing, he too had much of his thinking shaped by the depression. As a first-class Cambridge undergraduate in economics, he had been invited from his first year to attend Keynes's Political Economy Club and was thus exposed to the controversies surrounding Keynes's work. During his vacations he had helped to run clubs and camps for the unemployed and became aware, both in a practical and theoretical sense, of the problems of the depressed areas of Britain. He became interested in why the monetary mechanisms which facilitiated real investment seemed to have failed, a subject which he pursued in post-graduate work. It was concern with structural unemployment that thus led him to become a financial economist. In 1962 he was a Fellow and Bursar of Corpus Christi College, Cambridge, and University Lecturer. Melbourne was indeed fortunate that he was prepared to undertake the challenge of setting up a research institute.

Although it was to be located at the University of Melbourne, Henderson saw the Institute of Applied Economic Research as a national body. It should therefore deal with national issues and be guided by an Advisory Board drawn from a wide range of personnel. He undertook to establish an on-going review of the state of the economy within five years—a project which, in his opinion, would of itself be sufficient justification for the existence of the Institute. However, because he disapproved of the way in which the publication of a similar review had dominated the National Institute of Economic Research at London, he determined that there should be applied studies on the structure of industry and of financial institutions. Very soon, too, socio-economic problems of community health and of poverty were added to the agenda.[48]

In 1968 the first issue of the *Australian Economic Review*[49] appeared. It was prepared by Duncan Ironmonger, who had met Ronald Henderson while taking his doctorate at Cambridge. Ironmonger was prepared to relinquish a public service career as a statistician to undertake the

Institute's project. Edited by Ironmonger and closely scrutinised by Henderson, the *Review* assessed published statistical material and discussed current and prospective short-term trends. Aware that the credibility of short-term forecasting is quickly brought to account, Ironmonger tried to build comprehensive data bases (updated nightly on the University computer) and to consult with numerous working parties drawn from different sectors of the economy.

He became interested in the infant discipline of econometric modelling, a development made possible by the increasing sophistication of the computer industry. In 1969 Henderson and Ironmonger visited Harvard to attend a conference on modelling sponsored by the National Bureau of Economic Research. Here Ironmonger arranged to observe and compare the work of the NBER, the Brookings Institution and that of Lawrence Klein at the Wharton School of Finance and Commerce at the University of Philadelphia. In 1970-71 he spent time in Cambridge, centre of econometric modelling in England, and at the Wharton School with Klein, working on his own short-term model and collecting simulation models to bring back to Melbourne. The resources of the Institute, however, were not sufficient to sustain the necessary scale of this type of work, so that very limited and piecemeal modelling was built into the *Review's* forecasts.

Inevitably the *Review* opinion came to be perceived as an alternative or rival view to that of the Treasury, particularly in two respects. The Institute took a more Keynesian, or at least expansionary, view of the economy and it saw more merit in government initiatives for fostering manufacturing industry and for minimising the unemployment problems of restructuring. (Ronald Henderson had been dismayed by what he termed the 'killing' of the Vernon Report in 1965-66—a report which dealt with some contentious issues of Australian economic development.)[50] Undoubtedly public discussion on economic policy issues was greatly stimulated, thus increasing the demand for the public airing of economists' views.

The Vernon Report had been sharply criticised for the inadequacy of its statistical estimates and foundations for long-term projections of structural change. Probably such criticism hastened general progress towards econometric model-building. The 1970s saw the development of basic models of the economy, or sectors of the economy, by econometricians within the universities, Australian government departments and the Reserve Bank. Were these models compatible? Was one superior to another? Here was a fertile field for the testing of the limits of conflict and consensus on technical grounds. By the nature of the debate, public consideration of it was necessarily excluded, although policy recommendations flowing from the use of the models were still issues to be voted upon.

In 1972-73 the Institute expanded its work in this field. Originally sponsored by Telecom and by private industry, it extended its activities to the building of a long-term forecasting model, developed by Peter Brain, and to contract work based on modelling. In 1978 it joined the international LINK model, the project based on Pennsylvania's Wharton School and concerned with forecasting world trade flows on an annual basis.[51] Professor Henderson did not become involved in this second stage of the Institute's work, or in publicising it. That was left to Duncan Ironmonger.

Henderson had greatly raised the public profile of the Institute through research on socio-economic problems, which absorbed an increasing proportion of his time. In 1964 he had initiated, with Downing, an investigation into the extent and nature of poverty in Melbourne. Preliminary findings were released in early 1967 and *People in Poverty: A Melbourne Survey*[52] was published in 1970. During the same years, research within the Institute by John Deeble and Richard Scotton was producing a widely discussed blue-print for the reform of health insurance. Work was undertaken in the delivery of social services. Public attention was focussed on the Institute and practical consequences followed. In 1972 popular pressure led Prime Minister McMahon to appoint Ronald Henderson to head a Commission of Inquiry into Poverty. This Commission was expanded by the Labor government and reported in 1975, the chief recommendation (not implemented) being the introduction of a guaranteed minimum income. In 1975 Medibank was introduced, the first of a number of such schemes, all of which have been controversial. Ronald Henderson became much preoccupied with this work on poverty and with related issues of social reform. He has remained so, even since his retirement in 1979, in his capacity as honorary consultant to the Victorian Council of Social Services.

In some ways the death of Downing and the retirement of Henderson coincided with the end of an era, not just in Victoria, but in the world. The long boom had ended, and the Keynesian era was drawing to a close. Economists everywhere have now accumulated much experience in their endeavours to influence the natural workings of economies, and in the process have become less enamoured with such a role. In their attempts to reach higher and higher degrees of precision in their answers to the basic questions of growth, structure and distribution, they have become more acutely aware of the problems of interrelatedness. They tend to give greater weight to the influence of market forces. So it is in Melbourne.

In the 1980s economists at the University of Melbourne have as yet no predominant voice in the public arena. As a body they draw attention to Australia's vulnerability in a world economy which is undergoing rapid structural change. They stress that choices are hard and must be based on sophisticated levels of theoretical and empirical knowledge and expertise. They stress that the sharp conflicts between sectors of the economy must be understood and moderated. It is an environment in which Douglas Copland would instinctively feel 'at home', but one in which he would not feel fazed. Recognising that change and uncertainty are the stuff of life, he would exhort Victorians, in this their sesqui-centenary year, to approach the future with courage and confidence. He would say (with Horace), as he said so many times in his public life: *'cras ingens iterabimus aequor'*. (Tomorrow we set out once more upon the boundless sea.)

Notes

1 NLA, MS 3800, Copland Papers, B1-6
2 See A. Marshall 'The Present Position of Economics' (1885) in A. C. Pigou (ed.) *Memorials of Alfred Marshall*, London: Macmillan, 1925, p. 174
3 Adam Smith *An Inquiry into the Nature and Causes of the Wealth of Nations*, London: Strahan and Caddell, 1776
4 J. K. Ingram 'Presidential Address to Section F of the British Association', August 1878 in *Report of the British Association for the Advancement of Science, 1878*
5 J. E. Cairnes *Essays in Political Economy: Theoretical and Applied*, London: Macmillan, 1873, p. 239
6 W. E. Hearn *Plutology*, Melbourne: George Robertson, 1863
7 ibid. p. 444
8 D. B. Copland *W. E. Hearn: First Australian Economist*, Melbourne: Melbourne University Press, 1935, pp. 11-12
9 'Royal Commission on the University of Melbourne: Minutes of Evidence on Administration, Teaching Work, and Government of the University of Melbourne', *Papers Presented to the Parliament of Victoria*, 1903 (Second Session), p. 83, quoted in Craufurd D. W. Goodwin *Economic Enquiry in Australia*, Durham N. C.: Duke University Press, 1966, p. 572
10 Harriet A. Jevons (ed.) *Letters and Journal of W. Stanley Jevons*, London: Macmillan, 1886, pp. 151-52
11 See W. S. Jevons *The State in Relation to Labour*, London: Macmillan, 1882, and *Methods of Social Reform*, London: Macmillan, 1883
12 Alfred Marshall *Principles of Economics*, London: Macmillan, 1938, p. 28
13 Ernest Scott *A History of the University of Melbourne*, Melbourne: Melbourne University Press, 1936
14 Copland Diary, 19 June 1926, Copland Papers, B. 38
15 D. B. Copland *The Public Finances of Tasmania*, Hobart: Mercury Press, 1922
16 D. B. Copland *Costs of the Australian Tariff*, Hobart: Mercury Press, 1930
17 Copland Papers, B. 50-51
18 N. Lewis, Preface to Copland *The Public Finances of Tasmania*
19 W. L. Raws 'Review of D. B. Copland: *Commerce and Business*', *The Economic Record* vol. 1, November 1925, p. 122
20 D. B. Copland, 'The Trade Depression in Australia in Relation to Economic Thought', paper delivered to the Sixteenth Meeting of the Australian Association for the Advancement of Science, Section G, Wellington, 1923, p. 32

54 Victoria's Heritage

21 D. B. Copland *Credit and Currency Control*, Melbourne: Macmillan, in association with Melbourne University Press, 1930, p. 26
22 A. Hodgart *The Faculty of Economics and Commerce: A History, 1925–75*, Melbourne: Mimeo, 1975, p. 7
23 Copland Papers, B. 1–4
24 F. J. Riley 'Copland: An Appreciation' *The Economic Record* vol. XXVI, March 1960, p. 161
25 D. B. Copland *Wheat Production in New Zealand: A Study of the Economics of New Zealand Agriculture*, Auckland: Whitcombe and Tombs, 1920
26 Copland Papers, WEA lectures in B. 47, 48
27 Copland Diary, 1926
28 Copland Papers, B. 58–59
29 D. B. Copland to J. B. Brigden, 3 December 1928, Copland Papers, B. 58, F2
30 L. G. Melville 'Way Back to Prosperity' *Adelaide Advertiser* 9 July 1930
31 'Report of the Under-Treasurers and Economists upon the Possibilities of Reaching Budgetary Equilibrium in Australia', Appendix II of the 'Report of the Conference of Commonwealth and State Ministers' 25 May to 11 June 1931, *Commonwealth Parliamentary Papers*, 1929–31, vol. II
32 Sir Herbert Gepp 'Professor and Premiers' Plan' Melbourne *Herald* 15 March 1933 (The phrase was echoed by other newspapers)
33 H. W. Arndt 'R. I. Downing: Economist and Social Reformer' vol. 52, September 1976, p. 300
34 Letter from L. F. Giblin to Secretary, Board of Research Studies, Cambridge, 16 August 1937, Giblin Papers, University of Melbourne, Faculty of Economics and Commerce
35 J. M. Keynes *The General Theory of Employment, Interest and Money*, London: Macmillan, 1936
36 R. I. Downing 'Sir Douglas Copland: A Personal Memory' *The Economic Record* vol. 47, December 1971, p. 466
37 R. I. Downing 'The Uses of Social Accounts in the Australian Economy' in N. T. Drohan and J. H. Day (eds) *Readings in Australian Economics*, Australia: Cassell, 1965, p. 43
38 *Commonwealth Parliamentary Papers*, No. 11, Session 1945–46, vol. IV
39 R. I. Downing 'The Planning of Public Investment in Australia' in B. H. Higgins (ed.) *Public Investment and Full Employment*, Montreal: International Labour Office, 1946
40 R. I. Downing *National Income and Social Accounts: An Australian Study*, Melbourne: Melbourne University Press, 1951
41 D. B. Copland 'The Full-Employment Economy, with Special Reference to Wages Policy' in *Oxford Economic Papers, New Series* vol. 5, October 1953, p. 221
42 Under Richard Randall, Deputy Secretary to the Treasury, 1956–66
43 Interview with R. Henderson by M. Harper, Victorian Council of Social Services, 22 March 1985
44 R. I. Downing 'Social Reconstruction, Social Welfare and Self-Reliance', George Judah Cohen Memorial Lecture, University of Sydney, 21 November 1974, p. 1
45 R. I. Downing 'Growth, Security and Stability' in R. I. Downing (ed.) *The*

Australian Economy: A Manual of Applied Economics, London: Weidenfeld and Nicolson, 1973, pp. 184–85
46 Arndt 'R. I. Downing: Economist and Social Reformer', p. 289
47 ibid. p. 288
48 In 1969 the Institute became the Institute of Applied Economic and Social Research
49 Institute of Applied Economic Research *The Australian Economic Review* 1968
50 'Report of the Committee of Economic Enquiry', 6 May 1965, *Commonwealth Parliamentary Papers*, 1964–65–66, vol. XII
51 Institute of Applied Economic and Social Research *Annual Report, 1982*, Melbourne, 1983
52 Ronald Henderson, Alison Harcourt and R. J. A. Harper *People in Poverty: A Melbourne Survey*, Melbourne: Cheshire, 1970

4

The cabbage garden and the fair blank sheet: *an historical review of environment and planning*

J. M. POWELL

One of the unchallenged precepts during my own basic training in the liberal arts and sciences was that all geographers must possess a stout pair of boots. Over the years similar injunctions have been thrust at hosts of students enrolled in several other subjects, including history. And rightly so: far too much of our learning is second-hand. Every age should be made an age of discovery, in our formal education as in life itself. Although we remain conservative and inhibited in this area, something more than lip-service is at last being paid to the hallowed fieldwork principle in Australia's schools and tertiary institutions. For that reason alone this paper may at least provide a tangential reinforcement of the ideal in some quarters, and I confess that it has been consciously designed, in part, to suggest the need for a bold extension of the old maxim to our Victorian community as a whole. The primary intention is, however, more modest and straightforward—to examine some of the efforts made over the last 150 years by an increasingly urbanised, immigrant society to appraise and manage the state's dynamic 'natural' and 'built' environments.

Suspending the old lessons for a moment, the subject under review is plainly under-researched and, whether or not we have reached the age of consensus, in all such interdisciplinary areas it is still wise to tread very lightly. Perhaps we need to begin with a comment on the selection of an odd title, which may be striking the wrong chord, or none at all. Although I intend to use a relatively simple chronological framework later, the main title is actually a convenient composite of two descriptive statements taken out of context and in reverse historical sequence.

The particular variant of the 'cabbage-garden' jibe I had in mind was a note published in the *Geelong Advertiser* at the end of 1856, about six weeks after the first Victorian parliament had met. Signed 'Policy and Public Justice', it protested bitterly against the growing attacks on the squatters' supposed monopoly over the public lands, and argued that the pastoralists had good reason to complain about the incompetence of their opponents 'whose knowledge of land and ideal of a country has been formed in the culture of a cabbage garden or flower pot of a city suburb'.[1] Twenty years earlier, Mitchell's great exploration resulted in a confident proclamation of a veritable *Australia Felix* in what was shortly to become the vast sheep-walk of the Port Phillip District, later Victoria. And naturally, since the published report appeared a few years after the expedition, it was laced with cautions as well as promises.

> This territory, still for the most part in a state of nature, presents a fair blank sheet, for any geographical arrangement, whether of county divisions—lines of communication—or sites of towns etc. etc. The growth of a colony there might be trained according to one general system, with a view to various combinations of soil and climate, and not left to chance, as in old countries—or, which would perhaps be worse, to the partial or narrow views of the first settlers.[2]

So my liberty-taking is intended to signal an attempt to sketch out the efforts of an immigrant culture—materialistic, innovative and derivative, pretentious, frequently confused—to write its own enduring signature across the Victorian landscape. There is no point in saying at once that it has failed to do so, or that a poor appreciation of the environments of our own state is part of a continuing identity crisis, and so on. The story is too complex, too relevant, for such lightning dismissals. For there has truly been an abundance of effort, which is our inheritance, and it is immaterial that in so many cases the striving produced only an ephemeral and marginally legible graffito. The inescapable demands of modern citizenship require a large improvement in the current low levels of literacy where Australian environmental history is concerned, and for Victoria it is high time we intensified our endeavours to decipher and communicate what must always be a living document, a document for living. Accordingly, the present focus on environment *and* planning emphasises significant social-ecological transactions and relationships. The story is certainly no more than indicative, but it cannot be premature.

1834–80: Frontiers and domestications

Beneath the flummery, 1834, 1835 and 1836 remain only dates, mainly symbolising our Eurocentric concerns and limited understanding of prominent themes in the analysis of environmental change. Over the past few decades archaeologists, biogeographers, geomorphologists and others have shown that neither the mysterious whaling and sealing era, nor the succeeding squatting occupation which brought rather more widespread ecological disruptions, worked on a 'fair blank sheet'. The earliest anthropological accounts were necessarily imperfect records of communities which were already transformed, but in contrast, reconstructions based on the physical evidence point unequivocally to profound and extensive ecological changes over thousands of years. The use of fire, discriminating gathering, hunting and trapping which may deserve the title 'farming', and a greater concentration of population and durable settlements than was previously thought possible, are now known to have contributed massively to the highly successful adaptations characteristic of Aboriginal cultures. Above all, the great savannahs and grasslands which were so admired by Thomas Mitchell and his contemporaries—'A land so inviting, and still without inhabitants!'[3]—were to some extent not 'natural' but *anthropogenic*. Furthermore, it is quite appropriate to describe the Aboriginals' exploitation of their own community territories not only as the reflection of a deeply spiritual identification with each region and its constituent places but also as the product of a hard-won approach to resource evaluation and environmental management. Constituent elements of that approach included some emphasis on thrift and on traditional decision-making procedures for resource use, together with social rituals and taboos based on or related to the appraisal and use of the environment. The result for Victoria was a system of community-based regions, the Aboriginal territorial areas, within each of which a sophisticated style of planning has evolved as an integral part of local ways of living: at once comprehensive and comprehensible, its sources of authority and experience were autonomous and local, not superimpositions from a remote and centralised bureaucracy. That is another small extravagance, admittedly, and by definition it cannot be extended to claim an indigenous structure of decentralisation or devolution. Instead, for our present convenience it might be concluded that degrees of sovereign control and community assent, involvement and responsibility are implied, and that other common threads are the identification with place and a preference for comparatively low levels of exploitation, maintaining a dynamic equilibrium with nature.

Nor is it strictly true to say that the white invaders actually believed they were working with a 'fair blank sheet': for example, the frequently violent dispossession of the Aboriginal inhabitants was scarcely the result of unconscious efforts. Furthermore, the interruption in continuity suggested by the term is not entirely acceptable. Firstly, although pioneer pastoralists completed an astonishingly rapid occupation of an area almost as large as England in the fifteen years or so before 1850, in the early phases especially that occupation was patchy, even tentative, and remained so in more remote and difficult localities. Accordingly, there was an overlap with the indigenous management system, a social and ecological transition which still warrants close investigation. Secondly, the squatting mode of settlement was characterised at the outset by autonomous decision-making frameworks over vast areas; in a sense, within the confines of an extensive territory centred on their home base, station managers replaced the local Aboriginals as the guardians of significant environmental knowledge. That does not say that there was any transfer of the mantle previously described; as a rule, Aboriginal expertise was not sufficiently consulted, though there must have been exceptions. The introduction of capitalism constituted the real break, but the early administrators could not ignore the local and regional evaluations developed by the squatters' insistence on careful reconnaissance and empirical testing.

It will always be a good deal easier to describe Aboriginal environmental management in general terms than to display accurately, and in orthodox graphical terms, the regional contexts within which that traditional management was conducted. We know rather more about the employment of expedient regionalisations during the early colonial administrations. Armchair geography in Britain and Australia was obviously influential. It resulted in crude definitions of Settled, Intermediate and Unsettled Districts, which reflected a confidence in the imposition of government control over the style, pace and direction of settlement, and borrowed from wider imperial experience in (for example) Ireland and North America. Beyond the coastal districts favoured by the authorities for planting the nuclei of intensive settlement—that is, the bases for a progressive advance, an orderly penetration hinting at a safe return on investment—the administrative frame also served to monitor the results of a vigorously independent squatting occupation. So we now call the old squatting district of Portland Bay the 'Western District'; Gippsland more or less retains its original pastoral boundaries, as does the North East (originally the Murray district), but the Wimmera squatting district included today's Mallee as well. As I have argued elsewhere, the resemblance to today's vernacular and administrative regions is not accidental: mobile and opportunistic commercial livestock enterprises had sketched out a simple anatomy of environmental differentiation in quick time, and the squatting mode of occupation yielded not only a durable regionalisation but also a host of closely textured local appraisals developed by trial and error, and offering quantifiable but comprehensible measures.[4] Unfortunately, carrying capacities for livestock could not be readily translated to deliver an efficient guide for the kinds of small-scale 'yeoman' farming envisaged by Victoria's land reformers. There is no doubt, however, that they provided one of several inputs to locational decisions incorporated in the important land legislation of the 1860s.

Most of these observations require more elaboration than space permits. Briefly, the squatting example illustrates very well that each of the principal modes of European settlement contains a wide range of contributions to our environmental heritage—positive and negative offerings, both tangible and intangible—and I have dwelt on some more positive aspects. The rapid introduction of millions of cloven-footed animals to Australia is often cited as a triggering agent in accelerating soil erosion, but that says very little about the mismatch between opportunistic, trial-and-error stocking densities and the inscrutable synchronisations in the natural world. Similarly, the diffusion of European grasses, accelerated of course when the pastoralists obtained a stronger hold over much of their land in and after the 1850s, need not be separated from the effects of the selective grazing of natural pastures. Deliberate and accidental introductions of innumerable pests and weeds were probably inescapable accompaniments to the nineteenth-century elaboration of Europe overseas, notably in its New World variants, and the squatters' inspirations in acclimatisation were surely more practical in the longer-term than those of sentimental suburbanites—rabbits, deer and foxes notwithstanding. And again, in a pioneering period largely characterised by markedly insecure tenures, forest clearing activities were more often than not deemed expensive indulgences, while the unavoidable improvement of fodder and water supplies must have done something to balance an otherwise relentless attack on native wildlife.

Conservationists find it peculiarly difficult to strike a balance where the 'robber economy' of Australian mining is concerned, and will not establish a respected intellectual base in our emerging modern culture until they address such contentious themes in their multifaceted historical, geographical, and other contexts. Victoria's goldminers cast as long a shadow in our environmental history as they do in our social and political affairs, but until recently the scholarly preference inclined towards the latter.

The environmental destruction wrought by our celebrated miners was awesome. So many of the goldfields were situated in wooded hills, valleys and ranges where fine mutual adjustments of slopes, drainage and vegetation cover seldom survived the ravages of axes, fire and all the aggressive paraphernalia associated with hydraulic sluicing. The wilderness succumbed to the locusts: 'Every tree is felled', wrote William Howitt, 'every feature of Nature is annihilated',[5] and we are hard pressed to find any redeeming features. Is it stretching a point to suggest that one may be found in the reaction to these onslaughts, at the time and later? One of the most unfortunate characteristics of environmental management in the latter half of the nineteenth century was that great and small mining interests were permitted so much control over Victoria's forest and water supplies before the economic and ecological significance of those resources was understood. Mining condoned reckless, exploitative attitudes but—stretching the conservationist line—the industry made lasting enemies, not only among Victoria's early foresters and environmental scientists. Can we retrieve anything of more immediate value from the wreckage? I think so. Water rights were critical on every mining field and official moves towards a democratisation of water management produced moderately enterprising experiments in decentralised control; there was also an emphasis on the public ownership of Victorian water resources which was elaborated later in innovative legislation for irrigation settlement, ultimately fuelling many a debate on the demand for recreation space in the twentieth century.

The bulk of the miners poured into our remote periphery from the Empire's urbanising, industrialising, cabbage-garden hearth, and they mightily influenced the land legislation which occupied Victorians in most walks of life for more than 30 years. For the first Selection Acts the declared sequence of settlement was partly determined on the basis of popular and official appraisals conducted during the squatting era. In ambitious support, an intricate survey hierarchy had been prepared (suggesting a severely rational intensification of land use and settlement), the hierarchy ranging from 'counties', the largest units, through 'parishes', 'sections', and within the latter, allotments. But the survey plans were mostly paper tigers and thousands of pioneer farmers seemed condemned to become gamblers by act of parliament. Hatched by urban radicals gorged on a diet of romantic agrarian idealism, the Selection Acts were certainly badly flawed on environmental and economic grounds, and all the windy rhetoric about 'yeomen farmers' and 'little Englands in Australia' probably merited the contemptuous criticism doled out by experienced settlers. Overriding political interests and the pressing needs of an infant treasury did nothing to ease the burden of successive mazes of rules and regulations, and the pioneer communities were not directly involved in the planning process until the late 1870s.

Casual designations of 'failure rates' and the like still appearing in the 'land settlement' literature should be instantly discarded. More reliable local and regional reconstructions question such loose terminology and identify critical processes of geographical and social mobility which were profoundly influential in management decisions. For instance, adjacent farms in the Western District, initially alike in all respects except one—the main occupant's perceived position in a kind of mental map of a locational/career decision path involving buying, selling, renting, staying on, moving on, moving out of farming—mây have been managed in entirely different ways. One farm, let us say, is managed for short-term goals since the new frontier of the Wimmera is beckoning; the other is itself a destination, not a staging post. In this hypothetical situation conservative and exploitative land uses may be closely juxtaposed, an exceedingly common occurrence in pioneer settings where more orthodox explanations are unsatisfactory.

Management decisions in situations overloaded with uncertainties levied social and environmental penalties which still resound. Parsimonious government investments in agricultural research, credit facilities, marketing, transportation and technical education did nothing to assist those struggling pioneer families who, like so many of the squatters before them, mainly survived by learning from their own mistakes. Perhaps the worst of the resulting injuries were truly 'ecological' in the deepest meaning of that term, which must include the formation of those values, attitudes and associated behaviours which provide a very fulcrum for *relationships* between rural people and the land, primary producers and an increasingly centralised bureaucracy, country and city communities. The kinds of local and regional mobility already described were familiar coping strategies on New World frontiers during the nineteenth century, but the hallowed family farm was itself an extraordinarily robust institution in Australia and New Zealand, where it was inextricably linked with several variants of state socialism. Thus an ancient land and an immigrant people had become irrevocably locked in stressful co-authorship. Instinctively, without pausing to examine the complex tale, most of us are content to empathise with the pioneer families, while modern conservationists prefer to note the passing of a land ethic which had ruled for a thousand generations.

In the 1880s extensions of a kind of welfare state idealism throughout eastern Australia offered larger and more secure 'home maintenance areas' and 'living areas', but similar relaxations, notably those applied to restrictions on maximum sizes, had already been introduced in Victoria. So much of it was laudable, and overdue. But it also represented narrow concepts of productivity and dominating economic views of 'property', 'standards of living'—in short, a final confirmation that a dangerous anthropocentric perspective had supplanted the Aboriginal ethos. It was seldom conjectured that neither individualised management nor even the most talented of hardworking family groups might be found too small to guarantee in themselves an adequate ecological stewardship over the large areas which came to characterise Victoria's new farming landscapes.

We say we are now more prepared to admit our inescapable roles as ecological agents, yet we remain reluctant to analyse more than a miniscule fraction of the labyrinthine web of interactive contexts which provide the foundations for decision. Since most of those foundations were built in the past, there is an urgent practical need for geographical–historical research. Thus far, too many of the roads we have taken converge, again and again, in self-delusion.

1880–1939: Urban progressives and the genesis of planning

Abbreviations easily mislead and of course, 1880 signifies little more than present convenience, the beginning of the second of our nominated sections. During the 60 years before the outbreak of World War II, the Victorian population was increasingly concentrated in Melbourne and the main provincial centres; by 1891 over four in ten were accommodated, often badly, in the capital alone, and this metropolitan proportion rose to about 55 per cent by the early 1930s. Melburnians dominated the discussions on 'wise use' conservation and its relationship with alternative development programmes, and the local debates became more sophisticated, far better informed about international trends. Yet it is important to remember that the exploitative mode of the earlier period had also had its critics, upon whose work important later challenges were built. My condensed account omits those senior public servants who are seldom dealt a hand in our orthodox histories. Mention may be made only of two broadly representative individuals.

Ignored by modern scholars, Clement Hodgkinson (1818-93) was patently the Lands Department supremo for over a generation. While scores of mere politicians came and went, Hodgkinson planted deep roots and stamped his own indelible mark on land reservation policy. With insufficient recognition, Hodgkinson laboured long and hard in the absence of effective guidelines from his parliamentary paymasters and the result, as Wright has recently shown, was a host of large and small reservations in rural and urban areas.[6] His work provided Victoria's first classified dossier of public reserves in an age which was otherwise preoccupied with more exploitative land uses: with all its faults, it was an impressive piece of landscape authorship, a text for later scrutiny. His famous contemporary, the Government Botanist Ferdinand von Mueller (1825-96) is still cast too flippantly in the role of an irascibly eccentric or egocentric, very foreign bachelor, but he was more complex and far more significant than has been allowed. Mueller's advocacy of improved forestry practice showed the early Australian impact of Marsh's seminal book, *Man and Nature* (which first appeared in 1864) and cautioned his fellow colonists to heed the important work of the Empire's foresters in India, South Africa and elsewhere. With Brough Smyth, Hodgkinson and a few other leading public servants, Mueller pressed hard for a more generous experimentation with 'novel industries' in rural Victoria. Their recommendations included exotic forest plantations and an improved management of the official State forests, and the introduction of vines, olives, dried fruits, silk, tobacco, opium, perfumes and dyes. Their report was handed down in 1871. Its connection with this later section is signalled in its 'improving' zeal, a concern for 'efficient' resource management and a moralistic tone—the intensive work demanded by the new crops would be 'highly beneficial in training the young of both sexes in the habits of frugality and care, which so essentially mark the rural population of those countries where such industries exist', and in some cases might be well suited to the 'destitute or orphan boys or girls who are maintained at the expense of the State'.[7]

In the 'eighties enthusiasms generated by irrigation and refrigeration, combined with technical advances in the dairy industries and in cereal production, were interwoven with a renewed debate on the principles and practice of land disposal and land management. Two great

64 Victoria's Heritage

Melbourne exhibitions (in 1880 and 1888) proudly announced the projection of Australia onto the global stage, but for some individuals they must have served the additional purpose of underlining the timidities of parochial thinking. Certainly the search was on for useful international exemplars, whether by established 'cultural cringe' approaches to imported experts or by rather more dignified but still unsatisfactory study tours of favoured overseas regions. The first fruits were brought on more quickly by the droughts and rabbit plagues which were particularly devastating in the semi-arid Mallee country— the official establishment of irrigation colonies and a heightened interest in the correction of old errors by the 'closer settlement' of repurchased estates; substantial reforms in land tenure systems; a precocious introduction of fairly detailed cartographical inventories for the classification of the remaining public lands, which anticipated more celebrated measures taken in the United States by over twenty years; a rejection, albeit temporary, of the monopoly previously exercised by the freehold ideal over the hearts and minds of older radicals.

Leasehold tenures had the virtue of providing opportunities for government intervention and were therefore critical ingredients in the development of a seed-bed for modern planning. Put differently, it was understood that they might be used to assert the wider community's right to ensure appropriate economic and environmental management in the marginal country still available for settlement. In 1883 and 1884 discussions leading to innovative legislation produced distinct regulations governing extensive pastoral and mixed farming enterprises, mining, the setting aside of over 600 000 hectares (1.5 million acres) in State forests and timber, water and other reserves, the introduction of Crown land auctions to defray the costs of railway construction, and the reclamation of Kooweerup and other wetlands. Reflecting this new administration, the official design for Mallee settlement merits brief attention. Although it was quickly broken down by popular opinion and bureaucratic confusion, the original spatial model is nonetheless intriguing since it resembles one of those focussing 'schemata' which occur so frequently in the artwork of twentieth-century planners. As I tried to show in *The Public Lands of Australia Felix* (1970), the plan acknowledged the existence of a major region with special needs and challenges, and provided for an intra-regional separation of 'fringe' and 'interior' styles of subdivision. The large interior 'blocks' mainly differed from the fringe 'allotments' in the maximum sizes allowed— from 155 to 1300 square kilometres (60 to 500+ square miles) and their repetitive subdivision into alternate 5- and 20-year leaseholds. This hazard-prone region—larger than either Denmark or Switzerland, and twice as large as Wales, we should be reminded—had fully extended two generations of pioneers. Yet we see again a nagging preoccupation with crudely engineered forms of landscape domestication: essentially, despite its useful punctuation for our historical review, the model remains another product of heroic drafting. It is, however, directly relevant to today's environmental concerns in the incorporation of water frontage controls over the subdivisional arrangement, and in its allocation of the largest blocks to inferior farming country in the central-west—that is, the 'Big Desert' and 'Little Desert' areas.

The display of 'progressive' notions of efficiency and technocratic expertise in country Victoria was stronger still in redoubled efforts to promote 'closer settlement'. Gradually, systematic approaches were developed to evaluate and subdivide repurchased estates in Gippsland and in western, central and north-eastern Victoria, and improvements in dairy farming gave an added impetus to the settlement of Crown land in these regions, especially in the Otways, the South Gippsland hills and other wooded districts enjoying moderately reliable rainfall. Some of these initiatives were hasty and opportunistic. They were scarcely good advertisements for national planning, but our criticism should also weigh three qualifying features, or handicaps: popular and political demands resulting from the 1890s depression; nationalistic–imperialistic confidence in increased rural production in the early twentieth century; and a broad preference for a style of intensive farming dependent upon hitherto unfamiliar woodland systems. In the worst instances, rapid clearing activities destroyed pristine habitats for some commensurate returns in human misery, as another appalling tally of bankruptcies, forfeitures and abandonments was compiled. An ill-conceived process stranded its victims in remote areas without essaying a supporting infrastructure, not even in the form of elementary means of access. And the bush fell victim too when virgin hills, stripped bare of their protection, rapidly succumbed—settlers were trapped in quagmires, and the water courses were choked with the very soil that was to sustain the new social system.[8]

The contrast with the planned irrigation settlements of this period is irresistible. Their neat chequerboards were declared the very apogee of a progressive engineering investment in landscape change and social improvement. Much of the credit—sometimes too much—goes to America's Elwood Mead, a gifted civil engineer and professor of rural institutions who directed Victoria's State Rivers and Water Supply Commission (SRWSC) from 1907 until 1915. Mead (1858–1936) was already an international expert on water management before he accepted his Victorian appointment; he was then particularly well known at the highest political and public service levels in the United States, and there is good reason to suggest that the rapid expansion of Victoria's irrigation economy reflected his driving personality and the force of his social vision.[9]

Mead convinced his new employers that government-funded irrigation schemes could never be justified as a side-line on large holdings. An insistence on small-scale settlement would ensure more and better use of water so expensively supplied, and the levying of a compulsory charge for water rights on every holding according to its size would persuade farmers in specified irrigation districts to take proper advantage of the resource, or make way for others who were prepared to do so. These and similar measures were incorporated into new regulations issued under the Water Act of 1909, by which landowners in irrigated areas were required to pay for the water allotted to them whether or not they chose to use it. The clear message was a desire to bring the irrigation projects into a more inclusive closer settlement programme and, under Mead's direction, the SRWSC became highly skilled in promoting, designing and administering new and established irrigation settlements along the Murray and in several other parts of the state. As it transpired, it was one of those situations where there was at once too little and too much.

For example, Mead was sufficiently experienced to stress the importance of extension services in pioneer settlement, yet Victorian progress in those areas continued to be comparatively slow by North American standards. Marketing and transportation problems were addressed, but continued to pose large problems. On the other hand, the costly promotional efforts attracted many new settlers and the high priority given to engineering approaches seems in hindsight circular, perhaps a self-fulfilling prophecy. A righteous celebration of small-scale settlement, preferably of horticultural scale, hid the need for continuous and detailed economic-agronomic surveys; far too much water was applied to the land, far too little was done to improve local drainage, and in consequence existing difficulties with salting took on new dimensions. In recent years this old feature of 'desertification' has been identified as a multi-million dollar issue affecting vast areas of Australia's semi-arid plains. And the best known reaction from the engineers has been to suggest further heroic surgery for our threatened landscapes.

Neither Mead nor his colleagues should be charged with laying an early foundation for these social and environmental problems. Apart from any other consideration, the SRWSC inherited a run-down system and was obliged to make it pay its way. And in this case it is neither fair nor reasonable to emphasise a contemporary mental set favouring single-discipline approaches to complex interactions in the human and physical environments: it has already been said that the Commission's operations were comparatively broadly based. Certainly there was a cool paternalism in Mead's progressivism which may have produced a few hard decisions during the routine management of the various 'closer settlement' estates in his portfolio, and that was oddly characteristic of high-flying progressives. Again, the apparent neglect of historical analyses of the geohydrological features of Victoria's riverine plains was then common throughout Australia's irrigation regions. It may indeed reflect some under-utilisation of a geological profession which had performed sterling service in the mining industry and in the description of artesian water resources, yet once more I suspect that is a hasty observation. How often must we agree that more information is required? Scholarly histories of the SRWSC and other major instrumentalities were recommended several years ago in the confused approach to our sesqui-centennial and bicentennial celebrations, but I think that idea, like so many others, must have fallen on barren ground. If we can ever persuade Australia's geographers and historians to pull together for a change they will find a good and useful story in the early involvement of the Commission. The identification of ancient (or 'prior') streams which belonged to hydrological regimes entirely different from those of today has been shown to be a powerful tool in explaining the local mosaics of soils, topography and drainage characteristics which govern the intricate texture of irrigation farming. The recognition of those features was not particularly influential until after World War II, yet it would be extraordinary if we found no evidence of vernacular or official knowledge in earlier years. Mead's reportedly zealous insistence on intensification from the time of his arrival is also worth pursuing. It is interesting to note that he viewed the extensive or partial irrigation systems far more favourably in later years, in New South Wales and California.[10]

Closer settlement on dry and irrigated estates and individual new farms was increasingly aided in this period, without doubt, by transportation improvements, government-sponsored agricultural research and valuable extension services, yet the social underpinning of pioneer settlement—or of any other form of rural living—was badly neglected. 'More and smaller is better' still described the unquestioned ideal, and insofar as that became a consuming passion, the back-patting description of rational modes of rural planning was embarrassingly overdone. Furthermore, the authorities probably achieved more success in improving their own low standards of bookkeeping than they did in advancing the cause of applied social and environmental syntheses. In this context the distressing example of Victoria's 12 000 soldier settlers may be cited as a test of the government's capacity for rational management policies. Land—what else?—seemed the obvious answer, both sentimental and reasonable, to the problem of how to repay the 'debt of honour' and, under relentless popular pressure, the government ceded most of its control over the location of settlement opportunities. Saddled with huge mortgages set in buoyant times, and faced with declining prices for rural produce and allotments which were in many cases far too small to cushion the blows of changing circumstance, yesterday's heroes fell at last on home ground. And the pity of it is that the stunt was botched again—in the worst instances, embittered veterans remained to divide those same communities which had sent them off in pride and had shed tears at the prospect of guaranteeing local rewards for home-bred sons. Canada's bureaucracy was often accused of an overbearing paternalism in its handling of the settlement of returned soldiers on the prairies, but the Canadian authorities worked a good deal harder than their Australian counterparts on the social aspects of pioneering.[11] On the evidence compiled thus far, there was too little imagination, let alone compassion, in the Australian schemes: precious little allowance was made, for example, for the fact that the collective war experiences of those soldier settlers who were condemned as 'failures' were probably reasonably representative of the full profile of the AIF's disastrous imperial prostitution. The psychological dimension was never grasped. It was planning without people, again.

The ambiguous display of 'progressive' notions of efficiency and technocratic expertise in country Victoria was repeated in the efforts made to monitor and direct the expansion of Melbourne, and if it was difficult enough to influence the management of sparsely populated regions by doodling with simplistic lattices at an office drawing-board, then it was impossible to expect any such schemata to pin down a highly mobile metropolitan population of a little over a quarter of a million souls in 1881, with almost double that total at the end of the decade. Nevertheless, towards the end of the 1880s Melbourne's wider urban area became the focus of ambitious attention as a planning region, only a few years after the plans for the Mallee were launched. It was not exactly a novel departure, since early theorists had recognised the importance of more comprehensive, interventionist approaches to urbanisation in their rudimentary designs, but the new move was accompanied by the creation of a single powerful authority for the metropolitan area—another confirmation of the bureaucratic ascendancy in Victoria's affairs.

From its inception in 1890 the Melbourne and Metropolitan Board of Works was a controversial instrumentality, one of several shaky compromises made in Australia's capital cities between the 'unification' and 'federation' approaches to metropolitan government. An excessive fragmentation too often pitted the Board's municipal representatives against each other and set them in competition with central government agencies. Yet the MMBW's power continued to grow: was it in spite of, or a result of, the prevailing chaos?

Judged only on a commonsense appreciation of the natural unity of hydrological systems, the Board's disarmingly naive charter contained the promise of prodigious growth. It was simply required to administer water supply and sewerage for the metropolis and for that purpose its control over the Yarra and other public waterways in the urban area was restricted to commercial and recreational uses. In practice, the extensive construction of reservoirs and sewerage outlets meant that the wide reach of its operations embraced mountain catchments and bayside beaches. Within the intermediate built-up area the disruption of natural drainage caused by housing, industry and paved roadways gradually increased the problems of urban flooding and water pollution; local councils were unwilling or unable to correct a deterioration which any piecemeal action might, in any event, seriously aggravate. Accordingly, in 1923, the Board's urban functions were augmented to include drainage and therefore flood control. With its unusually broad geographical base, an accumulation of expertise in administration, engineering, legal and financial matters, and a cross-sectional executive representation drawn from several political and bureaucratic levels, the MMBW was destined to become an unrivalled institutional force in the changing landscape of Melbourne.

We have strayed too far from individuals and groups, and the critique of mechanistic emphases understates definite gains in various areas of reform. Social conditions fired the thinking of most progressives and, although there was some lack of coordination in the fields of environment and planning discussed thus far, in Melbourne the reformers contested energetically the specific issues of public health, education, and housing. The opthalmologist James William Barrett (1862–1945), whose name is so closely associated with these campaigns and with the continuing development of Melbourne University, now provides an obvious example. Students of wildlife conservation know that most of the period I have reviewed was essentially barren—wildlife remained 'game'—but they will remember Barrett's own committed writings in natural history, and the historic essays he edited in 1926 — *Save Australia: a plea for the right use of our flora and fauna*. (In these areas his contribution was not eclipsed until the appointment of the late Jock Marshall as Foundation Professor of Zoology at Monash University in the early 1960s.) The following brief account of a selection of Barrett's activities attempts to locate them in a wider context which also engaged the attentions of lesser-known Melburnians.

Michael Roe has shown how Barrett's Rooseveltian faith in nature's 'vitalist' inspiration outshone that of most of Victoria's progressives in its enthusiasm for Australian variants of the country life movement.[12] In the early inter-war periods Barrett's volumes of collected essays, *Twin Ideals*, showed expansive nationalistic interests overflowing into agrarian idealism, decentralisation and a passion for cultivating new organisational forms to produce a better 'rural civilisation'. In the latter regard, contemporary North American and Irish movements achieved far more but their Australian impact was obvious, and lasting. For our purposes, however, Barrett's specific involvement in conservation and town planning is very significant.

Barrett was an ardent promoter of outdoor recreation, and his long association with the great progressive educationist Frank Tate helped to ensure the place of nature studies and the celebration of Arbor Day and Bird Day in Victoria's schools. Outdoor pursuits were coming into vogue in an increasingly leisured and better educated metropolitan society, and even before the turn of the century the wider Port Phillip region was regularly scoured by earnest naturalists. Improvements in

70 Victoria's Heritage

Figure 4.1 Excursion venues, Field Naturalists' Club of Victoria, 1884–1916

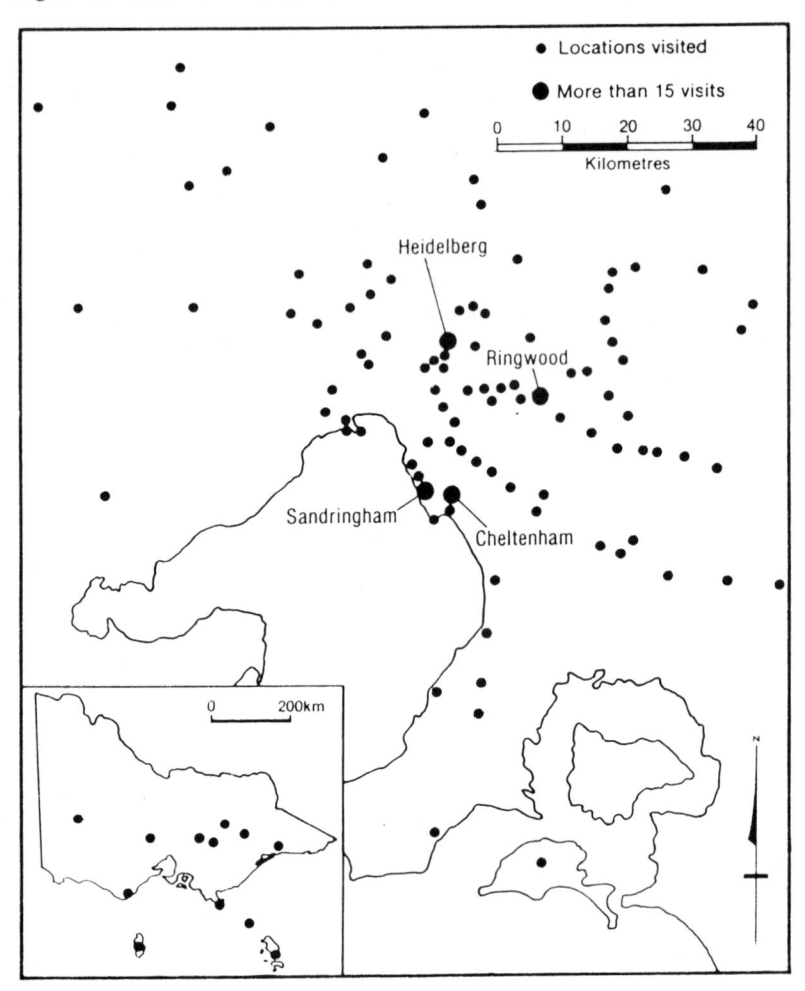

Source: Bardwell, *National Parks in Victoria*, 1866–1956.

public transport and rural roads, together with the cult of the bicycle and later of the automobile, extended the range of naturalists and other less specialised recreationists into most parts of Victoria. Barrett was a leading participant in these developments. As Secretary of the Victorian National Park Association he played a major role in the protection of Wilson's Promontory, which was fast becoming a favourite haunt of migratory suburbanites (see Figure 4.1). The reserve was created in 1898 and was gradually extended, often as the result of well organised public pressure, in 1905, 1908, 1909, 1918 and 1928—by which time it occupied an accumulated area of over 49 000 hectares (122 000 acres), then roughly half of the state's national park reservations.

But Barrett's was a late contribution to the parkland saga: Baron von Mueller had made several appeals for such reserves over the previous half-century, and Walter Baldwin Spencer (1860-1929), the distinguished Professor of Biology at the University of Melbourne from 1887 to 1919, brought the Field Naturalists' Club of Victoria, the Royal Society of Victoria and his own considerable reputation into the infant park movement some years before Barrett's entry. It may appear that Spencer was rather more inclined to an élitist view, preferring the reservation of large areas as wildlife sanctuaries, but the appalling carnage had been accompanied everywhere by a rapid destruction of habitat. In a different sphere Edmund Fitzgibbon (1825-1905), Melbourne's Town Clerk from 1856 to 1891 and the first Chairman of the MMBW, fought long and hard for the protection and better management of municipal parks and gardens for the entire populace, and was sometimes equally prominent in the early battles over Wilson's Promontory.[13]

Building on these pioneering efforts, Barrett's visibility in the movement noticeably increased after his return from an overseas tour in 1912. His experience of the work of Britain's Garden City advocates encouraged him to press for thoroughly modern town planning legislation, and this quickly led to the founding of the Town Planning and Parks Association on 27 October 1914, with Barrett as President. A small success was recorded in 1922 with the establishment of the Metropolitan Town Planning Commission, but its report was handed down in 1929, just in time to be shelved for the duration of the depression. Furthermore, although the Commission analysed slum reclamation, traffic congestion, improved zoning and civic design principles, the provision of open space and the preservation of historic buildings, there was also a disappointing preoccupation with the protection of property values and a naive assumption that it would be enough simply to ask (not *direct*) local councils to prepare their own plans for the consideration of a central authority. All of that was in keeping with the Barrett strain of progressivism—the State was invoked but positive (we might say 'big') government was reviled: reformers provided the pivot and elected authorities should be limited to ancillary, manipulative actions.[14]

As Roe has indicated very well, these many-sided contributions were unified, resolved, in the man's vitalist philosophy. And therefore Barrett saw, of course, a continuum between the old country life movement and what came to be called 'town and country planning' for 'complete' living: it was not yet a matter of cold technology. When he retired officially from the University's medical school in 1937 his active community interests placed him on 28 committees, but for all his gifts and social eminence he had effected few tangible changes in the Melbourne landscape. In practical terms, he did see the emergence of a more coherent body of professional town planners and his original proposal for a Garden City at Fisherman's Bend, made in 1913 before the Joint Select Committee upon the Housing of the People of the Metropolis, eventually won grudging approval. Part of the trouble was that his progressive beliefs extended in representative fashion to a disdain for orthodox political allegiances, therefore guaranteeing him minimum political influence; some of it was due to wartime interruptions and the claims made by the 1930s depression, some to what might be described as an intense individualism, very widely deployed over several fields of inquiry.

Fisherman's Bend, officially opened in 1927, is more properly described as a Garden Suburb, and even then the title is generous. Freestone accurately describes it as little more than a conservative facsimile of a British council estate, a mere showpiece which was devoid of shops or well-treed expanses for years, and was denied the saving grace of accessible opportunities for the 'deserving poor'.[15] Planning was still in its infancy, still struggling for acceptance. The profession only began to hit its straps over the next two decades, and so the depressed 1930s offered little prospect of any debate on the need to democratise a process which was manifestly inchoate. For city and country Victoria alike, we can merely point to marginal gains in environmental and planning sophistication, ending in an unwanted respite from full-bored exploitation. And in social terms the planning trajectory, such as it was, continued to follow a downward stroke.

1940–84: Regionalism and environmentalism

It is not difficult to show that Victoria's administrators have tinkered with regional structures with varying degrees of success since the beginning of European settlement in the State. The comforting promise of such elementary order was hard to resist in confusing and rapidly changing situations, yet we have seen that these designs were not only expedient refuges for harassed bureaucrats. However simplified and imperfect, they were certainly relevant to community affairs and frequently subsumed important popular appraisals. The regional concept was given further intellectual respectability during the establishment and elaboration of professional planning: for example, in the inter-war years it was assisted by the contributions of progressive education to an extension of planning interests beyond the narrow limits of architecture and engineering, into cognate fields of tertiary study such as geography, economics and sociology. And, during this final period in our historical review, the commencement of a war in which Australians actually found their own country under attack and threatened by invasion added new urgency to an approach which had been revived in various guises during the depression.

The Australian States maintained their constitutional powers to legislate for control over land uses, and although much of the impetus for radical change came from the increasingly intrusive federal sphere, some of the foundations were already laid. Throughout Australia considerable interest had been aroused by the ecological and social catastrophe on the Great Plains of the USA, and by the resulting 'comprehensive' planning schemes of the renowned Tennessee Valley Authority. Though they were far less dramatic, dust-bowl conditions were not unfamiliar visitations in Victoria, where over-clearing and bare fallowing had produced serious soil erosion in and beyond the hazardous north-west: in North America the dust bowl has been cited as an undeniable proof of the ecological insensitivities of a capitalistic culture, but our own mixed economy fared little better. A Soil Conservation Board was established in 1940 to initiate and coordinate inter-departmental measures, and in 1949 it was replaced by a separate organisation, the Soil Conservation Authority. Plainly this was not another case of *ad hoc* institutional growth, but the kinds of regional structuring favoured by this and other government agencies, new and old, were not quite the powerful planning tools envisaged at the national level. Following the lead of New South Wales Premier W. J. McKell and his colleagues in 1941, Prime Minister John Curtin convened a conference of Commonwealth and State ministers in October 1944, and this launched the first grand Australia-wide strategy of regional planning.

The regional method was particularly well supported federally by Ben Chifley—later Prime Minister, but then Minister for Post-War Reconstruction—and by 'Nugget' (H. C.) Coombs, who directed that Department until 1949. Contemporary statements and to some extent the resulting structures themselves still smack of military-style 'preparedness', with notions of decentralised deployment and hints about the need for local self-sufficiency and increased self-reliance. At times the early emphasis on the production of intricate physical, social and economic surveys appeared to be seeking intelligence which was no less appropriate to guerilla warfare than to an acceleration of peaceful development. Even today, such observations are not fanciful: there is no doubting the protean nature of regionalism. But in wartime Australia it was strongly charged with democratic sentiment, as had been shown in previous decades in 'new States' and secessionist movements, the Murray Valley Development League, and so on. Forty years on Coombs wrote that this had been perceived as a watershed for modern planning in Australia; it seemed to promise a rational form of sustained development based on sound ecological and social strategies, drawing deeply on public participation.

74 *Victoria's Heritage*

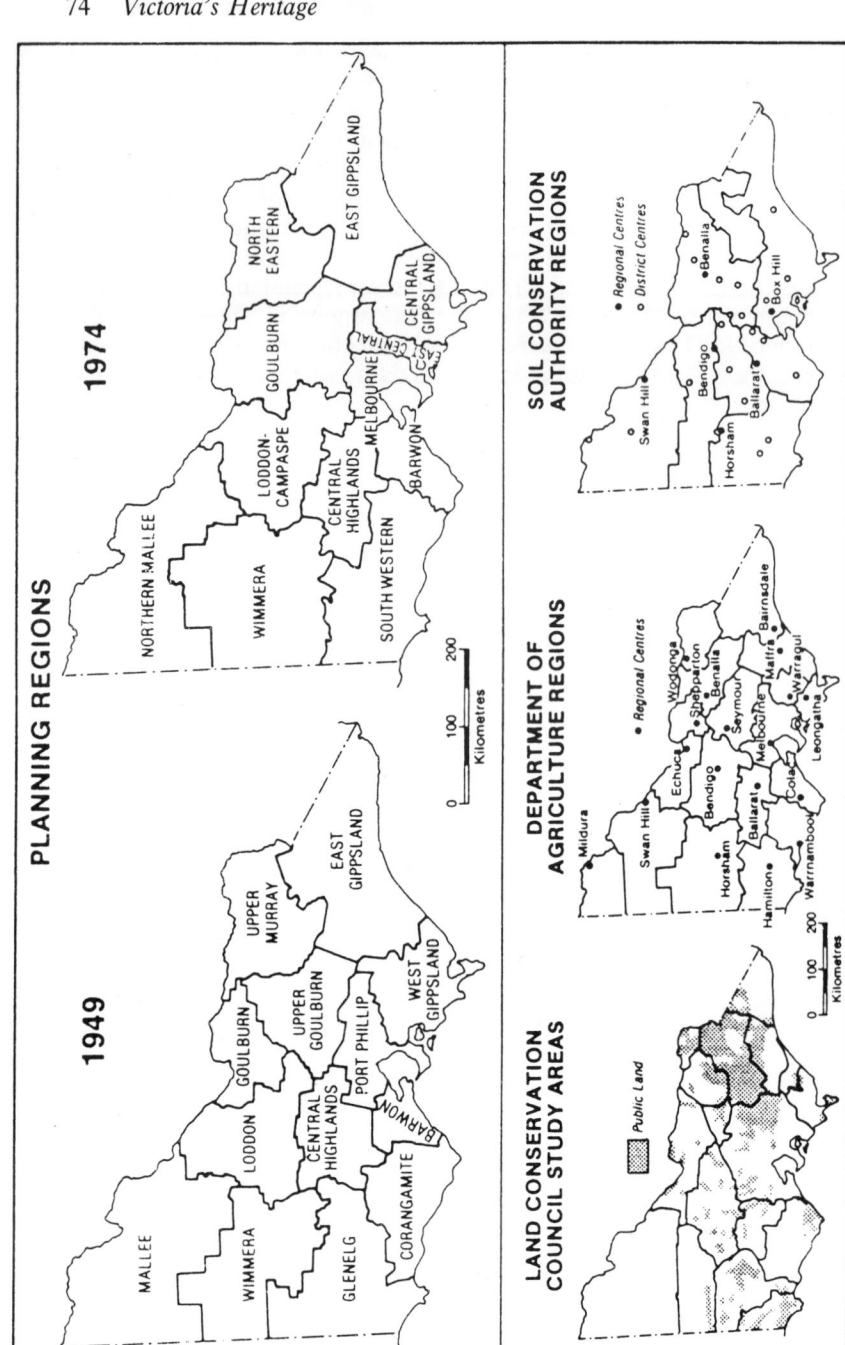

Figure 4.2 Selected regional planning structures

Source: J. S. Duncan (ed.), *Atlas of Victoria*, Government Printer, Melbourne: 1982, pp. 196–98, and official maps.

It is difficult in retrospect to recapture the intellectual excitement which these ideas generated. Many believed that they provided the means by which the potential of modern technology could be placed at the disposal of communities —not as a framework constraining and determining their lifestyles but as a force capable of liberating their imagination and giving scope to their creative energies.[16]

Progressivism again, and slightly coloured by hindsight. The federal Labor government had used the threat of withholding housing funds to argue that the free-wheeling market system had fostered land uses which favoured profit-making by the wealthy minority, and insisted that the States introduce planning laws to rectify the situation. While town planning, if that be the term for it, remained the province of State legislatures, regional planning became the joint responsibility of Federal and State authorities. Beneath the rhetoric there was no supportive statutory basis and that proved to be one of its fatal flaws—no matter that it was masked for a time by the boost to public service planning. In Victoria thirteen regions were determined and Regional Committees, mainly controlled from key municipal offices, were placed under the coordinating supervision of a Central Planning Authority (Figure 4.2). In a few powerful circles regionalism became a veritable gospel of efficiency to which all public service departments should be required to adhere. The immediate results were mixed: large utilitarian inventories, a welcome updating of statistical and cartographical materials, wider circulation of the planners' lore. Although in practice the Committees became fully extended in the production of this bland material, a process which was still exasperatingly incomplete after more than two decades, it was repeatedly affirmed that their most pointed advice would be welcomed—that there should indeed be an upward flow of ideas, in the spirit later eulogised in Coombs's autobiographical sketch.

The slow progress may be ascribed to inertia and territorialism within the public service, but it is also explained by the return to *laissez-faire* government. Modern planning has always drawn on reformist ideologies and in practical terms it suffered a downgrading during the post-war decline of the Victorian Labor party. Despite all superficial appearances, however, Australian society was not insulated from contemporary questioning of the traditional faith in the development imperative throughout the Western world. In the late 1960s and early 1970s, when the Lake Pedder, Blue Mountains and other landmark disputes were also raging, a related controversy over the proposed extension of farming into the 'Little Desert' finally stripped the facade from Victoria's much-vaunted planning structures.

It is over ten years since my own analysis of this complex affair was published.[17] In retrospect I still believe it is wise not to simplify such drawn-out events, which accommodated so many different actors with widely varying interpretations; even then it was clear to many planners, however, that we had reached a cultural divide. The 'Little Desert' fracas exposed the anachronisms in the Victorian polity in the sensitive interface between environment and development, and a complacent government was stirred into reluctant action. In the early 1970s Ministries for Conservation and Planning appeared, and the new deal was underlined by the establishment of an Environment Protection Authority and a promising new advisory body, the Land Conservation Council—of which more in a moment. It was a great time for Environmental Impact Statements and the like, which succeeded in diverting public attention from the fact that the assessments were usually taken after the main decisions were already made: the logical inclusion of a 'no go' option was not conceded for some years. Mountains of economic and ecological data, and a much smaller but rapidly increasing amount of social data, were nonetheless accumulated—on Port Phillip and Westernport bays, for example, and on the Newport Power Station proposal—and from our present perspective it is clear that we were then headed towards more purposive 'environmentalist' action.

The Land Conservation Council began as a cobbled, multi-agency organisation, drawing most of its membership from the executive heads of government departments engaged in land and water management, and with a small representation from outside the public service, including voluntary conservation bodies. Unfortunately, as certain nuances in the 'Little Desert' episode had shown all too well, several of the bureaucratic agencies were not only poles apart in their views on conservation and development. In addition they were old rivals for financial support and administrative authority—for example Fisheries and Wildlife, and National Parks were soon set against Agriculture, Minerals and Energy, and Forests, and a monolithic Lands Department which called on lengthy experience in confronting an infant National Park Service. At the same time, each of the parliamentary parties found it difficult to adapt to a new social movement which transcended traditional allegiances. While the Liberals stalled, old stagers in the ALP had become interested in 'growth centre' proposals but were often uncomfortable with conservationism and conservationists. The Australian Democrats' gravitation to a fluctuating central position began to attract the conservation vote, but it remained a small political force. Country Party stalwarts dug in, as expected: they resisted the dominance of metropolitan decision-making, challenging every effort to close off opportunities for development and increased employment in rural Victoria—helping, and in the process to spray impotent 'decentralisation' schemes around every corner of the State.

Proceeding from this fragile foundation, the LCC was required to supply detailed advice on the use of existing Crown land and on the improvement of soil and water manangement. Regional surveys were to be compiled, this time with the particularly well-publicised aim of

Figure 4.3 National parks and related reserves in post-war Victoria

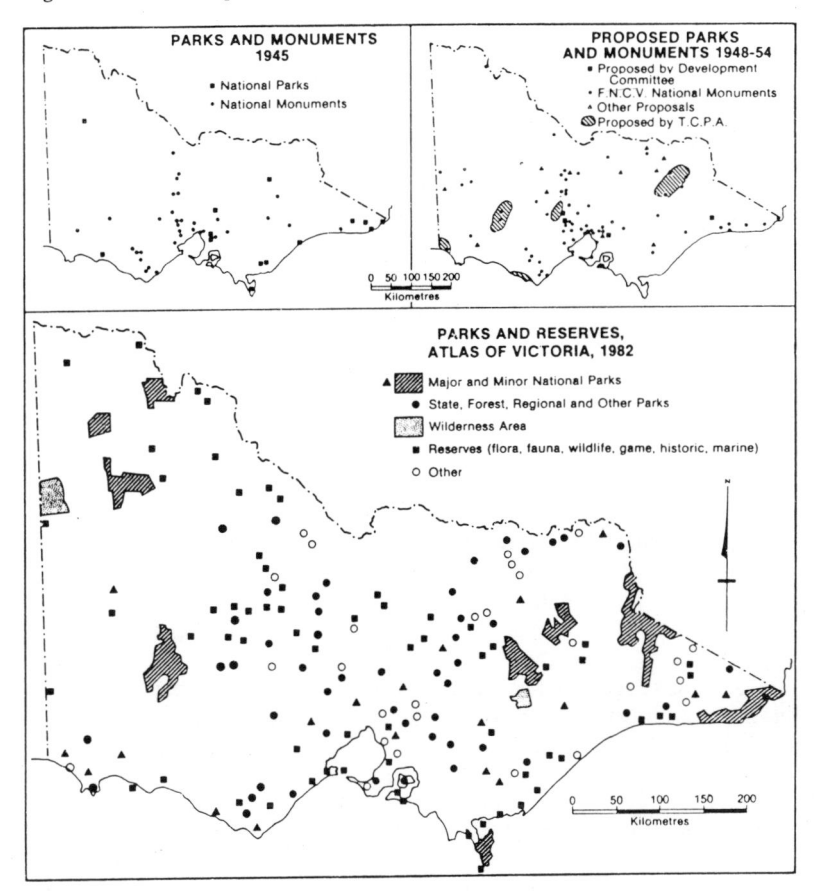

Source: Bardwell, *National Parks in Victoria, 1866–1956*, and J. S. Duncan (ed.), *Atlas of Victoria*, 1982.

soliciting wider community involvement, and for the servicing of recommendations for new and expanded reservations on scientific, amenity and other grounds. Much of the recent overdue increase in national parks and other reservations may be generously entered in the LCC's account, but the very insistence on a controllable bureaucratic response is also interesting. As my colleague David Mercer noted in 1979, the National Parks Association and other voluntary groups had been presenting well-considered submissions for about 30 years, and the creation of the LCC was in part an exercise in the 'politics of expertise' insofar as the government was declaring, in the face of competition from the non-official experts, that it had a monopoly over technical competence for national decision-making.[18] In the event, the LCC's proposed independence was deemed farcical and its hesitant proposals for the alpine region were opposed alike by conservationists who wanted an extensive, unbroken Alpine National Park and by commercial grazing, mining and timber interests. Victoria's foresters also came under attack from conservationists over this and other regional disputes, yet in fairness it should be stressed that undervalued 'utilitarian' foresters had themselves fought many a battle against crude exploitation.

By the early 1980s Victoria had 30 national parks with a combined area of about 686 000 hectares (about 1.7 million acres), and a further 299 000 hectares (about 739 000 acres) were set aside in 33 other types of park—undeniable progress, for which both official and voluntary bodies should be paid due credit (Figure 4.3). It constituted an increase of almost eight times the area so reserved in 1956, when Crosbie Morrison became the Foundation Director of the National Parks Authority. But those achievements were no more significant than the notice boldly served in this alpine dispute, as in the city's green bans and freeway controversies, and in the extraordinary spectacle of a revolt by highly respectable rural voters against the routing of a high voltage power line to Portland's dubious aluminium smelter. In each chapter the message rang out that, where governments prevaricated, the new age of participatory democracy might be ushered in by citizens' action movements.

Planning's earlier self-image had been founded on an easy acceptance of the possibility of objective technical expertise, reinforced by the notion that there was an equivalent acceptance in the community as a whole that the vast majority was destined to benefit from the promised improvements in amenity, convenience and health. It is now described as the 'consensus' view of society. By the later 1960s that outmoded concept was replaced by a better grasp of the inevitability of conflict in modern communities. As Logan puts it, planners could no longer claim to be acting for *the* public interest where many different sectional concerns were being forcefully presented.[19] The 'plural' society demanded that mediation and advocacy be included in the planners' repertoire.

Melbourne's own frustrating rounds of on-again, off-again metropolitan plans may be loosely described as official responses to expressions of public demand, combined with schematised assertions based on rationalisations of changing demographic and economic circumstances (Figure 4.4). The MMBW's first modern plan, presented in 1954, was later criticised for its 'static' modelling. The plan was predicated on low-growth assumptions which were soon proved incorrect, and the pressures for continued rapid expansion at the fringes undermined its credibility. Several enduring landscape contributions are often overlooked, however—the decision to concentrate growth in the eastern

Review of environment and planning 79

Figure 4.4 Selected metropolitan plans: inset, generalised expansion of the built-up area

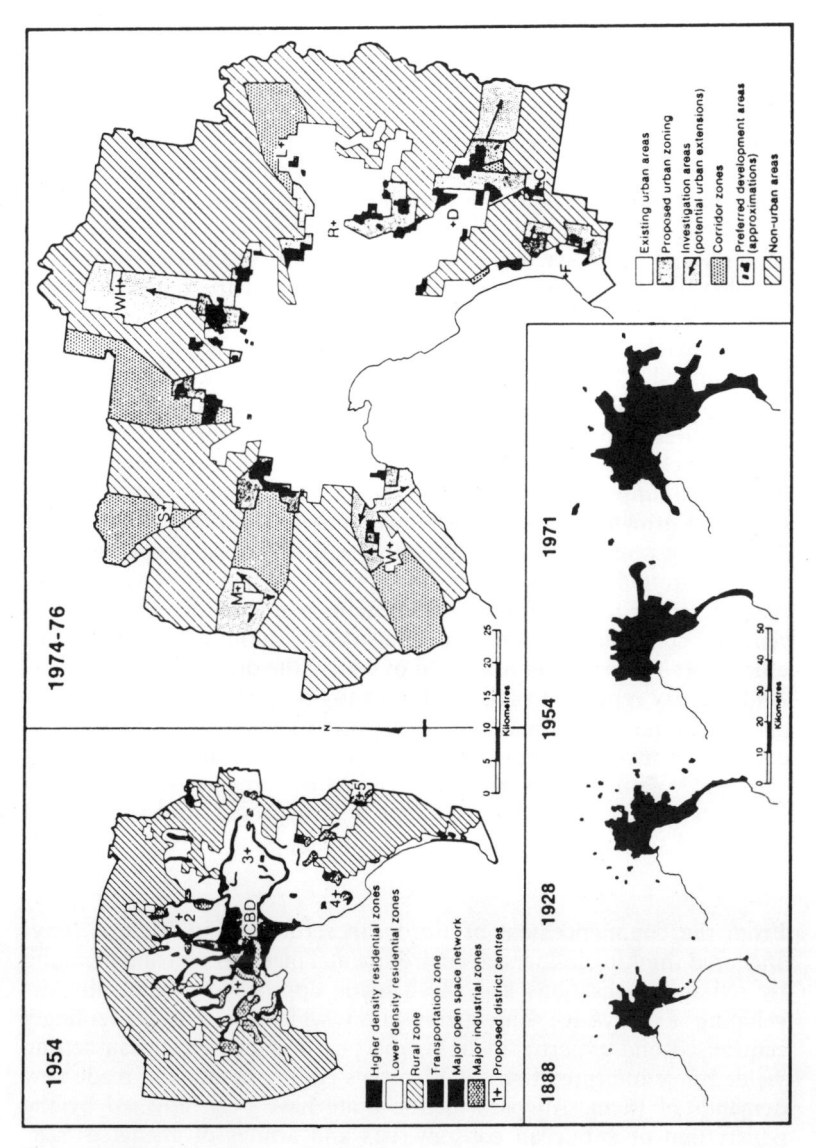

Source: MMBW official plans.
Note: 1954 scheme: 1—Footscray; 2—Preston;
3—Box Hill; 4—Moorabbin; 5—Dandenong. 1974–6:
W—Werribee; M—Melton; Wh—Whittlesea; L—Lilydale;
R—Ringwood; D—Dandenong; C—Cranbourne; F—Frankston.

sector reflected engineering advice and sample surveys of residents; the definition of a peripheral rural zone with minimum subdivision sizes was expected to limit profligate expansion; intra-metropolitan decentralisation leading to a polynuclear city was envisaged in the creation of new industrial nodes; inner city decay was recognised in a planned redevelopment focussed on high-rise Housing Commission blocks. The second plan was not the MMBW's child. In 1971 the Liberal government confidently sketched out a design based on high-growth assumptions, providing for satellite or new town development, urban corridors and some redirection of growth to the north-west and west. The MMBW and the Town and Country Planning Board were consulted in drawing up the design, however; both confirmed the popular preference for low density living and predicted a metropolitan population of approximately five million by the year 2000. The final structure incorporated a new freeway system which threatened to raze inner suburban neighbourhoods, and this and the notorious corridors provoked bitter public reaction. The ensuing debates articulated a fundamental challenge to the planners' presumptuous assertions, arguing that social impacts had not been taken into account and that the predicted growth rate was itself unacceptable. In 1974 and 1976 the MMBW responded, not insensitively, with modified proposals. The merry-go-round continued, with the appearance in 1980 of yet another plan returning to low growth assumptions and urban containment; it reflected continuing debates on intra-urban equities and management efficiencies for urban services, and of course the dreaded energy crisis. And the city remained as divided as ever—between neglected western and northern suburbs and the remainder of the metropolis; between an expensively dying central city marketed by politically influential fat cats, and volatile outer suburbs which had been dangerously forgotten in the video wastelands, and were still expected to survive in a car-bound surrealistic addiction to giant shopping centres.

From the commencement of European settlement in Victoria, city-anchored thinking influenced environmental management and planning by remote idealisations and mechanistic approaches, eventually developing a pervasive bureaucratisation which became increasingly centralised and expert-ridden. In the post-war era the urban setting yielded new interpretations of Victoria's environments and made new demands of them. All parts of the State have been affected by the penetration of suburban consumerists and armies of alienated 'self-actualisers' who differ markedly, not only in their sheer numbers, from the 'excursioning' groups of naturalists of earlier generations. But the urban influence is neither all-conquering nor uni-directional, as we have seen. The ubiquity of the city also diffuses its own paradoxical mixture of aggressive and caring attitudes. The high visibility of

Review of environment and planning 81

Figure 4.5 Distribution of Victorian Membership, Australian Conservation Foundation, 1983

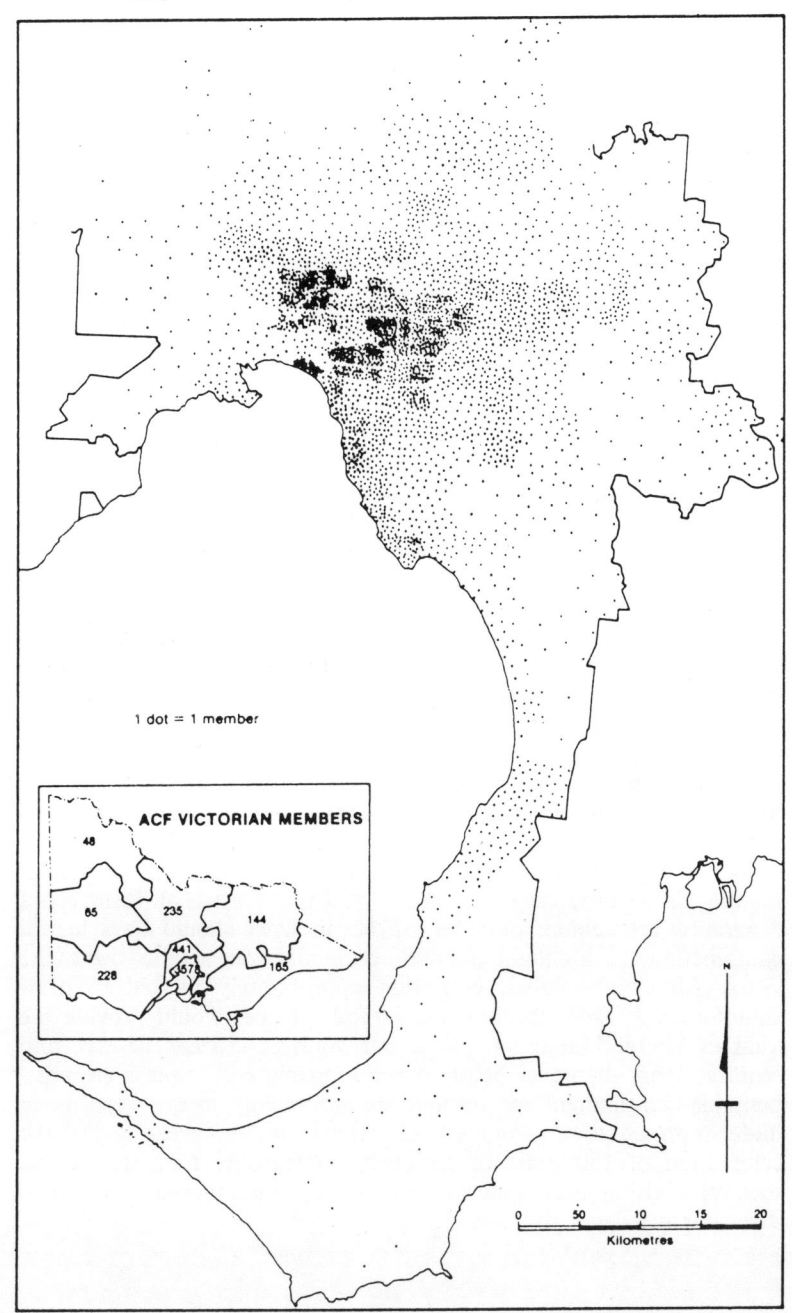

Source: Compiled from ACF files, courtesy of the Director, and based on postcode areas in J. S. Duncan (ed.), *Atlas of Victoria*, 1982.

Victoria in the Australian Conservation Foundation, our largest and most broadly based activist organisation in environmental affairs, is well known. The dominance of metropolitan membership in the ACF (Figure 4.5) has been a prominent feature from the outset, but the spatial association with middle-class suburbs, taken in conjunction with the close individual correlations with higher educational qualifications, outlines an unusual blend of radicalism which helps to signpost the future.

Conflict is now deeply engrained in our society and, if it is not to be seen as an end in itself, then it is reasonable to suggest that we become more open to ways of improving the dialogue—on matters connected with environment and planning as on other primary issues. Similar concerns have been expressed in the past, forming a valuable and underestimated part of our heritage on which we may draw. Barrett's progressive role offers good examples. During his busy participation in Melbourne's centennial celebrations he may have reflected for a moment on one of his earlier efforts, in 1910, to establish regular fieldwork activities in the school curricula. With the winning of shorter-term conservation goals and the promotion of good environmental citizenship in mind, Barrett had hoped to broaden the education programme by familiarising the students with the principles and purposes of national parks. The idea was no doubt premature, considering only the prevailing social and economic conditions. But we have had fewer excuses, surely, especially during the past twenty years. Direct field observation, which can bring the emancipation of seeing for oneself, is still scandalously neglected in Victorian schools, and by international standards our children are still disadvantaged in this respect, despite recent improvements. Again, despite the cant about our 'search for identity', all too few advanced students study our own history and geography. Comparable complaints are that higher level geography courses have been emasculated by the discarding of regional synthesis and the under-representation of concepts and information relating to the physical environment, and that Australian history and geography are seldom pursued *together* in what should be a logical combination, to highlight our environmental transactions down the years. An environmental education appropriately located to draw simultaneously from the humanities and sciences would provide the kind of liberal foundation *all* of our younger citizens deserve and require. More than ever before, environmental education is an indispensable requirement for responsible citizenship, and its continued under-representation in our schools offers a major caveat against the celebration of 150 years of European endeavour. In a democratic society, environmental deterioration reflects our ignorance and measures our indulgent divisions.

Notes

1. 'Policy and Public Justice' *Geelong Advertiser* 30 December 1856. For a discussion see J. M. Powell *The Public Lands of Australia Felix. Settlement and land appraisal in Victoria 1834–91 with special reference to the Western plains*, Melbourne: Oxford University Press, 1970
2. T. L. Mitchell *Three Expeditions into the Interior of Eastern Australia* 2nd edn, vol. 2, London: Boone, 1839, p. 333
3. ibid. p. 159
4. J. M. Powell *Environmental Management in Australia, 1788–1914. Guardians, improvers and profit: an introductory survey.* Melbourne: Oxford University Press, 1976, especially pp. 21–32
5. W. Howitt *Land, Labour and Gold; or, two years in Victoria, with visits to Sydney and Van Diemen's Land* vol. 1, London, 1855, p. 252
6. R. Wright, Space and the Public Purpose. Crown land reservation in Victoria, 1834–1880, unpublished PhD thesis, Monash University, 1985
7. Progress Report of the Royal Commission on Foreign Industries and Forests *Victorian Parliamentary Papers* 3, nos. 21 and 24
8. S. M. Legg, Arcadia or Abandonment? The evolution of the rural landscape in South Gippsland, 1870 to 1947, unpublished MA thesis, Monash University, 1984
9. D. J. Pisani 'Reclamation and social engineering in the progressive era' *Agricultural History* 57, 1983, pp. 46–83
10. J. M. Powell 'Elwood Mead and California's state colonies: an episode in Australasian–American contacts, 1915–31' *Journal, Royal Australian Historical Society* 67, 1982, pp. 328–53
11. J. M. Powell 'The debt of honour: soldier settlement in the Dominions, 1915–1940' *Journal of Australian Studies* 8, 1982, pp. 64–87
12. M. Roe *Nine Australian Progressives. Vitalism in bourgeois social thought 1890–1960*, St Lucia: University of Queensland Press, 1984
13. S. Bardwell, National Parks in Victoria, 1866–1956. 'For all the people all the time', unpublished PhD thesis, Monash University, 1974
14. Roe *Nine Australian Progressives* p. 71
15. R. Freestone, The Australian Garden City: a planning history 1919–1930, unpublished PhD thesis, Macquarie University, 1984
16. H. C. Coombs *Trial Balance*, South Melbourne: Macmillan, 1981, pp. 59–60
17. J. M. Powell ' "Action analysis" of resource conflicts: the Little Desert dispute, Victoria, 1963–72' in J. M. Powell (ed.) *The Making of Rural Australia*, Melbourne: Sorrett, 1974, pp. 161–79
18. D. C. Mercer 'Victoria's Land Conservation Council and the alpine region' *Australian Geographical Studies* 17, 1979, pp. 107–30
19. T. Logan *Urban and Regional Planning in Victoria*, Melbourne: Shillington House, 1981, p. 13

5

Literature in Victoria: *from the wild white man to the carnival of language*

CHRIS WALLACE-CRABBE

In setting out to write about that regional phenomenon, or dilly-bag full of phenomena, entitled 'Literature in Victoria', I am aware that we hover on the brink of a curious pun, an oddly misleading slide of language. Many of us have encountered it from time to time when noticing some reference to Victorian painting, or Victorian architecture, or Victorian writing. In a way which would amuse our teasing neighbours north of the Murray, the historical adjective blurs with the regional adjective; the result suggests by association that culture in this state is a bit dated, a bit puritanical, a bit passé. In my general observations about this district, later this colony and, later again, this state, I shall not be offering any such views of our stodginess. Far from it, indeed: even though I do recognise something familiar in the New South Wales poet, Les Murray's sly lines about the river which shares his name:

> The culture, on both banks, is pure Victoria: the beer, the footy, the slight earnest flavour, the cray.

Looking over the kinds of literary production which this state has engendered, or played nurse to, I do not think that Murray's 'slight earnest flavour' emerges as characteristic of their style. On the contrary it would seem that writing in this state has displayed more than its share of the hectic, the verbally mixed, the colloquial, the lairy and the experimental demeanours. Playfully subversive writing has commonly found a home here.

Let me leave such general speculations for later on. It would seem a good idea to begin by suggesting some of the particular phenomena which are covered by my title. What are its beginnings and its range? Perhaps a neat, if meagre beginning could be made with the journal of the Reverend Robert Knopwood, Chaplain to the short-lived Sorrento settlement of 1803–04. Not surprisingly, Knopwood's diary entries are quite without ambition or flourish.

Why not begin, then, with the songs, legends and stories of the Aboriginal people of this south-eastern corner of Australia? They have lived here, after all, a hundred times as long as the white ascendancy. My answer is in part narrowly logical and in part a simple confession of my limitations: narrowly logical, that is to say, because myth, oral narrative, worksongs and folklore are not strictly speaking, *literature*, which is the realm of letters and the lettered; and a confession of my limitations in that I know so little about the long millennia of the Aboriginal culture of our land. I am well aware that this ignorance is something for which I and many of my contemporaries will be blamed by future generations, but I have somehow come too late to the Aboriginal world-picture which for so long invested this land with its profound web of meanings to do more than glance over it from the hill of amateurism.

A year after Victoria's separation from New South Wales there was published in Hobart a book which strikingly symbolises the bridge or passing over from the Aboriginal millennia to white culture. The book is *The Life and Adventures of William Buckley* (1852). Buckley, 'the Wild White Man', has long been a familiar figure to our imagination, at once escaped convict, Crusoe, man of two disparate cultures, and link between the 1803 settlement and the Melbourne (or Bearbrass, its quaint early name) of 1835. No wonder that the phrase, 'Buckley's chance', most likely formed later from the firm of Buckley & Nunn, has drifted backwards and attached itself so firmly to the hulking escapee, wandering around the shores of Port Phillip until he took on a tribal identity which served and preserved him for decades.

In his preface, John Morgan stresses that he has written up this book from interviews and conversations with the illiterate Buckley, compares his role with that of Defoe, and stresses that author and protagonist are to share any proceeds from the book. Much of the writing is marked by the kind of authorial whimsy that we find in the following coy passage (on page 68 of the 1979 edition):

> It appeared that the cause of their attack upon us was some very old grievance about the women. I am sorry to say it, but these dear creatures were at the bottom of every mischief. From Adam, that old root digger, downwards, it has always been the same in every clime, and nation—then why fancy my very pretty looking, slightly clad venuses to be worse than others?—on their part, I repudiate the imputation.

The Life and Adventures does not always maintain such a European distance from its materials, however. One passage offers very shrewd insights into the problems of mutual incomprehension raised by the Aborigines' 'sale' of their land to white settlers, informing readers that there could be no chiefs with any right to dispose of tribal lands. But

William Buckley, remarkable bulk of a figure though he was, is only the ghost of an author, or the shadowy speaker behind a ghost writer.

We are all preoccupied with beginnings. Despite William James's warning that origins prove nothing, we all tend to feel that a first occurrence is, if not definitive, at least predictive. Accordingly, let us turn to some landmarks signalling the beginnings of literature in Victoria.

The first novel written by a Port Phillip resident was Thomas McCombie's *Arabin, or the Adventures of a Colonist in New South Wales* (1845). In the same year Richard Howitt published his melange of a book, *Impressions of Australia Felix during four years' Residence in that Colony: Notes of a Voyage round the World: Australian Poems, etc.* Howitt is at pains to emphasise the clarity of his disillusioned view, asserting his distance from the falsely beguiling prose of emigration books; indeed he speaks, in the dedication to his brother, Godfrey, of emigration as 'exchanging substantial good and imaginary evil, for real evil and imaginary good'. His verses fall, thematically and stylistically, into obvious conventions of poesy. Yet there is some interest in the fact that he can modulate from hard to soft primitivism as he moves from poem to poem. Thus while 'Primitive Native Condition' is as harsh as its prosy title, 'Tullamarine' tries to feel its sympathetic way into an Aboriginal mother's lament over her dead son, whom she compares to the tullamarine flower. As a rule, though, Howitt tends to contrast the unsung blankness of colonial experience with the articulated world of his British origins: 'O, what a place of birth was ours, The Land of Memory and Time!' ('Old Impressions').

The first three works of fiction which explicitly draw upon life in Victoria were published in the one year, 1854. They are Mrs Ellen Clacy's *Lights and Shadows of Australian Life*, George Haydon's *The Australian Emigrant* and *A Boy's Adventures in the Wilds of Australia, or Herbert's Note Book* by William Howitt, brother to Richard and Godfrey. Both Clacy and Haydon had published emigrant memoirs before turning their experience into fiction; while William Howitt's book is essentially an assemblage of descriptive materials about the colony with a few simple narratives thrown in. It may not surprise us that Mrs Clacy's memoir, *A Lady's Visit to the Gold-diggings of Australia* (1853), is livelier and more particular than are her novelettes, which seem utterly conventional. The humorously factual eye of *A Lady's Visit* has its effect in such passages as the following (on pages 127–28 of the 1963 edition):

> In every window—milliners, baby-linen warehouses & c., included was exhibited the usual advertisement of the gold buyer—namely, a heap of gold in the centre, on one side a pile of sovereigns, on the other banknotes. The most significant advertisement was one I saw in a window in Collins Street. In the middle was a skull perforated by a bullet, which lay at a little distance as if coolly examining or speculating on the mischief it had done. On one

side of the skull was a revolver, and on the other a quantity of nuggets. Above all was the emphatic inscription, 'Beware in time'. This rather uncomfortable-looking tableau signified—in as speaking a manner as symbols can—that the unfortunate skull had once belonged to some unfortunate lucky digger, who not having had the sense to sell his gold to the proprietor of this attractive window had kept his nuggets in his pocket, thereby tempting some robbers—significantly personified by the revolver—to shoot him and steal the gold.

Turning back from this description of early conceptual art, we may note that Haydon's *The Australian Emigrant* was the first real Victorian novel, for all that it was at the same time a blatant piece of propaganda on behalf of the region which he had already written about as Australia Felix. It is a jovial story and, inter alia, speculates suggestively on the motives involved in giving names to new properties and settlements. Perhaps the way in which we read all these works will remind us of Mandelstam's dictum that instruction is the central nerve of prose.

Ah, but this raises the larger procedural question of how we are to go about reading a body of regional literature, how we are putting it together as a demonstrable field. For in offering to discuss something, or some things, entitled 'The Literature in Victoria', I am constructing that literature in accord with some set of principles and/or prejudices. As far as possible I shall lay those principles out plain and clear, but they will continue to entail contradictions for all that. So, in seeking distinctive features in that writing which has been engendered by the area between Bass Strait, the River Murray and the South Australian border, I shall not only display the goods but try to describe the kind of show window in which they are being marketed.

Mind you, were I presenting my views in the privileged robes of a poet and not in the sober suit of a critic, I might sweep all of Victoria together in some bold knot of metaphors, as Bruce Dawe does in 'Life-Cycle', and hang the expense. This hyperbolic poem begins with the claim that 'When children are born in Victoria they are wrapped in the club-colours,' and sonorously ends thus:

> And the tides of life will be the tides of the home-team's fortunes—the reckless proposal after the one-point win, the wedding and honeymoon after the grand-final...
>
> They will not grow old as those from more northern States grow old, for them it will always be three-quarter time with the scores level and the wind advantage in the final term,
>
> That passion persisting, like a race-memory, through the welter of seasons, enabling old-timers by boundary fences to dream of resurgent lions and centaur-figures from the past to replenish continually the present,
>
> So that mythology may be perpetually renewed and Chicken Smallhorn return like the maise-god in a thousand shapes, the dancers changing
>
> But the dance forever the same—the elderly still loyally crying Carn...

Carn... (if feebly) unto the very end, having seen in the six-foot recruit from Eaglehawk their hope of salvation.

Incidentally, this splendid poem puts me in mind of how seldom our literature makes reference to that game of which Melbourne is the world capital.

The simplest, and no doubt the most monotonous way of discoursing on the literature of Victoria would be simply to mention individual works in metonymic chains or long queues. Thus, if we take up the prose of instruction and information about the colonial years, we could proceed from the memoirs of Richard Howitt and Mrs Clacy to Sir Roger Therry's *Reminiscences of Thirty Years' Residence in New South Wales and Victoria* (1863); from there we could pass on to Marcus Clarke's extremely vivacious essays, in the course of which he distinguishes between Melbourne's higher and lower Bohemia, the latter being typified by those battered *clochards* who lived in the parkland along St Kilda Road. Still on the frontiers of journalism, we could move on to Edmund Finn ('Garryowen') with *The Garryowen Sketches* of 1880 and *The Chronicles of Early Melbourne* of 1888. Although 'Rolf Boldrewood's *Old Melbourne Memories* (1884) sounds like a similar work, its jaunty, hard-riding chapters are nearly all concerned with the author's experiences in rural Victoria; English-born himself, the high-spirited Boldrewood was not above a bit of Pom-bashing, as when he compared 'some under-sized Anglo-Saxon, with no brain power to spare' with some of the Aborigines he had known in the early days of Western District settlement, 'grandly-formed specimens of humanity, dignified in manner, and possessing an intelligence by no means to be despised, comprehending a sense of humour, as well as a keenness of perception, not always found in the superior race' (page 40 of the 1969 edition).

From there we could turn naturally enough to other memoirs by squatters or settlers, to E. M. Curr's *Recollections of Squatting in Victoria* (1883) and to *A Homestead History*, edited and published in 1942 by G. F. James from the papers of Alfred Joyce, who had settled in the Victorian Midlands in 1844 and had finally gone bankrupt in 1886. It is late editing that we also have to thank for that vivacious work, *Georgiana's Journal*. Georgiana McCrae's grandson, Hugh, the amorous poet, edited this volume in 1934, and its flavour emerges nicely in the following extract from the day of the opening of Prince's Bridge (on page 206 of the 1966 edition):

> A day full of surprises and excitement. At 6 a.m. the saxhorn band began to play a reveillee outside "The Châlet": a performance which had been kept secret even from Mr La Trobe himself, who now appeared in a flowered dressing-gown, straining his eyes at the window. He held my sleeve while some of the gentlemen put down their horns to sing "Hark, Hark the Lark!" in a key that was too high for them; yet it sounded better than the French *aubade* which immediately followed. After this they recovered their

instruments and gave us stirring polka tunes, although poor Madame, who had one of her neuralgic headaches, would gladly have foregone that part of the programme. Mr La Trobe then walked out onto the veranda to put an end to the music, but with the opposite effect, for, no sooner did the performers behold him, than they joined, some with voices, some with saxhorns, in a tremendous rendition of the national anthem. His Honour bowed, and they would have gone through it again had I not led him into the house.... So they marched away, still playing polkas.

The aftermath of this resonant morning was that Georgiana had to stand in for the Governor's wife during the public events of that stirring day, November 16, 1850.

Well, in a similar way we could trace a sequence from the first published play, Francis Belfield's *The Bottle or the Drunkard's Curse: a Temperance Drama* (1849), trusting that it would finally lead us to the modern plays of Hibberd, Romeril and Williamson. Or we could look at the first two woman poets, Mrs C. S. Perry and Miss Susan Talbot, both of whom published books of verse in 1857, wondering if lines like 'Melbourne! thy name hath waked my slumbering lyre,' can take their place in a line which will lead us down at last to such poets as Jennifer Strauss and Doris Brett. Surely, though, it was in the next generation that Victorian writers began to become distinctive, began to show the kind of stamina and confidence in their dealings with a text, in such a way that makes us want to examine the innards of what they are up to. In this regard, it strikes me as either a happy accident or a piece of stern historical causation which ensured that Joseph Furphy, Ada Cambridge, Marcus Clarke and 'Tasma' were born within five years of one another, in the 1840s.

Such talk as this obviously brings me on to a second principle or procedure by which to talk about our literature. This—and it is one by which we all behave frequently—involves taking some note of hierarchies of value. However creaky our reasons for doing so, we all know that some books are better than others, and usually prefer to hear the better books talked about than the worse.

It is surely striking, then, to see how quickly Victorian literature in Victoria, if I may double the term again, pressed on to produce that large, stony, powerful novel of convict life and death, *His Natural Life* (1870–72) and, at the opposite extreme of the emotions, 'Tasma's' *Uncle Piper of Piper's Hill*, in which we find the kind of social comedy which will later become central to Martin Boyd's novels. It is a sign of a new age that society in *Uncle Piper of Piper's Hill* is not simply shown as raw, rude and pioneering, but is capable of generating *ennui* and, more than that, of containing a sympathetic female character who is unconventional and irreligious. Even the narrator opines at one point that, 'The remark that Voltaire made about the great Russian Empire, when he compared it to a pear that was rotten before it was ripe, might be applied with equal truth to many a Victorian township' (page 184 of the 1889 edition). Much of the indubitable wit of 'Tasma's' novel springs from her imaginative sense that the Victoria which she portrays is no longer a new society, having its fixities and its developed quaintnesses already.

Joseph Furphy, a contemporary as I have noted of Clarke and 'Tasma', transformed himself into a precursive modern, not only through his subversive, eclectic, zany, omnivorous performance as an anti-novelist, but more simply by failing to publish a novel until he was 60 years old. It was in 1903 that his labyrinthine comic masterpiece, *Such is Life*, appeared, over the pen name which is the real—that is to say, fictitious—name of its officious narrator, Tom Collins.

I have written on *Such is Life* several times, and can best summarise my present view of this remarkable book by quoting from an account which I offered to an American audience some three years ago:

> Early in their negotiations (May 2, 1897) Furphy wrote to [A. G.] Stephens that 'the plan of the book is not like any other I know of,—at least, I trust not.' What he devised, with great labour, was a new kind of novel which would, on the one hand, recreate the life of bullock drivers among the Riverina sheep and cattle stations with great fidelity and comic richness; but it would also be able to entail and present Furphy's views on causation, belief, the acquisition of value systems and the arbitrariness of acts of choice; further, it would incorporate reflections upon itself and on the nature of the fictive art. This reflexiveness has, of course, become a common feature of the twentieth-century novel, but it sprang from great conceptual daring in an unknown provincial writer of the 1890s.
>
> The tropes and tricks of *Such is Life* all proceed comically in quest of reality, of the 'suchness' of life in a universe where all belief systems are relative, provisional, fallible . . .
>
> The reader is at the end of a shifting chain of connections.

If hierarchies of value in literature are what we are talking about, then I am obliged to record my view that *Such is Life* is the greatest novel which this country has produced. To which I shall, of course, be asked what I mean by calling it the greatest. What I mean has a simple subjective component: that there is no Australian book which I can reread so often without ever exhausting the pleasures of the text; but, more seriously, it seems just to say that this novel is one which can be read under entirely different critical and historical dispensations, but however different the methodologies which are brought to bear on it, it comes up as full of interest, worthy of extended comment, worthy of analytical argument. This is the only meaning of literary 'greatness' which could at all be called objective.

Thus *Such is Life* has been read as a loose federation of yarns ('federated' was the author's own term), as realistic, as politically radical, as an epistemological endeavour, as existentialist, as an anti-novel, as post-modernist before its time, and as plain bloody funny. It stands up very well to the different regimes of critical fashion.

The other most powerful and abiding novel to have been produced by a Victorian is surely Henry Handel Richardson's *The Fortunes of Richard Mahony*. Richardson wrote this sustained and harrowing novel over a couple of decades, from around 1910 until 1930. Apart from her one fact-gathering trip back to Australia in 1912, she wrote the book entirely in London. Like various earlier novelists, and like Martin Boyd after her, Richardson assigns considerable dramatic importance in her novel to the effects of travel to and fro between the old world and the new. But to say this is only to scratch the surface of the book. Like *Such is Life*—a book which it resembles about as much as chalk resembles cheese, or horse-laughs resemble heart attacks—*The Fortunes of Richard Mahony* has been the site for a host of different readings. Its commentators have focussed on its meticulous historical naturalism, on its tragic or pathetic vision of Mahony, the idealistic, thin-skinned Anglo-Irish doctor at odds with his environment, on the balance between Mahony and his pragmatic wife, on the book's involvement with historical ideas, and on the narrative as a fictional quest into the life and fate of the novelist's father, Dr Walter Richardson.

Nothing else in HHR's work has the weight of *Mahony*, although *Maurice Guest* (1908), set in Germany, treats powerfully the fringes where music and romantic love feather one another. And Melbourne readers have long had a soft spot for *The Getting of Wisdom* (1910), a shortish, jauntier book in which she lightly fictionalised her school experiences at PLC, East Melbourne. Its irony wears well.

The lives of Richardson and of the poet, John Shaw Neilson, cover the same years. But she was a pianist and a professor's wife, while he remained an uneducated farmhand, poor of purse and poor of sight. But from sources which must have been largely oral he forged a kind of poems, or perhaps we might call them songs, which reassembled traditional metres and images in a voice which was entirely his own. It is harder to analyse Neilson than to quote him. Even a little-known poem of his can offer a sample of his unique plangency; 'To a Runaway Sound' will serve as an example. Notice how its simple images play over an experience as delicate and dodgy as anything in consciously Symbolist poetry:

> Nay, but I love you not. Who set you free?
> From what mad prison came you to hasten the cool heart of me?
>
> Go away out then, where lovers would sweeten the ground;
> No law will heed you, for you are a runaway sound.
>
> You would have angels to listen where thought cannot climb.
> Fall away over white dresses in holiday time.
>
> Did you lie deep in a forest or down in dark sea?
> For all your light step you call up slow things to me.
>
> Go away out of the colours, rattle the ground,
> But stoop not my dull heart to hasten, you runaway sound.

As in Neilson's better known lyrics, we have here a conventional, even a naive-seeming diction, and metres which sound as though they belong to some quite traditional mode of ballad or jingle. Yet the experience, like the sound being addressed, slips away. It has to do with excitement, with evanescence, with sexuality: but it is not demonstrably any one of these things. And, which is not uncommon in his poetry, its evocation has to do with synaesthesia, that strange kernel of the Romantic heritage. Here, as in 'The Orange Tree' and 'May', Neilson is the most poetic of poets, and the hardest to pin down. Distinguished later poets like Vincent Buckley, Bruce Dawe and R. A. Simpson were able to learn nothing from him.

While it was in Melbourne that Australian drama at last changed and burgeoned, starting from Betty Burstall's initiatives at the La Mama Theatre, Carlton, in the late 1960s, it is difficult to say now how much of that drama has substance as literature, rather than as occasions for theatrical performance. While the plays of David Williamson enjoy the widest popularity on stage, only the work of Jack Hibberd is sufficiently dense and complicated in linguistic texture to fall unmistakably under the heading of literature. From *A Stretch of the Imagination* (1973) to the as yet unpublished *Odyssey of a Prostitute*, he shows himself to be a writer for whom language is an intoxicant, and a pun the fatal Cleopatra. His demeanour stands somewhere between Brecht, Beckett and Sidney J. Baker's *The Australian Language*; that is to say, he uses his great vernacular range, not in the interest of realistic character depiction, but for estrangement and displacement. Thus, in *See You Tomorrow at Maxim's* the battered Cec Poole enumerates his complaints for Dr McRob (see page 210 of Hibberd, *Squibs: a collection of short plays*):

    Poole: I can't sleep. I get these pains in the khyber. The dooks tremble. I got no feeling in me plates of meat. I drop bombs. Burp. Dry retch. Then there's me phosphate gland. Clive, my mate, who I owe a fiver, I call him Clive of India, reckons I'm a monte for the yellow jack. I know my lungs are bronical. (*proudly*) I hack up stacks of phlegm. The colour of asparagus. Tinned.
    Pause.
    McRob: Anything else?
    Poole: I have a coat of black fur on my brewer's bung.

Anyone who so relentlessly foregrounds the language he uses is clearly a writer for the page as well as for the stage. Hibberd's is a very distinctive talent, but it belongs, as I shall suggest later, in a perceptible Victorian tradition.

Again, one could discuss literature in this state in terms of its eccentricities, its odd phenomena, its twists and quirks. The two dramatists called Louis, for instance—Esson and Nowra—who both found themselves excluded from success in the local dramatic scene. Or that unique and overwhelming comic figure, Barry Humphries, about whom I dare not say anything, except to observe that many writers would seem to have been influenced at one point or another by his devastating monologues. Or the larrikin light verse of C. J. Dennis, its acute historical timeliness for the generation of World War I and, hence, its extraordinary popularity: *The Songs of a Sentimental Bloke* sold more than 66 000 copies, a very large figure for poetry in the twentieth century. Or, while we think of narrative poetry, the very long, political, conversational stories in verse of Alan Wearne, among which *The Nightmarkets*, still in progress, bids fair to be the longest poem ever published in this country: it should certainly test the readership for narrative poems. And, sometimes forgotten, there is that sudden early bestseller, Fergus Hume's *The Mystery of a Hansom Cab* (1886). Making use of that rising genre, the detective story, and drawing on people's interest in what Clarke had called the lower Bohemia, Hume sold a rapid quarter of a million copies of this Melbourne-based thriller.

Early settlers aside, nothing has been said here about commentators and critics in other fields, in whose writing some personal force, some eccentricity of utterance, or simply a consistency of timbre which betokens the author's personal vision would lead one to call their books 'literature'. Into this swaying category I would have to gather the architectural criticism of Robin Boyd, Nettie Palmer's shrewdly analytical *Fourteen Years* (1948), Sir Walter Murdoch's essays and Maie Casey's family memoir, *An Australian Story* (1962), to name only a few. But over all these would tower the massively subjective, high-flying and rhetorically unique histories of Manning Clark. It is surely true that we read Clark's histories very much as we read a novelist or poet, that in reading him we take imaginative personality first and method only second. Even those who cavil at his historiography would have to admit that Clark is a massive presence in literary Australia, a tone of voice which we cannot escape. Like Bernard O'Dowd, like Katharine Susannah Prichard, like Hal Porter, Clark is a prime example of the Author as Character.

There is one aspect of literature in Victoria during the first half of the twentieth century which might be merely a disquieting curiosity but may well be a larger general truth about local culture. If we leave aside Richardson, continuing her writing career overseas, and Prichard, who lived in Western Australia after the First World War, hardly any of the acclaimed literature was produced by women; or, if you want to put the matter another way, Victorian women were somehow excluded from literary success between Federation and the early 'sixties. They wrote histories or biographies, a representative career being that of Nettie Palmer who fell silent on the 'creative' front after 1915. Elsewhere, Miles Franklin, Kylie Tennant, Christina Stead, Ethel Anderson, Eleanor Dark and Eve Langley were producing notable fiction, but what was happening on this side of the Murray? Again, the contents of Harry Heseltine's *Penguin Book of Australian Verse* do not list a single woman poet from this state; nor has Heseltine been a jaundiced anthologist, on the evidence of other collections of Australian poetry.

I do not, alas, have a ready sociological explanation for these decades of exclusion from the talent stakes which our women plainly suffered, in sharp contrast to New South Wales in particular. But there are suggestions which might be followed up in a speculative article on the visual arts by Bernard Smith. In his 'Two Art Systems', published in *Meanjin* in 1981, Smith sees the arts in Melbourne as having long been associated with academies and institutions, while Sydney art was connected with trade and pleasure:

> ... I suspect that Melbourne art seeks to assert a public function, aspiring to the conditions of classicism, that in Sydney art is regarded as a more private concern and continually reverts to a condition of decor, an embellishment of the artist's personality or the collector's residence.

If such a contrast holds true in the verbal arts as well as in the visual, it could well help to account for the restricted success of women in literature here, for much of this century. But things may be changing for the better at last: over the last 25 years we have seen the fiction of Criena Rohan, Glen Tomasetti, Beverley Farmer and, above all, Helen Garner, who has recently followed up *Monkey Grip* (1977) and two disciplined novellas with a splendidly shapely and plangent novel, *The Children's Bach*. I would also wish to draw readers' attention to the bizarrely experimental prose poems of a Polish migrant, Anita Walwicz: in these pieces Walwicz turns her ethnic and linguistic displacement into a tool with which to dismantle our expected formations of language or narrative. She is like nobody else.

We all hanker after generalisations. Whether or not writers can have been formed by their first fifteen years being spent in this state, or their first 25 years, or their floruit, after a childhood somewhere else, we all want such discourse as I am engaged in to throw up generalisations about Victoria and its writers. Now, there is a well-known line of speculation which derives particularly from an article by Manning Clark in Peter Coleman's *Australian Civilization* (1962), but which has been adumbrated and embroidered by a number of subsequent commentators, including the present writer and those who contributed to the *Meanjin* 'St Petersburg or Tinsel Town'. debate. I shall not amplify it: merely remark that according to its rough typologies writers from 'our' side should have a tendency to be responsible, historically minded, socially concerned, meliorist, even radical. And by radical here is meant politically radical, not formally experimental or wildly anarchist.

In terms of this sketch, one can readily draw a line of succession among our writers. It begins with one facet, or one reading, of Furphy, and continues down through Bernard O'Dowd, Prichard, Vance and Nettie Palmer, Judah Waten, John Manifold, John Morrison, Frank Hardy, Criena Rohan and John Romeril. The poets and playwright on this list lock together rather less neatly than do the writers of fiction. Most of the latter could have been, for part of their careers at least, gathered under the umbrella of social realism, or socialist realism, if you prefer: Manifold with his cavalier wit, his brisk jauntiness and his balladry, was stylistically the odd man out, despite his adherence to the Communist Party. Their fiction has had a disposition to dwell on the plight of the dispossessed and disadvantaged, to stress socio-economic forces, to alert itself to class conflict, and to eschew resolutions achieved through metaphor or symbol. If it has been politically forward-looking, the naturalism of its narrative methods has been extremely traditional.

To this, however, I would add another reading, another line, another tradition, which while not necessarily superior to the other strikes me as more distinctively a Victorian tradition. This is the line of writers who have jubilantly used mixed diction, breaking decorum, scrambling idiolects and subverting the very genres which they have practised. If we may call the first kind of radicalism the School of Verity we may dub this company members of the Carnival of Language. They, too, spring from Furphy, but from a Sternian or post-modernist reading of that versatile imagination.

The poet who most demonstrably belongs to this carnivalesque line is Bruce Dawe, especially in his earlier work. There one could find—as in 'Life-Cycle'—the reckless combination of a fine ear for the idioms of middle Australia with the most rhetorical kind of literary diction, the transitions often achieved quite abruptly, even in the worst of taste. The different kinds of diction are cheerfully foregrounded by a poet who is so natural that he has no qualms about revealing the artificiality of his art, no qualms in making the narrator in his monologue, 'A Victorian Hangman Tells His Love', speak like no imaginable human being: the poem is as rhetorical as Shakespeare; it is also genuinely queer.

Jack Hibberd and Hal Porter are other writers given in this way to stirring the language-pot wildly, to mixing the modes in the interest of more expressive kinds of subversion. Porter is an interesting paradox, being the only member of this team who combines his linguistic larrikinism with conservative social postures. Nevertheless, in the best of his short stories and in the arresting first book of his autobiographical trilogy, *The Watcher on the Cast-Iron Balcony* (1963), he produces a new kind of jazzily gothic metonymy, stringing the past on gilded chains of language.

But the central inheritor (if he would not object to the word, central) of the Carnival of Language in its more revolutionary forms is surely Peter Mathers. In his two novels and one collection of short stories, Mathers works furiously to ensure readers that he offers nought for their comfort, if much for their restless diversion. It is not only our expectations of some linguistic decorum that he goes about dismantling, but also our sense of what character might be, what narrative traction might be, even what might be normative in human behaviour. One cannot represent in miniature Mathers's interruptions, derailments and acts of literary arson, but one can offer a little of the peculiar flavour of *The Wort Papers* (1972, pages 272–73).

> The Epistle of Bernard Oats, of Burnt Gum via Uppersass.
>
> In the glare of the workshop lamp and the flickering candle I held the rocker box over the tappets the way the Bishop of Christ holds the crown over the man to be made King but instead of a tumult of bells I heard the rumble. Was this dawn to see the day of wrath? Has it, at last, come? Is this to be it? Whirlwind and firestorm? Pray let it not be. Is the dwelling of Our Father of Paspalum to be laid waste?
>
> The bomb has fallen. Pyres hiss and rumble on every continent. How long will it be before survivors stream up to Uppersass and will they be welcomed or warned off? If we Uppersassians survive shall we set up camps on the outskirts of cities to succour them or will it be roadblocks and firearms to confine them?
>
> The wife, busy preparing provisions for our pilgrimage, called from the house: Bernie, quick! I laid the grey rocker-box cover on its new cork gasket and ran to the house kneading cotton waste as far as the mulberry then losing it, telling myself I would get it later.

If I choose to end on so bizarre a note it is largely because this latter strain of radicalism in our writing has had so much less comment than the other strain with its overtly socio-political comment. It is also because a sesqui-centenary is in danger of being an inherently and excessively solemn occasion. Further, it pleases me to end by asserting that whatever distinguishes the literature of this state, it is not aestheticism, and it is not charm.

Bibliography

Thanks are due to Susan Bye for her assistance in discovering and snapping up unconsidered trifles.

'Boldrewood, Rolf' (T. A. Browne) *Old Melbourne Memories* ed. C. E. Sayers, Melbourne: Heinemann, 1969

Clacy, Mrs Ellen *A Lady's Visit to the Gold-Diggings of Australia* London: Hurst & Blackett, 1853

Clacy, Mrs Ellen *Lights and Shadows of Australian Life* London: Hurst & Blackett, 1854 (Recent research casts doubt on the existence of Mrs Clacy)

Coleman, Peter (ed.) *Australian Civilization* Melbourne: Cheshire, 1962

Dawe, Bruce *Condolences of the Season: Selected Poems* Melbourne: Cheshire, 1971

Furphy, Joseph ('Tom Collins') *Such is Life* Sydney: Angus & Robertson, 1944

Garner, Helen *The Children's Bach* Melbourne: McPhee Gribble, 1984

Haydon, George Henry *Five Years' Experience in Australian Felix* London: Hamilton Adams & Co., 1846

Haydon, George Henry *The Australian Emigrant: A Rambling Story Containing as much Fact as Fiction* London: Hall, Virtue, 1854

Hibberd, Jack *Squibs: a collection of short plays* Brisbane: Phoenix, 1984

Howitt, Richard *Impressions of Australia Felix during four years' Residence in that Colony: Notes of a Voyage round the World: Australian Poems, etc.* London: A. Hall, 1845

Howitt, Richard *A Boy's Adventures in the Wilds of Australia, or Herbert's Note-book* London: A. Hall, 1854

Hume, Fergus *The Mystery of a Hansom Cab* new edn, London : Remploy, 1980

McCrae, Georgiana *Georgiana's Journal* ed. Hugh McCrae, 2nd edn, Sydney: Angus & Robertson, 1966

Mathers, Peter *The Wort Papers* Melbourne: Cassell, 1972

Morgan, John *The Life and Adventures of William Buckley* new edn, Sussex: Caliban Books, 1979

Murray, Les A. *Ethnic Radio* Sydney: Angus & Robertson, 1977

Neilson, John Shaw *Witnesses of Spring: Unpublished Poems by John Shaw Neilson* Sydney: Angus & Robertson, 1972

Porter, Hal *The Watcher on the Cast-Iron Balcony* London: Faber, 1963

Richardson, Henry Handel *The Fortunes of Richard Mahony* new edn, London: Heinemann, 1954

Smith, Bernard 'Two Art Systems' *Meanjin* 40, 1, 1980, pp. 26–41

'Tasma' (Jessie Couvreur) *Uncle Piper of Piper's Hill* Melbourne: Nelson, 1969

Wallace-Crabbe, Chris 'The Legend of the Legend of the Nineties' *Review of National Literatures* 11, 1982, pp. 64–84

Walwicz, Anita *Writing* Melbourne: Rigmarole, 1977

6

Popular entertainment in Victoria

FRANK VAN STRATEN

This is an unashamedly nostalgic ramble to the Victoria of the years following the turn of the century to around the First World War. Sometimes we'll sneak up to the end of the 'twenties.

We've all heard elderly people tell 'what it was like then'. For this talk, I've gathered a host of recollections from many elderly people. I started recording oral history tapes with veteran theatre people 22 years ago. The collection has grown, and it is now part of the Performing Arts Museum's collection, and is supplemented by tapes made by other members of the Museum's staff.

These tapes sometimes make tedious listening, but if you start to distil, to select, then you start to get a pattern. That's what I've tried to do for this presentation: not to worry too much about dates or chronology, but to concentrate on what people remember, on the things that were important to them as theatre people.

The theatre people we're going to meet were all involved in popular entertainment in this state, in the years before and immediately after the First World War.

Vaudeville

If you were out for a night on the town in Melbourne at the turn of the century, you went to Bourke Street. Bourke Street was always the centre of Melbourne's popular entertainment; in fact our first theatre was established there in the 1840s. The most popular theatres were the vaudeville houses, and Bourke Street had many of them. In the 1900s, a vaudeville bill was not just one act after another. The first half was a remnant of an old minstrel show. Essie Jennings made her appearance in such a minstrel 'first part' or 'sit-around' at Rickards' New Opera House (later the Tivoli) in 1902:

The four blackface cornermen sat two on each side and a whiteface interlocutor—Charlie Waite, he was there for years—sat in the centre and announced the items. The soubrettes sat round in all their frilly little doo-dahs and big picture hats. But, they never *walked* on. I was number one and Mr Rickards wouldn't let me sit down because I wore the tight-fitting Gibson Girl dress, and he said I looked too stately to get up off a chair! He always made me walk on from the side . . . And I was there for two years.

Essie Jennings was one of the few people I have met who knew Harry Rickards. He was the king of Australian vaudeville. He had come out here in 1871 as a coster singer from England, and stayed to found a vaudeville empire that spanned the continent. His niece had some fascinating memories of what 'Uncle Harry' was like:

I hardly like to say it, but he was rather showy! He used to strut around the theatre with his big chest sticking out with diamonds all the way down the front, instead of buttons. He brought out a Rolls Royce car from England and he had to bring the chauffeur out with it: in those days you bought the chauffeur as well as the car! Everything had to be just right.

Rickards built the New Opera House in Bourke Street in 1901, replacing the old one demolished a couple of years before. It was there that great Australian comics like Roy Rene ('Mo'), Jim Gerald and George Wallace went for inspiration—and then they did their acts at Fuller's Bijou Theatre, almost next door. Here's Jim Gerald reminiscing about the New Opera House:

It used to be sixpence in the gallery, a shilling upstairs and two bob and three bob downstairs. They had all the big stars there, like Cinquevalli the juggler, Peggy Pryde, Wilkie Bard and a famous English comedian called Nat Clifford. He had a song that I sang for many years afterwards, 'The Grand Hotel':

I live in grand style,
At a grand domicile,
It's known as the Grand Hotel.
It's cheap so to speak,
Only ten quid a week,
Of it's qualities I'm going to tell.
They've only one guest,
They've poisoned the rest.
Now what could a man wish for more?
Though I sleep in a shed,
I've got a nice bed,
It's a down bed—right down on the floor!

At the Grand Hotel, at the Grand Hotel,
Where all kinds of strange insects dwell
Where for tablecloths they use the sheets
from your bed,
They don't give you meat, but there's plenty
of bread.

> They've a graveyard of their own
> Where a few of the old boarders dwell . . .
> But the landlady's daughter
> Brings my shaving water—
> And that's why I stay at the Grand Hotel.

Essie Jennings remembers the songs that she sang at the New Opera House:

> I sang all those sentimental songs—'If Those Lips Could Only Speak', 'Love Me In September As You Do In May'—all those crying ballads. Then I was the first to introduce the illustrated slides. The slides came on as you sang. And I was the first to do 'Sweet Adeline' with the four cornermen. They used to join in the harmonising chorus. It used to tear the house down; it was a terrific sensation.

How did you make a start in vaudeville? People came from all walks of life. George Wallace was a canecutter from Queensland; Charles Norman's background was quite different:

> Every second house had a piano. It was the joy of the home. You could buy them for five shillings down and two bob a week! So as lads growing up we used to go to each other's houses, especially Saturday nights, and have sing songs. It was a natural entertainment. And then I met a lad named Ernie Eade. He had a gift of harmony and we could sing well together. So we put some stuff together—one or two corny jokes, some songs. The Hawaiian songs were very popular and they were easy to harmonise: 'Goodbye Hawaii, I'm leaving, I'm coming back to you' was one of the first.
> We went to a vaudeville show at the Recreation Hall in Box Hill run by a man named Caley. There were all these erstwhile showmen around the suburbs here. Mr Howard had the Prahran Town Hall, May Downs had Port Melbourne. Footscray was a tough date. Almost every night of the week you could work if you had some sort of act. We took in this scene and Caley said, 'Go and see a man called Willie McKay at the Temperance Hall in Russell Street'. So we went in and met Willie. He was a nice little man, he'd been a comic singer in the old days and he said, 'You'll have to come in and study. I'll help you'. He'd helped no end of acts. So we'd go in a couple of nights a week and get a few songs down. Then he said, 'You need a dance; you must have one of those simultaneous dances'. So we found Alice Uren on the other corner of Bourke Street. She taught us one or two tricks: a neck roll, a nip up, handsprings. Ernie and I put a nice little soft shoe act together. We worked in full evening dress—top hat, white gloves, silver-topped canes were the thing!
> The audiences in those days were softer, kinder, they understood the business more. They understood what you were trying for. When you went on they knew something about it. It set a standard. So there was always a cameraderie between audiences and performers then, especially around the suburbs, where they had three bob 'top' at the most, and probably a shilling at the back.

If you 'made it' you had your fans. Winnie Trevail was a glamorous and popular soubrette:

I remember the gallery girls. They used to come all the time. They'd pick out their favourite performer and they'd wait at the stage door for you to come out. They'd give you beautiful gifts. I got quite a few!

It wasn't all plain sailing. There were some vaudeville houses that were notorious for their rough audiences. Jim Gerald:

They loved you no matter what you did. The Bijou was a very rough theatre. The Tivoli was 'posh', and Fuller's Bijou was 'number two'. All the comedians came from Fuller's. There they'd throw bottles—anything—at you. But if they loved you, they *loved* you. If they didn't love you, God help you!

Charles Norman again:

Friday nights at the Bijou were very rough. All the boys would be packed in the gallery. They'd all been paid, so Friday night was the big night for the shows. They'd all be full of fun, all wanting to join in the act. They'd join in alright—and if they didn't like it much they'd call out, 'What? No work?'

Addie Marsden's mother, Addie Pearce, had a drama school, and put on shows all around the Melbourne suburbs:

Mum always had two policemen in attendance, especially at South Melbourne. That was a very big audience. We never had any disturbances, but other companies did. Footscray had an exceptionally bad reputation for rowdiness, and so did Moonee Ponds. We performed there a couple of times and had no trouble.

Jim Gerald recalls a typical song of the pre-First World War era:

The type of song that Roy Rene and I sang was something like:

In our little garden subbub
Far away from the noise and hubbub
When you're tired of the pubbub
And you're tired of the clubbub
Take a little drop in the garden subbub
There you can grow stewed rhubbub
Bath in the old wash tubbub
So when you're tired of the hubbub
And the clubbub and the pubbub . . .

I can't quite remember the finish of it! But that's the type of song that the comics in those days used to sing. Not dirty, but they all had that funny way, so the words didn't matter as much as what you did with the 'business' of the song.

Material was always a problem for Australian performers because there weren't any recognised writers in this country. A lot of material was stolen from overseas artists, who found that when they visited Australia, their acts had been well and truly exploited by the locals. Eventually, when the Tivoli engaged an overseas act, notices were posted backstage prohibiting unauthorised use of that artist's material until the conclusion of their tour. This situation led to a great deal of reliance on adlibbing. Charles Norman:

> You were always scrounging for material. There weren't the writers around that you could go to then. We didn't get writers till much later on. Even the top comedians were always looking for material. Of course, it made you improvise more, it developed your talents. You had to survive, so ad lib became the thing with Australian performers.

The most famous and probably the greatest of all Australian comedians was Roy Rene, 'Mo', and he was notorious for his ad libs. His widow, Sadie Gale, worked with him in many sketches:

> We used to enlarge upon things, Roy and I. I was able to ad lib with him in a way other people couldn't. They couldn't take the liberties, they wouldn't dare. But if I could see an opening for a line, I'd go on with it. We used to do a sketch called *The Stage Door*. It originally was 2½ minutes. Over the years it gradually got to 12 minutes with all the adlibbing and different things that had crept into it. If we put in a line and it got a laugh, we'd keep it.
>
> He did a sketch called the *Queen Elizabeth*. He did the thing with white spats on and a full beard! You can imagine what it was like, all the different antics and facial expressions when he sat on the throne! I used to make my head go from side to side to say 'Enough's enough!'
>
> Years ago they used to say that Roy used to be so dirty that the police were brought in. That's a lot of rot! They wouldn't have been allowed to do half the things people said Stiffy and Mo did. But now they get away with murder. Stiffy and Mo weren't even allowed to say 'God', 'damn' or 'hell'—but Roy did use a few 'bloodies' in the finish!

Melodrama

Melodrama was the most popular form of dramatic entertainment, and several major melodrama companies trundled around Australia for years. Melodrama was the first form of live entertainment to fall victim to moving pictures, so the great melodrama companies had mostly disappeared by about 1910. Memories of them are rare. Addie Marsden again:

> There was a weekly-change melodrama season at the Princess Theatre. We used to go there quite often. Then William Anderson built the King's Theatre and he put on awful melodramas like *The Face at the Window*. Eugenie Duggan was his wife and she wasn't much of an actress. Mum used to enjoy laughing at them!

As a young boy, Reg Fowler acted in his father's company:

> Dad first started off with real drama: *East Lynne, Mother Machree, Uncle Tom's Cabin*. But then the problem of royalties came into it and he started writing his own plays so he wouldn't have to pay royalties. There was a play we used to do a lot called *Home, Sweet Home*. It started off with:

'Jerry, Jerry! I wonder where that boy has gone! He's never about when you want him, and if you don't want him, you can't get him out of the way!'

Addie Marsden played juvenile lead in her mother's production of *Uncle Tom's Cabin*:

> I loved playing Topsy because it was a comic part, apart from having to blacken myself up and wear a bag with holes cut in it for my head and arms! Then mum did *East Lynne*. There are two little boys in *East Lynne*. My little brother was one and I was the other, Willie. In the death scene where the mother's disguised as the governess and Willie's dying of consumption, I'm in a cot on the stage and crying like anything because the acting was so realistic!

Nellie Stewart was probably the most popular actress this country ever produced. She is best known for *Sweet Nell of Old Drury*, which she first played at the Princess Theatre in 1902. Her daughter, the late Nancye Stewart:

> The play suited her, but she had such a magic herself. It was the sort of thing that Ellen Terry must have had. She was a charmer. They adored her no matter what she did. But it was the first time she'd ever done dramatic work. She'd always done musicals, Gilbert and Sullivan, opera—she had played *Faust*—and she wanted to do *Sweet Nell*. George Musgrove said 'You've never done a straight part, we'll have to get somebody else to play it.' She was furious. She made up her mind and she did it.
>
> *Sweet Nell* was an extraordinary play—everybody thought it was marvellous and it's so funny to read now. She used to sometimes stop in the middle and wonder 'What am I saying now, what is this part, what act am I in?'
>
> We had a lot of different scenery because they used to make small sets for our tours. We had a special train. I think we played 147 towns all over Australia and New Zealand. It was a tremendous success. Mother could put on *Sweet Nell* at any time, and always draw a house.

There were many companies touring Australia, bringing live entertainment to isolated communities. Reg Fowler:

> In the early days we travelled by train, but that was very inconvenient, because the timetables didn't fit in with the show business. Quite often the show would finish about 10.30 and then there was a mad scramble to pack everything up to catch an early morning train. You'd only travel 10 or 15 miles so you'd get to the next town very early in the morning, nobody awake, so you'd spend several hours sleeping in the waiting room.
>
> Then dad started using carriers. You'd hire a carrier in each town. In those days it was a horse and cart or a jinker and a dray. That was always inconvenient because you'd get to a town late and there'd be a mad scramble to get ready to show.
>
> Then dad hit on the idea of hiring a carrier in Melbourne to do the whole trip—about two or three months. That wasn't too good either—a lot of arguments about one thing or another. So dad bought his own bus, a Ford.

> We had it nicely fitted up. We'd put a tent on each side to make dressing rooms, because a lot of the country halls had dressing rooms up the front, not by the stage, and you would have had to walk through the audience to get to the stage.
> Usually we'd be in the country for three or four months. Once we went up to Queensland and we were away about eighteen months. Then we'd come back to town and the artistes who were with us would get employment elsewhere and we'd look for someone else. It was hard to get people to travel in the country for any long period so dad changed his cast quite a lot.
> There's a town in the Western District where we played several times—Chatsworth—and there was a big shearing station just outside the town. All the employees had their own little houses which made quite a little village down the bottom paddock. We showed there four or five times in a shearing shed. Everybody came along with their own seats—sometimes butter boxes or kerosene tins! At night you'd look out across the paddocks and see hurricane lamps coming across the hills as people came in from the neighbouring farms. That was the audience on its way! We used to pack that shearing shed out!

Musicals

Ronnie Shand 'paid his dues' with a small touring musical comedy company in the 'twenties:

> He's unknown today, but Lionel Walsh was an extremely astute businessman and actor-manager. He started out with touring dramatic shows and later turned to musicals. He had a miniature musical comedy company: a band of six or four, a ballet of six, and a handful of principals. He had the rights to put on these shows at least 40 miles away from the main cities. We did play Geelong. The year I joined him he was doing shows called *The Rise of Rosie O'Reilly* and *Little Nellie Kelly*. The year before he'd done *The Maid of the Mountains* and *Sally*. We rehearsed in Sydney and we travelled by buses—in those days we called them charabancs. They were International trucks fitted up with three rows of seats so they each held twelve people. There was a canopy over the top. He had two of these, his own car, and a truck. There was also another touring company run by D. D. O'Connor taking musical comedies through the country.

Illusionist Les Levante recalls touring in the early years of this century:

> When I first started in this business as a professional there were at least 50 touring shows in Australia—the Lynch Family Bellringers, West's Pictures. It was usual to travel from four to seven people. It was a big company that had a dozen.

Pantomime

The big spectacular shows were necessarily confined to the big cities. Every year J. C. Williamson would stage lavish pantomimes. Nellie

Payne started her career in one of J. C. Williamson's pantomime companies and remembers him well:

> He was very charming, good looking, and had a very nice manner. He was always interested in his artistes. The first time I met him I was playing in *Alice In Wonderland*. I was a lobster and I had to wear this shell with just a little three inch slit to see through, and I was feeling frightened. Mr Williamson knocked on the shell and said 'Are you alright?'
> We played the pantomime the whole year. Perhaps fifteen weeks in Melbourne and eighteen weeks in Sydney, and then went to New Zealand.
> I remember there was a big march scene based on drinks: the girl dressed as vermouth was all in lovely green and so on. I was a cherry cocktail! I had to put on the little hat so the cherry hung down the side of my head. You couldn't be individual—you had to wear everything as the designer meant it to be. Of course the one who got the most applause was the champagne girl—she was the most beautiful show girl.

'Modern' drama

After World War I tastes changed and modern American drama became popular. Nellie Bramley recalls her weekly-change drama seasons at the Palace Theatre in Bourke Street:

> I remember the long, long seasons we played there. Every Saturday night my mother and father and my darling sister sat in the box. They always put the house lights on for me to say goodnight to everybody, so I saw my audience. They were all permanent bookers. I'd look down and think 'Oh, it's Tuesday. The Coyles are there and their family. That's how the seaon ran so joyfully.
> It was hard, hard work. We did a new play every week. You were dedicated to the theatre. I didn't drink in those days—I don't dare!—and I didn't smoke. So I was able to concentrate on doing these new plays. The plays opened on the Saturday afternoon. It had to be a *performance*, not just a skim through. I had a routine. After the Saturday night performance I'd be handed the new play that we were to open the following Saturday. When the Monday night performance finished I'd start work on it. I had a standing order with the Misses Cobb. They had the sandwich shop next to the theatre. I don't know if it's there now—or the Misses Cobb! They're probably cutting sandwiches for heavenly actors —I hope so, they did them beautifully! So I'd take my sandwiches and a bottle of lemonade, go straight upstairs to my bedroom at the theatre, have a shower, get into bed, nibble my sandwiches, and start to learn the new play.

Some actors had trouble adjusting to the new style. Nellie Payne recalls being coached by Nellie Stewart:

> In this scene I had to be very cross—and of course I was: *very* cross. I thought that was good acting! I remember Nellie Stewart saying, 'No, dear, don't do that. You'll lose the sympathy of the audience.' That was so foreign to my outlook and nature. She wanted it to be more feminine. In those days

we weren't very feminine. We were very straightforward: straight dresses and so on. You'd call us 'ladylike'.
The people who were very feminine were the female impersonators. There were shows with ex-soldiers, and they had more charm and female mannerisms than we ever thought of!

Motion pictures

Films were first shown in Melbourne at the Opera House in Bourke Street in 1896 by a magician called Carl Hertz, as part of a vaudeville bill. Moving pictures rapidly caught the public's imagination and in 1900, Commandant Booth of the Salvation Army asked the Perry family to assist the Army in making films. Reg Perry was a very young lad at the time.

> In 1900 they started production of *Soldiers of the Cross*. This was mainly taken at an Army girls' home in Dandenong Road, Murrumbeena. The family were all recruited, amongst other Army officers, and it used to be quite a joke with us being kept home from school to go out to appear in the film.
> There was the famous arena scene where the Christians were supposed to be thrown to the lions. The women were kneeling in the centre of the arena and my brother Horrie and I were the lion. Horrie had two strings, one which moved the eyes and one which worked the lower jaw. I brought up the rear, as it were, with a string that wagged the tail. We got into this papier mache body and put huge things on our feet resembling the lion's paws and learnt to amble along. We'd go and clamp the jaws onto the poor Christians kneeling in the centre of the tennis court—probably one of my own sisters!—and there the movie sequence would finish. At the same time a slide was taken of that scene and at the performance in the Melbourne Town Hall that would be shown while dad changed the little reels of film. It created quite a sensation because nothing quite like it had ever been seen before.

It wasn't long before commercial operators realised the potential of films. T. J. West founded West's Pictures and a Bourke Street dentist called Dr Arthur Russell began Hoyt's. Addie Marsden recalls a visit to the dentist:

> He used to make a lot with his dentistry, but he was very interested in show business. He'd take a circus around the country and lose his money on that. Then he went to America for further training and he found that movies were taking on. He came back and got a few people to put in money to start Hoyt's. His surgery was way up the top of Bourke Street near the old White Hart Hotel. He had quite a bit of space at the back and one time we visited him he had rows of chairs for us to try to see if they were suitable for Hoyt's show. He opened Hoyt's in what was St George's Hall, across Bourke Street from the Opera House. They had a wonderful spruiker who had originally been at the Waxworks, Charlie Fredricksen. He was 'The Man Outside Hoyt's' for years and years.

Picture shows soon sprang up all over Melbourne. 'Frosty' Summers remembers some around the South Melbourne area:

> There used to be a picture show in the South Melbourne Town Hall. Another one in Clarence Street—there's a garage there now. It was run by Mrs Howson. She used to play the piano while the pictures were on. I think it was called 'The Globe'. Then they had pictures on the beach at the end of Victoria Avenue. They used to hire out deckchairs for you to sit on. The pictures didn't talk but they had this gramophone going and that told you what they were saying. The trouble was the picture went a bit too fast or a bit slow, and the talkie would be talking when it wasn't supposed to be!
>
> Years ago there used to be a bit of a show at South Melbourne football ground on Saturday night. They'd a stage there on wheels, and they used to push it over facing the grandstand. They'd have vaudeville there and the pictures were shown on a screen between the goal posts.

Reg Perry recalls his father's touring picture show:

> One of the old man's early pictures was called *Comin' Through the Rye*. It had a little boy in kilts walking through the cornfields with his back to the camera. At a certain stage he turns around, and smiles. Dad had it down to a nicety. He'd give a loud whistle and the boy would turn round, and they'd clap and cheer and yell, 'Put it on again!'. That was typical.
>
> Of course we used to have sound effects with the silent pictures. We had a chap named Sam Crewes. Sam used to 'operate'. We had coconuts for horses hoofs, and a thundersheet, all that gear. Mr Crewes would be stationed next to the projector in the centre of the hall and when he thought effects were necessary he'd sing out, 'Ee-fects!'. And a voice from behind the screen would yell, 'Awl-right!' and he'd make the appropirate noises. Then when Sam considered that there'd been enough he'd shout, 'No effects!', and there'd be another 'Awl-right!'
>
> Eventually we got a wonderful electrical contrivance from England that made every possible noise you could think of!

The Waxworks

The moving pictures forced the closure of many of the popular Bourke Street entertainments of less sophisticated years. Addie Marsden remembers Kreitmayer's waxworks:

> It was very well set up. There was a tableau of a woman who had killed several children and buried them under the fireplace. She was a dear little thing with a white lace bonnet—you'd never think she was a murderess! There were single figures of Bismarck and Queen Victoria and so on. And the carriage and horses of the Prince and Princess of Spain—they'd been assassinated. There was the Kelly Gang too. All these were set around a big hall. Upstairs there was a native camp. They also had a room downstairs with instruments of torture. The hall had a good stage with a nice proscenium. They had a good pianist and often a ventriloquist; I've forgotten his name.

Popular music

There was music everywhere: in the shops, in the streets, in the theatres and in the home. Songs became popular without records and radio to promote them. The most popular Australian song of them all was 'On the Road to Gundagai'. Jack O'Hagan recalls how he came to write it:

> As a matter of fact I wanted a river with a name of four syllables and I'd settled on Mississippi. Then suddenly I thought of Murrumbidgee and decided to make it Australian. So I got out a map and found Gundagai. I'd never been there, probably hadn't even heard of it before!
>
> The demand in Australia was enormous. It was a smash hit straight away. We used to print 20 000 at a time! They couldn't make records here, so finally they sent it to London and fortunately Peter Dawson sang it for the gramophone and it sold and sold.

'Gundagai' and many other popular songs of that era have entered our collective consciousness and have assumed the character of folk song. Their simple melodies have an extraordinary power to evoke memories of happy times and friendly faces. Let 'Frosty' Summers, at 85, have the last word:

> You know, they *were* good old days! I often think I had a darn sight more fun then, than I do now!

7

Visual Victoria: *waterfalls, tents and meat pies*

MARGARET PLANT

Although there were topographical painters from the earliest days of Victoria's foundation, and raconteurs of the goldfields—such as S. T. Gill—it was Eugene von Guérard who 'discovered' the landscape for painting.[1] Arriving in Melbourne in December 1852, and early disappointed at the diggings, he sought the patronage of Western District squatters, visiting the area by taking the Melbourne steamer to Warrnambool and then travelling overland. His travels were extraordinarily comprehensive: he kept the still-contemporary sense of discovery, of a first awed viewing of a new country.[2] Inculcated with a European sense of the sublime and the majesty of nature, he responded to the solemnity of the Victorian mountains: his view of the peaks has never been equalled. In the path of Sir Thomas Mitchell, and in the company of fellow painter, Nicholas Chevalier, he went to the popular site of Mount Arapiles with its adjacent Mitre Rock in the Western District, and painted those sandstone formations in 1863 (Australian National Gallery).[3]

In 1858, again with Chevalier and the noted geologist and surveyor Alfred Howitt, von Guérard climbed to the Baw Baw plateau via the now familiar peaks of the Dandenongs just out of Melbourne.[4] The expedition passed through the fern country, which von Guérard records in his 1857 *Ferntree Gully in the Dandenong Ranges* (private collection). The painting received an enthusiastic reception, its subject was described in the *Illustrated Melbourne News*: ... a little thread of water, touched faintly here and there with drops of light, steals through the opening and a couple of lyre-birds one of them perched (somewhat obtrusively) upon a mossy boulder, are the only living occupants of this sylvan solitude'.[5] Inevitably one recalls Henry Kendall's poem 'Bellbirds' (so long in the Victorian school childrens' reader):

109

By channels of coolness the echoes are calling, And down the dim gorges I hear the creek falling.[5]

The multi-green mountain bush, the tree ferns and mountain ash of Sherbrooke Forest in the Dandenong Ranges is, as a recent guide would tell us, 'a household name to Melbourne families'.[6] Among the most assiduous observers of the Dandenongs country (indeed of Victoria) was Fred Williams, who lived in Upwey in the 1960s and painted Sherbrooke Forest 'stands of saplings'; they became modernised bush, geometric, elegant, but dignified in dark traditional tones, an extension of the colonial views of fern and forest country.[7]

Nineteenth-century excursionists early discovered the attractions of the near-Melbourne terrain. Ferntree Gully was the first Victorian national park, established in 1882. Also popular was the area of Fernshaw. Many times devastated by bushfires, the 'little hamlet' described in the *Picturesque Atlas* of 1888 is now but public conveniences and a picnic clearing.[8] For over 25 years Fernshaw was much studied by artists. Louis Buvelot painted *Near Fernshaw* (Australian National Gallery) in 1873, Isaac Whitehead in detailed colonial style, painted *Fernshaw* (National Gallery of Victoria) in 1880; by 1900, John Ford Paterson's *Fernshaw, A Bush Symphony* (National Gallery of Victoria) is relieved of darkness, and with heightened colour is suffused with the mists characteristic of the *fin-de-siècle* period.

The colonial artists who staked out the repertoire of sites relished waterfalls, responding to their alpine parallels.[9] In his passion for the dramatic view, von Guérard went to the Wannon Falls in the Western District, one of the most painted of colonial sites, dramatically framed by rock in Nicholas Chevalier's painting (National Gallery of Victoria), picturesque in Thomas Clark's (Warrnambool Art Gallery), in expansive view by Louis Buvelot (Queensland Art Gallery).

Von Guérard's most spectacular waterfall, which has become something of a paradigm painting for contemporary artists, is *Waterfall, Strath Creek* (Art Gallery of New South Wales). The falls are located near Murchison, and are now known as the Murchison Falls, though painters still refer to it using von Guérard's name. The motif is given an exhilarating vertical format which dramatises the thin sheet of white water between dark rocks, and the sky is pushed away as the water pursues its relentless gravity. The drama of this painting has remained seductive to modern painters: the need may well be to find water in a dry land and accost the power still explicit in nature.

In the 1970s, Fred Williams set out with Sheldon Hill's *Physiology of Victoria* to relocate for painting the motif of the gorge and the fall. Some of Williams's most powerful paintings of that decade have falls as their subject, in and around the Werribee gorges and the falls of Gippsland.[10] Small gouaches after von Guérard's painting of Strath Creek Falls make explicit Fred Williams's interest.

Louis Buvelot, 'Wannon Falls', 1868

Arthur Boyd, another of the key visualisers of Victoria, recalls the colonial falls in NSW terrain at Shoalhaven, where he frequently paints the Fitzroy Falls, surely remembering von Guérard (although Boyd is now located north of the Victorian border).[11] Gullies with streams, bush ponds, are the setting for Boyd's neoclassical dwellers in the Australian bush.

As I hope it has emerged, among my purposes in this paper is to stake for Victorian art a tradition: not only in the rendering of its key places, but in key experiences, in the interconnections between artists across 150 years. These links are powerful enough to constitute a genuinely Victorian 'heritage'.

Of interest in the study of early 'circles' of artists, is the attention given by one of our notable colonial writers, Marcus Clarke, to the paintings of Chevalier and Buvelot. Clarke, in his position as Secretary to the Trustees of the Public Library of Victoria, prepared a text, in 1874, to accompany a volume of photographs of paintings in the National Gallery of Victoria. They were in fact the first purchases, and it might be noted that the National Gallery of Victoria was established in 1864, only some 30 years after the foundation of Melbourne.[12]

One phrase of Marcus Clarke's introduction to the paintings has become particularly famous, even over-quoted—his reference to the 'weird melancholy' of the landscape—and also worth noting is his description of the fumbling oddities of flora and fauna: '... strange scribblings of nature learning how to write ... birds that cannot fly, beasts that cannot walk on all fours'.[13] If, as has been claimed, Marcus Clarke saw the landscape as a projection of his own melancholia, that sombre mood has not been lost in subsequent renderings of the Victorian bush. Rejection of Clarke's sentiments arises from our ingrained affection for the Heidelberg School, from notions of the paintings of Streeton, Roberts and Conder, in characteristic, preferred sunshine.

Modern artists, seeking to counteract the ubiquity of the pastoral tradition in painting, inheritors, too, of a modern sensibility geared to stress and malaise, have sought a wider range of visual and emotional effects. The sinuous, even sinister coils of growth in the coastal bush at Cape Schanck project a Marcus Clarke melancholy into von Guérard's painting of that area in 1858.[14] Such country finds echo and amplification in Arthur Boyd's painting during the Second World War, in his important 'Hunter' paintings.[15] A bush menace results from the focus on gorges, thick growth, and humanoid inhabitants still supine and bound to the earth. First studied in drawings, Boyd's 'Hunter' country was a location near Bacchus Marsh.

But the attraction of sunlight, the comfortable and the lyrical persists, so potent has been the influence of the Heidelberg painters. They effected the transition from the sublime mode of painting, so appropriate to the sense of land recently discovered: the land partly domesticated and settled. The transition was in large part seen to be the achievement of Louis Buvelot, to whom the younger painters paid tribute: Frederick McCubbin said, 'We owe him much and should love him accordingly'.[16]

Buvelot, who arrived in Melbourne in 1865, certainly followed the colonial painters' path to the Western District; but he is persistently associated with country nearer to Melbourne, and the areas to be frequented by Roberts, Conder and Streeton. Within a year or so of his arrival, in 1866, the National Gallery of Victoria had purchased his *Winter Morning near Heidelberg* and his *Summer Evening near Templestowe*. Both paintings are prophetic of interest in the area of Heidelberg to artists' camps. The titles suggest Buvelot's preoccupation with mellow seasons and times of day, and attention to specific effects; winter, as well as summer, and the long shadows of the evening were to be increasingly painted.

Buvelot moved away from the grand peaks and distances of von Guérard in preference for closer viewed pastorales that showed the land accessible and partly settled. He responded to 'Marks of Improvement made in the Colony', to quote the subtitle of a study of 1859 by W. Kelly, called *Life in Victoria in 1853 and 1858*. Buvelot's most famous painting, it might be noted—*Waterpool at Coleraine* (National Gallery of Victoria)—was not painted near Melbourne, but in the Western Dsitrict; it subtly introduces minute marks of settling—the felled log and the axe in the foreground.

Buvelot's endearing vision is reflected in a 1960 painting by John Perceval, explicitly titled *Homage to Buvelot* (Ballarat Art Gallery), with two grand gum trees, heroic, and familiar at the same time, shedding

Eugene von Guérard, 'Waterfall, Strath Creek' 1862

their untidy bark, looped up in the thick modern paint.[17] Buvelot also painted at Dromana, at Fernshaw, Lilydale and Mt Macedon—all central sites for young Victoria. Mt Macedon, that often-painted mountain, had early been domesticated and turned English, and was notable for its gardens and extensive plantings of English trees.[18] It was the seat of Melbourne gentry, where the Governor had a retreat. Isaac Whitehead painted Mt Macedon in a grandiose colonial view in 1876. At the turn of the century it became the home of Frederick McCubbin, whose paintings sited there moved close into the bushland, relishing the crusty English-like textures and the rich greens mixed with more indigenous growth and glimpses of mountains.

The bayside beaches were early populated by Victorians (although, not surprisingly, von Guérard earlier preferred white-water coastline around Cape Schanck, Phillip Island, Wilson's Promontory). Closer to Melbourne, the grazing country and flood plains of the Yarra, as it was then, around St Kilda, was painted by Thomas Clark. *The Coast Near St Kilda* has a bullock in the foreground, a tent on the foreshore, and a steamer out towards the heads. But the seaside as resort was soon developed, peopled, and painted—in line with new fashions in Europe.[19] Brighton was painted in a watercolour by Henry Burn (State Library of Victoria) in 1862, with a row of edifices on Beach Road, and a fine sweep of beach, sea and sky.[20]

The Mornington Peninsula, prime holiday belt for today's Melburnians, was early discovered, following Matthew Flinders's ascent of Arthur's Seat. Louis Buvelot painted at Dromana a view of Safety Beach and tracks in ti-tree, with, again, the symbols of settling, the man with axe on shoulder (National Gallery of Victoria).

But the promenade, the enjoyment of sand and bay, and not just the 'view', is uppermost in the paintings of Conder, Roberts and McCubbin, painting in the familiar beaches of St Kilda, Sandringham, Mentone, Rickett's Point and Half Moon Bay. It was Girolamo Nerli, who arrived in Melbourne in 1885, who seems to have introduced that light touch so appropriate to the beach vista.[21] Only briefly in Melbourne, Nerli presented a view that we recognise as 'characteristic': horizon smoke at Sandridge, now Port Melbourne, viewed across a flat stretch of sand and the flat, no-surf bay. Nerli's *Sandringham* (Art Gallery of New South Wales) views the opposite direction to the east and the less settled coastal area. The beach is an outdoor boulevard, site of elegant promenades.

Perfecter of the light style, Charles Conder in 1890 painted *At Rickett's Point* (National Gallery of Victoria), in which the children take over and the brushwork has that delicious summary quality so in harmony with its subject. Little has changed, if one adds the crowds and the windsurfers: this remains our characteristic beach vision.

In Conder's *The Holiday at Mentone* (private collection) pier and sea baths cast sharp shadows on the sand, and a neat spectrum of characters cast their shadows: a dapper gentleman staring out to sea, another prone on the sand, a woman reading with back turned to men and sea.[22]

Tom Roberts painted his *Mentone Beach* (National Gallery of Victoria) with dinghy sailing, and *Sunny South* (National Gallery of Victoria) with (daring) nude bathing. Fred McCubbin painted *Moyes Bay, Beaumaris* (Art Gallery of Western Australia), again with the child discovering the beach, playing with his boat.

In the Victorian tradition, the continuity of one family is conspicuous: the Boyd family, with Arthur Merric Boyd Sr beginning the lineage, painting in the foreshore area of St Kilda. His son Merric painted around Brighton, and Arthur Boyd, a major figure in current Australian painting, has returned to the earlier painted places with a persistence that might be called Proustian.[23] Arthur Boyd's first exhibited paintings were done in the company of his grandfather, in the Mornington Peninsula in the late 1930s when Arthur was in his teens. Paintings of his father, Merric Boyd, reappear in the paintings depicted as both potter and painter, through his opus. In 1969, in one such painting, Arthur Boyd painted his father painting at the beach at Beaumaris as a storm approaches.

Beside the lure of the beach, as everyone knows, is the bush sunshine, lyricism, the coveted perception of 'Australia Felix', and the camaraderie of artists which belong to the camp sites set up in the bush periphery of Melbourne in the 1880s by Tom Roberts, Arthur Streeton, Fred McCubbin—in Eaglemont, Box Hill, Mentone.

A marker at the spot at which the so-called Heidelberg School is deemed to have started, is today in suburban Summit Drive, Eaglemont (by courtesy of the Heidelberg Society), and one can still look across from that vantage point towards the Dandenongs and experience the warmth of the 'Golden Summer' terrain, which Streeton painted in 1889. Streeton, known in his circle as 'Smike', wrote to Tom Roberts ('Bulldog') in rapture at the rich scene with 'the warm blue far far away all dreaming and remote ... the wind float[ing] gently south like a stream of Turkey lollie spiders threads and making dim and large the one majestic Dandenong ranges'.[24] Streeton had in fact been down to the local pub—not the 'Old England' which still exists with its decor of old Heidelberg photographs, but to the Watts which was perhaps cheaper since records fail to establish that it had a licence.

The camaraderie of Streeton and Roberts—Smike and Bulldog—is celebrated in their letters. It was born, as such associations often are, in the places of instruction, in this case the young National Gallery School—again of astonishingly early foundation, in a young colony, in 1870. But the initial training given by the school was not to the taste of young painters. Tom Roberts recorded the training from sculpture casts in a painting of 1885 now in the Australian National Gallery, which is in marked contrast to the process enshrined in that icon of Australian painting, Tom Roberts's *The Artists' Camp* of 1888 (National

John Perceval, 'Merric Boyd', 1946

Gallery of Victoria).[25] This most famous of camps was at Box Hill in Davie Houston's paddock down on Damper Creek. Louis Abraham (whose father usefully provided the cigar box lids that were used in the '9 × 5' exhibition in 1889) is grilling the chops, bending over the fire with his grill on the end of a stick, with Fred McCubbin, the 'Prof', already settled with the beers to hand.

The artist's camp has spawned much mythology in Victorian paint-

Tom Roberts, 'The Artist's Camp', 1888

ing, giving to the tent the status, almost, of an icon, a symbol of artists' solidarity.[26] (But one must be mindful of the stretches of colonial painters' lives lived under canvas—Ludwig Becker's excursions, those mountaineer treks of Chevalier and von Guérard).

The tent is transitional, a first sign of settling, a residence still intimate with the country, as it is in Charles Conder's *Under a Southern Sun* (Australian National Gallery)—the land already cleared, the little girl playing, the washing strung from the tent. Many times the tent has been pitched and repitched in pictures and sculptures. In 1940 Sidney Nolan painted a tent prophetic of a new modernism—and that artist's peripatetic painting.[27] In the late 1940s, some young art students acquired a block of land in Lilydale, and pitched their tent.[28] We might assume that the concentration of Fred Williams on local landscape began at the Lilydale camp, even if it was not his regular practice until he arrived back from England in 1957.

Ti Parks, born in England and having come to Melbourne temporarily in 1964, may not have been fully cognisant of the Heidelberg tradition, but he used the tent as symbol of shelter in an exhibition at the Argus Gallery in 1968. Two tents were shown in apposition: one was a purchased two-man tent to which Parks gave a ridiculous ground sheet of plastic in suburban materials, on the same scale, but an outline only in knitted blue mohair, with a ground sheet of an acrylic bathroom rug. In a gesture of artists' solidarity, this latter tent was gifted to the National Gallery of Victoria by fellow artist, Dale Hickey.[29]

The tent is a symbol of temporary settlement, but (as the waterfall elicits the power of nature) the tent is frail protection for the artist exposed to the elements; it also indicates his dogged exposure, however. So Arthur Boyd, in a fluent series of paintings of 1972 to 1973, shows the artist at his landscape task, chained like an animal with blackened billy and fragile tent pitched in the bush; or the tent is reduced to a structure more primitive than a humpy: a basic triangle of wood.[30]

Of a different generation, and with a younger sculptor's sense of literal presentation, Tony Trembath installed 25 Telecom tents at La Trobe University, in 1978, where he lived for two weeks. The tents contained the paraphernalia of living, and also of the artist's life: his tools and his models, exposed to public view.[31]

Conscious of their illustrious art history, the Heidelberg Historical Society in 1985, the sesqui-centennial year, set aside 'Pegg's Paddock' as a site to receive a commemorative work of sculpture. Tony Trembath's controversial design is in four parts—with a watchtower, a pavilion, a disappearing galvanized roof that echoes the perennial geometry of the tent, and a boat (symbol of building, arrival, departure). Here are the marks of arrival and settling, of tent and house, of suburbia and fringe country.

In the 1880s, Fred McCubbin, Tom Roberts, Arthur Streeton and Charles Conder enjoyed shelter beyond the tent's canvas, as a tiny sketch records: Conder's painting of *Roberts and Streeton on a Wet Afternoon* (Australian National Gallery), where they stand in the Eaglemont hut lent to them by Charles Davies. A sketch of Streeton's *Golden Summer* is on the wall; their beds, as recorded, are of saplings and flour sacks. This painting contributes to the continuing history of Victorian tradition, since it was owned by Fred Williams before he gave it to the Australian National Gallery. Also famous in the Heidelberg annals of cameraderie is the profile portrait, the 'friendship' portrait of Arthur Streeton aged 24, painted by Tom Roberts, *Smike to Bulldog*, 1891 (Art Gallery of New South Wales).[32]

For later generations, both artists and viewers, the Heidelberg paintings, whether they were executed in Box Hill, Mentone, Eaglemont, or Chartersville (where the summer school of E. Phillips Fox and Tutor Tucker St George became legendary) are a high point of Victorian (and Australian) painting. But Heidelberg conventions reach a nadir in the 1920s and 1930s, when the pastoral tradition seemed class-bound and repetitive. The painting of the 1880s and 1890s has kept an innocent lustre, however, and has been reaffirmed as primary inspiration for recent painters and sculptors.

Fred Williams attests to the inspiration and the challenge of the Heidelberg painters. In 1970 his work was shown with Arthur Streeton's in 'Heroic Landscape', an exhibition at the National Gallery of Victoria. Williams has painted his 'answer' to the taut rock formation of Arthur Streeton's *Fire's On* (Art Gallery of New South Wales)—and those Streeton rocks surely affect Arthur Boyd's river face paintings of Shoalhaven. Arthur Boyd has claimed that 'all Australian paintings are in some way a homage to Tom Roberts. The actual mood goes from the cold hard midday light to the soft pink evening or morning light'.[33] Fred Williams expanded Roberts's hillside angles—the horse-back angles—into aerial view. Swerving horizon lines and hillsides turned on orbital edge were first evident in Williams's painting of the hillside country of Lysterfield in the Dandenongs, and then in the series of paintings of the You Yang Ranges—the dry mountains that rise from the flat plains near Geelong, and have formed a subject for many Victorian artists.[34]

The moods of the Victorian landscape—from melancholic and sinister to sanguine and luxuriant—were splendidly staked in the Victorian nineteenth century. In the twentieth century that repertoire has been knowingly consolidated and expanded, with increased melancholy, with irony and humour, with impassioned observation, and mindful conservation. But moving into the twentieth century, Victoria stepped backwards as the key artists made their exodus, and the ponderous theories of Max Meldrum, with obsolescent hindsight, declared the safety of tonality, and of traditional subjects of portrait and still life.[35] (Though one must add that *one* pupil of Meldrum, Clarice Beckett, resident and painter of bayside Beaumaris, escaped the Meldrum dourness with her spare slippery paintings of the bay, the beach and the city of trams.[36]) The National Gallery School under Bernard Hall offered little better, with Velasquez uppermost; there was little concern for the particularities of Victoria. Melbourne modernism was inhibited, much more so than in Sydney, by the self-congratulatory activities of an older Streeton; there was lacking a father figure such as Sydney had in George Lambert to encourage 'newer' forms of paintings.

Painters William Frater and Arnold Shore understood something of the potential of post-impressionism (which was, after all, a firmly nineteenth-century movement); they essayed to find new 'modern' means of presenting local landscape. Whatever the tentative nature of modernism in the paintings of George Bell, his influence as a teacher was important from the 1920s to the 1940s, and he is firmly associated with the understanding of more modern and flexible attitudes to painting. His Bourke Street School (historically photographed by pupil Russell Drysdale) was a place of encouragement for such diverse talents as Russell Drysdale, Peter Purves Smith, Eric Thake, Fred Williams. 'He made us brave', Maie Casey said of her teacher.[37]

There were a few notably 'modern' figures emergent in the 1930s, such as Sam Atyeo and Adrian Lawlor (who appears—in post-impressionist mode—in a Frater portrait of 1930, and powerfully modernised in his own self-portrait of 1937). Lawlor took up a caustic pen to attack the reactionary mountains in Melbourne art: the *Addled Art* theories of Lionel Lindsay and the Australian Academy of Art, founded in 1938 as the reactionary brainchild of Robert Menzies. In opposition to the Academy, the Contemporary Art Society was founded in 1938 with George Bell as first president.[38] New circles, in close contact with the CAS, were cohering: a new vitality was entering Melbourne art. In Heidelberg, a house called Heide was the centre of one of the most influential circles, although it was only in the 1960s that its potency for Australian art was fully recognised.[39] The house of John and Sunday Reed was the gathering place of the artists and literati. Max Harris from Adelaide joined with John Reed to edit the journal *Angry Penguins* which has sometimes given its name to the circle. French symbolist poetry, surrealist, metaphysical and expressionist painting cut across the dreary, limp influence of post-impressionism, to liberate the imagination and method for artists Sidney Nolan, Albert Tucker, Arthur Boyd, John Perceval. Socially concerned subject matter and a new symbolist primitivism flourished together, with a new but precise sense of location. Thus Nolan's *Rosa Mutabalis* of 1939 accomplishes her post-symbolist flowering in front of a background of the Reed house at Heide seen across a paddock.

After Meldrumism, Dargieism and Bernard Hallism, the right-wing art domination of Melbourne was at last challenged. Young Melbourne artists staked a vigorous new field, recognised clearly in the 1980s as a generation (to use John Reed's phrase) of 'Rebels and Precursors'. But even prior to the 1940s, the impact of the depression and the politicising of art effected certain painters who worked as social realists with themes both passionate and pertinent, as painted then, as now, by Noel Counihan.[40] The city relinquishes all aura and glamour, becoming a scenario of slums and graffiti. Melbourne was less than marvellous; like most cities, it was equated, in the war years, with T. S. Eliot's *The Waste Land*, a site of evil as in Albert Tucker's *Futile City* of 1940 (Heide Park and Art Gallery), a city on fire with Flinders Street Railway Station and St Paul's Cathedral conspicuously going under.

Two immigrants to Melbourne played an important role in invigorating the urban subject. Danila Vassilieff, Russian wanderer, first came to Melbourne in 1932, left, and returned in 1983.[41] Possessed of a rough-shod style of painted-drawing, he was influential for the younger Arthur Boyd and John Perceval, turning them away from expectations of Arcady. Josel Bergner, a Jewish immigrant, painted around the Victorian market, and the Aboriginals in Fitzroy, and distinguished little between a European sobriety of tragic experience and its transplantation to Melbourne.[42] In this climate, between 1942 and 1944,

Albert Tucker's potent *Images of Modern Evil* were born, one of the most sustained and passionate series of paintings in Melbourne's history.

Albert Tucker, 'Portrait of John and Sunday Reed', 1982

Albert Tucker's paintings are a quite specific reaction to Melbourne in wartime. St Kilda—the old Sandridge of Nerli and the beach closest to Melbourne—took on a mixed mood of daytime versus evening. Tucker describes how his 'Images' came 'directly out of wartime Melbourne—beer and sexual contests along Swanston Street, all along St Kilda Road from Princes Bridge down to Luna Park and St Kilda'.[43] The ferry of modern evil is the green and yellow Melbourne tram which will take you to Luna Park, where Nolan painted the *Giggle Palace*, and Joy Hester, the grinning entrance of Luna Park, the *Fun Fair* (private collection) with a sacrificed female stretched like a rag doll in front of it, Port Phillip Bay dark behind. Daytime St Kilda, for Sidney Nolan, was a more innocent view of blue and gold, and bathing boys at the baths.[44] Tucker, with heavier hand, cast his sun bathers surreal as humanoids. Nolan, between 1942 and 1944 (posted in wartime to

Dimboola), painted the Wimmera landscapes, mostly small-scaled, incontestably 'modern', proferring a new contrivedly innocent view of the Victorian landscape.[45] Arthur Boyd and John Perceval, in those years, were heavy with themes of the slum-bound inner-city populated by animals and cripples, and the night life of a wartime Melbourne, with the hectic seediness of symbolic Luna Park not far distant.

That complex circle of Melbourne artists in the 1940s has been recalled in one of the most tradition-enriched exhibitions of recent years: 53 portraits by Albert Tucker, painted between 1976 and 1985, exhibited as *Faces I have met* and reassociated, as the catalogue text has it, with T. S. Eliot's 'Prufrock': 'There will be time, there will be time to prepare a face to meet the faces that you meet . . .'[46] The faces are *the* circle of the 1940s, artists and literati: the Reeds, Adrian Lawlor, Noel Counihan, Sir Sidney Nolan, coy now above his collar and tie, Joy Hester, glamorous and tormented against the sea; a genial Arthur Boyd, a disoriented John Perceval, and the face of the house at Heide remembering its symbolist days with a *Bonjour Monsieur Rimbaud* title. With a bull-dogged face, in a setting of an empty room, is Bernard Smith, in 1945 not yet living in Melbourne, but known as author of the seminal *Place Taste and Tradition* that mapped the history of Australian art convincingly for the first time in its relation to European tradition and to local subjects.[47] Hardly disinterested when it comes to the art of the 1940s—the then recent past—Smith attacked Surrealists and 'Apocalypts' for their failure to come to grips with the reality of the present.

Bernard Smith was to be a central figure in Melbourne in the 1950s and 1960s, not merely as a critic and art historian, but as the cohering figure of the 'Antipodean' exhibition of 1959, which endeavoured to stem the incidence of abstract painting in Australian art.[48] This exhibition, by bringing together a distinctive set of artists—John Brack, David and Arthur Boyd, John Perceval, Clifton Pugh, Charles Blackman (and Robert Dickerson from Sydney)—demonstrated the impressive variety and range of figurative painting, and, indeed, the power of specific reactions to place and face.

It is perhaps not realised how rich is the tradition of portraits of Melbourne artists and their circles, testimony, indeed, of the tenacity of those circles. Tucker, in the 1940s, already had a considerable repertoire, including self-portraits. Nolan painted Max Harris, Joy Hester (masked), and John Perceval. Arthur Boyd painted Max Nicholson, and the Perceval and the Boyd children, Frank Kellaway, and Charles Blackman. John Perceval painted Tim and Betty Burstall, the Perceval and the Boyd children, and, in a most sympathetic portrait of 1946, Merric Boyd.

The Boyd home, 'Open Country' at Murrumbeena, was as important as Heide was to the consolidation of modern art in Melbourne.[49] Here the Boyd's had an extended family, which included John Perceval (son-in-law) and the potters who developed their ceramic 'industry' after the war. Here the young architect Robin Boyd, son of Penleigh Boyd, built in 1938 a markedly modern studio for Arthur. In the paintings of Arthur Boyd and John Perceval, there is a shift from the emotionality of the war years, which found its summation in Boyd's *Melbourne Burning* of 1946-7—a view across the bay to old-time Sandridge, with a foreground jammed with mourners.

Boyd also painted the country near Murrumbeena around Berwick, with its rounded hills, orchards and market gardens, and at the Harkaway, home of his uncle the writer Martin Boyd, he frescoed the dining room with religious-themed paintings. John Perceval's subject matter became biblical and domestic, or a blend of the two, causing, for example, Christ to dine at Young and Jackson's—no doubt using Murrumbeena pottery tureens, as the barrels came rolling in and another party was accommodated beneath the infamous painting of *Chloe*. Perceval frequently painted 'suburban landscapes' with the now-defunct outer circle railway that ran via Murrumbeena, and the domestic pottery full of the blond-headed Boyd and Perceval children.

In the later 1940s and 1950s a relative tranquillity settled over Melbourne art. Some artists defected to the Centre: Russell Drysdale was among the earliest, Sidney Nolan the best publicised. Arthur Boyd's *Black Man and Bride* series, shown in the 'Antipodean' exhibition of 1959, was a reaction to experiences of Alice Springs in 1951. Albert Tucker left Australia for an extended period in 1947, but created home thoughts from abroad, in an explorer series, conquering Gippsland terrain—either Strzelecki or Angus McMillan, with flat hat, rifle, corrugated face (Queensland Art Gallery).

Sidney Nolan, while staying with the Reeds at Heide in 1946-47, before his exit from Victoria, painted his famous series of Ned Kelly paintings: 25 of the 27 were given to the Australian National Gallery by Sunday Reed in 1977. While Australians in general have been quick to adopt Ned Kelly as the anti-hero whose opposition to authority can be seen, somehow, as natural and useful, Nolan's first series were in addition a sustained response to the bush country of northern Victoria—the Kelly country in the Goulburn Valley—Glenrowan and Mansfield, Beechworth and Wodonga. It is country beautifully assimilated into a Kelly drama: muddy dams, blue skies, haze and dust, mountains, valleys, painted as if to suggest the pose, fluidity and variety of nature against which police and bandits are but droll puppets.[50]

In the 1950s, around Melbourne in the bush periphery, local *plein air* painting continued and flourished—around Hurstbridge, Cottles Bridge and Panton Hills. The bushland around Eltham and Warrandyte attracted new artist settlers.[51] Walter Withers had lived at Long's Hill at Eltham where he painted his 1909 *Silent Gums* (National Gallery of Victoria). Clara Southern, a pupil of McCubbin and a well-known name at Charterisville, settled at Blythe Bank in Warrandyte. Penleigh

Arthur Boyd, 'Nude Black Dog and Tent by a Black Pool', 1961

Boyd, resident at Warrandyte, is remembered for his wattle-laden paintings of the Yarra River (National Gallery of Victoria). In the 1970s Fred Williams made regular pilgrimages to St Andrews when the wattle was in full flower; John Perceval and Arthur Boyd also painted in the area. In 1971 Clifton Pugh began his Dunmoochin community of mud-brick dwellings which have been associated with the Eltham area since Justus Jorgensen's eccentric Monsalvat was raised in the 1930s, to reassert artists' affection for the land, and desire for its proximity to it.[52]

Closer to Melbourne, John Perceval 'discovered' Williamstown, and in a sequence of paintings from 1956 until the late 1960s, painted the ships, docks and swans on the Strand side, and the more informal jetties and rowing boats on the Rifle Range side. His *Gannets Diving* of 1956 (National Gallery of Victoria) introduces a local touch with the boatmen on the rocks garbed in Richmond football guernseys. The Williamstown expeditions redeclared the camaraderie of site visits. Harold Hattam went often, and Charles Blackman painted with Perceval. Not surprisingly, nineteenth-century artists had preceded them: Fred McCubbin, and Walter Withers, who had painted there around 1908-1909.

Seeking redress for the lesser recognition of sculpture, a potent group came together in the 1950s, first known as the 'Group of Four' and then as 'Centre Five', inspired in their work to make reference to local nature, and in their materials, to utilise local woods. Julius Kane, who came to Melbourne from Budapest in 1949, was a leading force until his death in 1962: his hollow wood sculptures, his 'Organisms', approximated for the first time in Australia to an expressionist carved tradition. Inge King, Clifford Last, and Vincas Jomantas have worked with local woods.[53] Lenton Parr turned an insect world, with classical overtones, into industrial formats. Inge King's recent work in monumental scaled black metal is exemplified by *Forward Surge*, commissioned in 1973 as one of Melbourne's most spectacular projects for the Performing Arts Centre (adjacent to the National Gallery in St Kilda Road), yet it recalls her 1960 *Bush Family*, a presence in the bush and an endeavour to challenge the environment, bush or city. Before Norma Redpath became expatriate to Italy, her bronze sculptures with their reference to geological formations staked for local work a new reference to nature, dredging up metaphors that pertain to the antiquity of the land.

Julius Kane, Inge King, Clifford Last—with his meticulous turned wood columns—might be seen as sculpture's colonials, bringing a much-needed conviction of modern practices and local references to that art (as did Lenton Parr, as an assistant for two years to Henry Moore), challenging at last the notion (alas, still lingering) that sculpture is for commemoration. Despite the poignancy and power of such work, the notorious incident of the commission—and expulsion—of Ron Robertson's *Vault*, installed briefly under protest in the new city square in Melbourne, is witness to the recalcitrance of the central city.

The country, the bush in proximity to the city, works on the city and its dwellers, who cannot be ignorant of its near presence. The vast tracks of suburbia had only been intermittently art's subject, more often castigated than celebrated.

In the 1950s, new commercial galleries opened (breaking the Melbourne tradition of exhibiting art in picture framers' establishments, antique shops and furniture emporiums). The Australian Galleries in Collingwood was established in 1956 by Thomas and Anne Purves. Georges and Mirka Mora arrived in Australia in 1951: the Mirka Gallery was established in 1953. Georges Mora was central to the revival of the Contemporary Art Society, and was proprietor of the Balzac

Restaurant in East Melbourne (with its 'decor' of John Perceval angels and mural by the Annandale Imitation Realists).[54] The Moras then opened a gallery and bistro in Fitzroy Street, St Kilda (with decorations by Mirka in her characteristic mermaid style). The Tolarno Gallery continues in South Yarra. In 1960 the Argus Gallery was opened, under the directorship of Ruth McNicholl, to be another centre for young artists and an 'avant-garde'. Violet Dulieu started the South Yarra Gallery in 1961. Gallery A was first sited in Flinders Lane by Max Hutchinson, with Clement Meadmore as sculptor-furniture designer and director. In 1962 it moved to a modern white warehouse in Toorak Road, South Yarra, potent for the display of new abstraction. The activity of John and Sunday Reed in the 1950s gallery revival was central, through the foundation of the Gallery of Contemporary Art in Flinders Lane in 1958, which became (alas too briefly) the Museum of Modern Art and Design. Today 'Heide II', the Reed home built adjacent to the first influential house in Bulleen Road, is a state gallery, consolidating the Reed collection and mounting exhibitions that are the direct expression of the Reed's interest and collecting.[55]

These were more than commercial venues. They were new 'salons' for the artists, confirming the variety, vitality and the assured professionalism of the Melbourne art world. At Gallery A, in the early 1960s, Janet Dawson commenced a print workshop and a school. RMIT had a print workshop evening each week where Tate Adams, Fred Williams and James Mollison worked together with a younger generation dominated by George Baldessin. The Crossley Gallery in Crossley Street off upper Bourke Street was a centre of a new dispersal of the art of etching and lithograph, with local artists and a strong and influential representation of Japanese printmakers.[56]

In 1960 Robin Boyd declared the ubiquity of 'The Australian Ugliness', and in his Boyer lectures of 1967 detailed 'the Artificiality of Australia'.[57] But a wry eye (and ear) for the particularities of Melbourne urban life emerged in the 1950s. Mrs Everage stepped out of Moonee Ponds;[58] John Brack showed the family touring, peeking from the windows of their FJ Holden (National Gallery of Victoria). Brack's line was merciless, finding new urban subjects—the *Barber's Shop* (National Gallery of Victoria), the *Menswear Shop* (Australian National Gallery), the woman in curlers in the phone box. His scalpel-sharp drawing of 1954 called *New Suburb* (Australian National Gallery) might be prophetically placed beside Robin Boyd's photograph of a new treeless suburb, all back fences and washing lines, called 'Arboraphobiaville' in *The Australian Ugliness*. In a famous image of 1959 Brack has the commuters at *Five o'clock in Collins Street* (National Gallery of Victoria) returning axe-faced to their suburbs, to the then-Premier Sir Henry Bolte's hymned duo of the block of land and the motor car. Brack's commuters pass within stone's throw of the Grosvenor Chambers where Tom Roberts painted, and the Melbourne chambers where Charles Conder once had his studio.

In an acerbic series of 1963-65 Brack extended his shop series to include the window of the period-piece, Roper's Surgical Store, then in Swanston Street, with its elastic stockings and range of walking aids. There is little doubt that Brack would see Melburnians also in need likewise of spiritual props.

In Brack's portraits, a wry contribution to the tradition of *amitié* in Victorian painting, the victim is pinned down on the floorboards and the painter's eye well peeled for variances of carriage and silhouette as he catches the mixture of pride and arrogance of John Perceval with his shelf of ceramic angels (National Gallery of Victoria) and the mediative roundness of Fred Williams.

But Melbourne painting has not lacked its aspirants to the spiritual, nor has the antipodean eye for the exigencies of suburb or scene worked against the achievement of the 50 painting years of Roger Kemp, seeking a unity of all matter, a freedom from the limitations of location, and inspiration through Gothic armatures and the black and blue of stained glass.[59] His 'configurations' and 'sequences' based on the circle and the square expand now to mural scale.

The 'tide' of abstraction entering Australian painting in the 1960s and 1970s appeared to some a merely imported American idiom, but in fact an older generation, epitomised by Roger Kemp, had already demonstrated abstraction's spiritual roots. A younger generation, in part inspired by the steely eye of John Brack, was finding in abstraction a tool for urban exposure, drawing on the sharp abstract modes of hard edge and minimalist art.

The positive and ubiquitous geometry—or monotony—of suburban fences, brick walls, weatherboards, and mohair knitting (a fashionable preoccupation of the 1960s) became the teasing modules of a sequence of large-scale urban abstracts of the 1960s. In the fences and walls of Dale Hickey's paintings, the knitting patterns—the 'Superknits'—of Robert Rooney, together with the cut-out collectibles that featured on cereal packets, the walls and bathroom tiles of Janet Dawson, the suburb was present, but distanced. Ti Parks, creator of 'tents', had a stranger's sharp eye for the urbanities and made radiograms, tiles, plastic cafe doors and woolly acrylic the subject of localised paintings and collages. The subjects, midway between the grandiose and the absurd, took up the 'featurist' details described by Robin Boyd as endemic suburban bad taste, but they were, and are, the reality of the suburbs. James Doolin, another temporary and influential resident from West Coast America painted in the 1960s a series of 'Artificial landscapes', in the shadow, or sunshine, of Boydian critiques of 'Artificial Australia'.[60]

Bruce Pollard, a young gallery director in empathy with the new art, established Pinacotheca, first in St Kilda, then in a disused Richmond factory, with battered cinema seats and a baronial wooden ceiling, and the requisite white walls. Again a new salon was formed. John Nixon, an active Melbourne artist, began Art Projects with a valuable (and not widely popular) bias towards conceptual art, in the studio territory of the west end of the city, towards Spencer Street, just ahead of the demolition hammer.

In 1983 the Australian National Gallery in Canberra gathered up the icons of Melbourne suburbia in an exhibition called 'A Melbourne Mood: Melbourne Cool'—a name that will doubtless adhere (and one hopes will find as beguiled an audience as the Heidelbergers).[61] The work ranged from Eric Thake's 1950s witticisms on local themes and John Brack's shops and commuters, to younger artists working in multiple areas of canvas, construction, video and discotheque.

The recognition, in humour and irony, of the reality of the suburb prompted much art in the 1970s. Suburban themes became the stock of series of photographs: Robert Rooney turned from painting to photographing scorched almonds, the palm trees in front of Luna Park and the FJ Holden. Already used as bona fide illustrations to life in suburbia, Jenny Watson's heavily painted series of 'Houses where I have lived' depicted a series of eastern suburbs double-fronted brick veneers, with intact Yates-style gardens and Dulux trimmings, set down in luxurious paint as if they were as sensuous as any bush artefact.[62]

On the side of the bush, the Mildura Sculpture Triennial, established in 1960 in the Riverina city on the banks of the Murray, merits a positive note in the records of the state's art history, as it has provided Australia-wide a sustained venue and breeding ground for sculpture.[63] In 1975 it became a 'Sculpturescape', recognising the international current of outdoor environmental installations, moving sculpture out from gallery rooms and neat irrigated lawns to sprawl and burrow along the Murray terrain.

At Mildura, in 1973, sculptor John Davis laced a set of trees along the river with various canvas wrappings. He has since focussed his art on a 'sense of place'—the You Yangs, the Hattah Lakes in Kulkyne National Park—drawing the materials of his sculpture from those sites, using twigs, stones and branches bound together to construct tentative primitive dwellings—preceding the tent—or gathering together materials as outdoor altar-pieces.[64]

While a new regionalism of international endorsement consolidated in the 1970s (and still remains potent), the pursuit of irony and the awareness of the equity of the image were to attract a new generation of artists, confidantly aware of local art and social traditions while sophisticated in international theories of semiotics and structuralism. A knowing audience was staked by the appearance in 1981 of *Art and Text*, edited by Paul Taylor, active as custodian of a 'New Wave' and of a 'Second Degree': a 'newer subcultural style' in touch with 'pop music, fabric design, pictorial conventions and social aspects of the body'.[65] In 1982 an exhibition, 'Popism', was shown at the National Gallery of

Victoria, marrying Andy Warhol's Campbell Soup tins to local Rosella.[66]

In another, and necessary response to the pluralism of the times, and in the wake of the delayed understanding of the 'Rebels and Precursors' generation of the war-year 1940s, a new expressionism surfaced, annexed to the international 'Zeitgeist'. A much publicised mentor was the older artist Peter Booth who had passed from a heavy form of abstraction in the 1970s to a heavy figurative nightmare style of painting, with stolid self and ferrety dog as central images.[67] Younger painters responded with a new primitive figuration and consciously *forged* a link with Melbourne 'expressionism' of the 1940s. In Melbourne, Roar Studios were set up in 1982 in an old shoe factory in Brunswick Street, Fitzroy, as a non-commercial collective, declaring their penchant for 'expressive artists, people who've got something to say'.[68]

At the same time, bush and countryside are still accosted *en plein air*. Fred Williams' last suite of paintings focussed on distant Pilbara country, but locally, in Victoria, he worked from 1975 to 1977 at the billabong in Kew that hides below the North Eastern Freeway.[69] In what is perhaps a necessary opposition to Fred Williams, the bush has relinquished its subtlety and becomes strident in the recent garish and unsubtle vistas of Jeff Makin (following Fred Williams' motifs) and the shrill Cottesloe geometries of Dale Hickey.

With urban deliberation, in pursuit of the immigrants' point of entry into Melbourne at old Sandridge, and with inspired earnestness and humour, Jan Senbergs turned to Port Melbourne. As a point of historical return and departure, he used the set of watercolours painted in 1875 by Wilberham Liardet.[70] Liardet was then in his mid-seventies, and his paintings reconstructed earlier Melbourne. Particular to the port area was the marker used by surveyor Darke, who raised up a beer barrel, to the delight of Senbergs. Liardet established his famous hotel directly on the beach at Sandridge and, at least for a time, had a monopoly on the ferrying trade from anchored ships and the passage to Williamstown. Senbergs's suite of paintings and drawings produced between 1979 and 1981 play droll havoc with the hoisted beer barrel and the modernisations of Port Melbourne: its Westgate Bridge exit, Senbergs's own demolished studio, and the residential high-rises along Beaconsfield Parade.

Finally it might be observed that Victorian artists have always been sensitive to the state's disasters, alert to register the destruction of man and land; the continuing vulnerability of landscape, of early explorer, of later settler.

William Strutt, Victoria's first history painter, was on the spot for the start of the Burke and Wills expedition from Royal Park in 1860: a competitive journey, liberally funded by the Victorian Exploration

130 *Victoria's Heritage*

Jan Senbergs, 'Liardet's Beach', 1980

Dale Hickey, 'Pie', 1974

Committee, which ended in the disaster of Cooper's Creek. Burke, 'Victoria's first hero' was to be the subject of a burial picture painted by Strutt in England in 1911 (State Library of Victoria), and the tragedy of Cooper's Creek was the subject of a large-scaled canvas by John Longstaff, fully entitled *Arrival of Burke, Wills and King at the Deserted Camp of Cooper's Creek, Sunday Evening, 21st April, 1861* (National Gallery of Victoria). Commissioned by the Public Library of Victoria and the National Gallery of Victoria, the work is indicative of the status of the heroes; Longstaff worked on it from 1902 to 1907.[71] The first major bronze statue to be cast in Melbourne (unveiled in 1865) was Charles Summer's plinth statue of Burke and Wills, originally sited at the intersection of Russell and Collins streets, but now gracing the city square. Now an ironic fall of water emerges beneath the reliefs that show the explorers dying of thirst.[72] In 1950 Sidney Nolan, with his impeccable sense of the modern audience for Australian myth, painted a series that shows the journey out from Melbourne, the explorers uneasily seated on camels, and the fate at Cooper's Creek.[73] Lost children were an early theme, painted by Strutt, and by McCubbin, whose *Lost Child* of 1886 and his later *Lost* of 1907, are well-appreciated paintings in the National Gallery of Victoria.[74]

But it is the bushfire that registers the shock of disaster in both country and city repeatedly throughout the history of Victoria. After his return to England in 1866, William Strutt painted his heroic-scaled *Black Thursday, 1851* (State Library of Victoria).[75] John Longstaff recorded the Gippsland Sunday Night fires of 1898 in a huge painting of 1907, and the fires have burnt into the later twentieth century in Clifton Pugh's views of crows and carcasses, Fred Williams's post-1968 paintings of fire in the Dandenongs and the new growth of ferns.[76] With Ash Wednesday of 1983, the inferno of land and of people was painted by the young artist, David Larwell (National Gallery of Victoria), and a sacrificial bush altar *Ash Wednesday* made by young sculptor, Fiona Orr.

Tragedy, sublimity, lyricism, melancholy; country, city, suburb—all have found their visual expression in Victorian art. No longer can one sustain the view of the critic who wrote in the *Argus* of 1867 with the 'complaint or regret often expressed in Australia, that its scenery, howsoever beautiful, has no human interest; that it wants as yet the consecration and the charm that we can connect with no mountain, valley, rock or river, the "extrinsic circumstance of record or tradition". The past owes nothing—as in other countries—to the present'.[77]

Recall, association, quotation, homage: all now have been practised. It might be claimed that tradition is often captured expressively in the genre of humour and irony that bring to the forefront the ordinary icons of local life. Thus one might end with a pendant 1974 picture by Dale Hickey of that accompaniment to many a luncheon and football match, the meat pie with sauce, and a poignant declaration by another child of Victoria—Barry Humphries:

> I think that I could never spy
> A poem as lovely as a pie
> A banquet in a single course
> Blushing with tomato sauce ...[78]

Notes

The notes are intended not only as an acknowledgement of sources, but as an amplification of the sites and circles mentioned in the text.

1. Alan McCulloch *Artists of the Australian Gold Rush*, Melbourne: Lansdowne, 1977; Geoffrey Dutton *S.T. Gill's Australia*, Melbourne: Macmillan 1981; Marjorie Tipping *An Artist of the Goldfields, The Diary of Eugene von Guérard*, Melbourne: Currey O'Neil 1982.
2. A map tracing the Victorian journeys forms the endpapers of Candice Bruce *Eugene von Guérard*, Australian Gallery Directors' Council, 1980.
3. Mt Arapiles is described in 1888 on page 194 of the famous *Picturesque Atlas of Australia* (ed. Andrew Garran, republished Lansdowne Press, Sydney, 1984) as

   ... a curiously fantastic mass of rock, one thousand three hundred and seventy-six feet high ... In its horizontal laminations and vertical fissures, it resembles the stupendous foundation walls of some vast edifice planned and commenced by Titans and then abandoned, leaving nature to adorn the ruin, according to her gracious wont, by crowning its summit with forest trees and weaving a robe of foliage about its feet. A little to the northward of it, surmounting a wooded mound, is another columnar rock, but of very much smaller dimension, with a cleft-crest, whence it has derived the appellations of the Mitre Rock.

   Mt Arapiles and the Mitre Rock were also painted by Nicholas Chevalier in 1863 (Australian National Gallery). Chevalier and von Guérard visited it together in 1868 (Bruce *Eugene von Guérard* p. 68). Von Guérard's painted *Mt Arapiles* (private collection) is dated 1874.

   Sidney Nolan, stationed at Dimboola during the Second World War, 1942 to 1944, painted *Wimmera from Mount Arapiles* (National Gallery of Victoria), one of a series of paintings in summary style and high-keyed colour. The series has been accorded an importance in the shift in Australian landscape painting to modernist concerns. See Richard Haese 'Under the sign of the plain and the sky' in *Sidney Nolan: the City and the Plain* National Gallery of Victoria, 1983, pp. 3-31, and Haese 'The Lost Wimmera years of Sidney Nolan 1942-44' *Art Bulletin of Victoria* vol. 24, 1983, pp, 5-19.

   Ian Burn offers some valuable counter observations in his review of the National Gallery exhibition (and catalogue) in 'Landscape and Life' *The Age Monthly Review* August 1983, p. 18ff.

   Arthur Boyd's paintings of the Grampians country and Wimmera farms follow from a visit to the area in 1950. His tempera landscapes favour rather humble rural establishments with stubble and wild grasses in the foreground, low distant hills, and bird life. See Franz Philipp *Arthur Boyd*,

London: Thames and Hudson, 1967, pp. 62–66. On page 64, writing of *Wimmera Landscape II*, 1950 (private collection), Philipp suggests that 'one might *cum grano salis* describe (it) as a classical Australian landscape: the flat wave of the distant hills with its purplish undertone mediating between the yellow brown of the plain', but in fact the Wimmera landscapes have some haunting and lonely quality that makes them unusual in the tradition of pastoral painting.

4   For the von Guerard expedition, and the quotation from the *Illustrated Melbourne News*, see Candice Bruce *Eugene von Guérard* p. 48, and Candice Bruce, Edward Comstock and Frank McDonald *Eugene von Guerard, a German Romantic in the Antipodes*, Martinborough: Alister Taylor, 1982. Susan Priestley, in *The History of Victoria, Making their Mark* (Melbourne: Fairfax, Syme and Weldon, 1984) notes on p. 125 that Thomas' 1868 *Guide for Excursionists* recounted walking trips beyond Lilydale to Healesville, into the Dandenongs to the small farming enclave of Harmony Vale (now Olinda), and to Ferntree Gully', and on p. 233 notes the decoration of Ferntree Gully in 1882 as 'The People's Park'.

5   Henry Kendall's evocation of the fern country and his landscape response in poetry is studied in Brian Elliot *The Landscape of Australian Poetry*, Melbourne: Cheshire, 1967, ch. IV. 'Channels of Coolness', p. 100 ff.

6   *Blair's Guide Travel Guide to Victoria and Melbourne*, Blackburn, 1984, p. 90

7   On return to Australian from Europe in 1957, Fred Williams painted at Mittagong in New South Wales, where his characteristic geometry and sobriety of colour became evident. Sherbrooke Forest paintings followed in 1959. He moved to Upwey in August 1963, and painted intensively in the Olinda-Sherbrooke area. He painted again in Sherbrooke in 1974. Bernard Smith claimed that Fred Williams took up where Tom Roberts left off, having in mind Roberts's Sherbrooke Forest paintings, circa 1924 (*Australian Painting 1788–1970*, Melbourne: Oxford University Press, 1971, p. 414). Fred Williams himself suggested that he 'repaints other people's paintings', and gives the example of *Bailed Up* (Craig McGregor *In the Making*, Melbourne: Nelson 1969, p. 103). While such articulate consciousness of Australian art indeed constitutes 'a tradition', Williams's assimilation of European modernism should not be forgotten. For Tom Roberts's Sherbrooke Forest paintings see Helen Topliss *Tom Roberts, A Catalogue Raisonné*, Melbourne: Oxford University Press, 1985, plate 226. In 1921 Arthur Streeton went to live at Olinda, writing to Tom Roberts of his proposed move in vein nostalgic for the Heidelberg days: 'I'm striving to buy, if I can get it cheap enough 3½ acres on top of Olinda. The top is cleared of all except about 10 fine Blackwoods, most beautiful trees (and the blossom, as you know, a soft yellow, like pale butter ...') *Smike to Bulldog, Letters from Sir Arthur Streeton to Tom Roberts*, ed. R. H. Croll, Sydney, 1946, p. 105. Tom Roberts returned to Australia in 1922, to settle in the Dandenongs nearby, at Kallista. See Helen Topliss, *Tom Roberts, A Catalogue Raisonné*, p. 25.

8   *The Picturesque Atlas*, p. 302. The famous Victorian photographer J. W. Lindt sited his studio and guest house, the Hermitage, above Fernshaw on the Black Spur. He died, and his house was wiped out in fires of 1926. See Jennie Boddington, 'J. W. Lindt, photographer (1845–1926)', *Art Bulletin of Victoria* 1975, pp. 23–27.

9 The motif of the falls (for Victoria and beyond) is briefly addressed by David Thomas in *'Thomas Clark' Bulletin of the Art Gallery of South Australia* vol 35, 1977, pp. 4–9. For Von Guérard, see p.10 (*Strath Creek*), p. 107 (*The Weatherboard Falls in the Blue Mountains* and *Waterfall Clyde River, Tasmania*) and—not included—the highest falls in Victoria, the Steavenson Falls, near Marysville (Australian National Gallery).

10 For Fred Williams in pursuit of gorges, see McCaughey *Fred Williams*, 'The Gorge, 1975–8'. The Gorge series consists of a large group of works painted mainly in 1976–77, in and around Werribee Gorge. Williams had painted at the Preston and Keilor gorges since late 1974, but it was only at the end of 1975 that Williams began to paint at Werribee Gorge, and the series began in earnest. The paintings were to form the bulk of his exhibitions in Sydney and Melbourne in 1978. Williams also painted Wild Dog Creek (a small tributary of the Werribee Gorge), the Lal Lal Falls and, in 1979, the waterfalls of Southern Victoria—Agnes Falls, Noogee and Port Welshpool in South Gippsland. Von Guérard had painted the Lal Lal Falls; see Marjorie Tripping *An Artist of the Goldfields*, p. 11.

11 For the Shoalhaven Falls, see Sandra McGrath *The Artist and the River*, Sydney: Bay Books, 1983, p. 196, p. 198 (where the waterfall is a background for Susannah's bathe before the Edlers) and p. 206.

12 Leonard Cox *The National Gallery of Victoria, 1861–1968, a search for a collection*, National Gallery of Victoria, Melbourne, n.d.

13 Marcus Clarke's text, which he reprinted as preface to the 1876 edition of Adam Lindsay Gordon's *Sea Spray and Smoke Drift*, is reprinted in Bernard Smith (ed.) *Documents in Art and Taste in Australia*, Melbourne: Oxford University Press, 1978, pp. 133–140. L. T. Hergenham, in a valuable article, emphasises that Clarke's view is 'private' and 'personal', and suggests that Clarke 'appears to be promoting the myth that the harsher, wilder areas of Australia (today generally represented in literature and art by the inland deserts) rather than the more habitable, gentler and picturesque areas of the eastern litteroral and other areas are the "real" Australia' ('Marcus Clarke and the Australian Landscape' *Quadrant* 3, 1969, p. 34.). In his catalogue essay for *Australian Art in the 1870s, an exhibition to mark the centenary of the Art Gallery of N.S.W.*, 1976, he suggests that Clarke's texts may have influenced painting of the 1870s, noting that 'Von Guerard and Clarke worked in the same building and both worked on the book of National Gallery pictures' (p. 13).

14 Candice Bruce observes of the Second Expedition of von Guérard to Cape Schanck that he produced

> ... one of his most significant paintings ... *Pulpit Rock, Cape Schanck, 1865* that can perhaps be regarded as the culmination of von Guérard's technical expertise on the one hand, and efforts at Romanticism on the other. It is certainly the fulfilment of his ideas on Australian landscape and seems to sum up everything that is best in his work. The strong geometry, the twisted and contorted trees, the symbolism of the bird and fox eyeing each other warily, above all the rhythm that pervades the whole composition, fills the painting with an energy that is sexual in its writhing.

15 For the Hunter landscapes of Arthur Boyd, see Franz Philipp's comment (*Arthur Boyd*, pp. 38 and 39): 'Arthur Boyd creates a new type of landscape ... from an impenetrable thick of river gums into a clearing where dead,

rotting trees intermingle with felled humans ... The primordial mountain bush landscape of 1944 was to play a focal part in the later development of Boyd's nature-myth ...'

16 Frederick McCubbin's tribute to Buvelot is republished in *Documents on art and taste in Australia* (ed. Bernard Smith, Melbourne, Oxford University Press, 1975): 'Some remarks on the history of Australian art', p. 269 ff. McCubbin's 'modern' rejection of colonial subjects and painters is of interest, since he claimed (inaccurately) that 'Where von Guérard and Chevalier went in search of mountains and waterfalls for their subjects, Buvelot interested himself in the life around him'. Contemporary reactions to the environment, mood and placement of Buvelot's paintings are presented in Jocelyn Gray 'A new vision: Louis Buvelot's press in the 1870s' in *Studies in Australian Art* (ed. A. Galbally and M. Plant, Department of Fine Arts, University of Melbourne, 1978, pp. 15-26. Buvelot's significance for Arthur Boyd is noted in Richard Haese *Rebels and Precursors, the Revolutionary Years in Australian Art*, Melbourne: Allen Lane, 1981, pp. 210-211.

17 John Perceval (unlike Fred Williams or Arthur Boyd) has eschewed mountains and waterfalls, in preference for what is traditionally taken to be the Buvelot closer country. At the same time, John Perceval's preference for painting knee-deep in the grasses and close to the woodlands carries the tradition of Fred McCubbin. See Margaret Plant *John Perceval*, Melbourne: Lansdowne, 1978, pp. 76-78.

18 *The Picturesque Atlas* presents Mt Macedon as an exotic region, with engravings of 'the Governor's residence'. On pp. 283-4 there is the following description:

> Enjoying a cool temperature at night in the hottest period of the year, presenting an endless variety of romantic scenery, and commanding a succession of prospects of great extent: this lofty region has been selected by many Melbourne residents as a place in which to spend the *villeggiatura* ... The southern slopes of Mount Macedon are dotted with villa residences, the highest in point of situation being also, by a piece of unusual good fortune, the most artistic in design ... '

For Fred McCubbin at Macedon, see Ann Galbally *Frederick McCubbin*, Melbourne: Hutchinson, 1981; for example, p. 105 reproduces *The Artist's Studio, Macedon*.

19 Susan Priestley notes in *The Victorians, Making Their Mark* that 'Victorian summer seasons encouraged greater enthusiasm for sea bathing during the 1880s' (p. 228), but notes the 'Victorian' structures placed on public bathing beaches until well into the twentieth century.

20 Helen Topliss presents the coastal sites of Brighton, Sandringham, Beaumaris and Mentone in *The Artists' Camps: Plein Air Painting in Melbourne 1885-1898*, Melbourne: Monash University Gallery, 1984, mentioning the Brighton home of the Boyds and John Mather, whose *Picnic Point*, painted in March 1886, she sees as prefiguring Roberts's *Mentone*, 1887 (National Gallery of Victoria), and John Ford Paterson, whose *Hauling the Seine Half Moon Bay* (Bendigo Art Gallery) was painted in 1888.

21 The painting of the beaches of Australia was established by Roberts and Conder at Coogee, NSW during Easter, April 1988. (See Ursula Hoff *Charles Conder*, Melbourne: Lansdowne, 1972, pp. 40-41, and Ursula

136 *Victoria's Heritage*

Hoff 'Arthur Streeton at Coogee' *Art in Australia* vol. 5, 1, 1963, pp. 40–44.) On Nerli's Melbourne participation, see Bett Currie 'Signor Nerli' *Art and Australia* vol. 16, 1, September 1978, p. 60. 'Certainly Roberts and Streeton joined Nerli to paint the Melbourne bayside beaches ... On the grounds of costume, weather and opportunity it seems the late winter or spring months of 1890 or the first months of 1891 are the likely dates for the many beach scenes for which Nerli is famous ....'

Nerli's view of Sandringham, looking towards the east (the opposite direction to Sandbridge), is compared by Ursula Hoff (*Conder*, p. 47) in a discussion concerning Conder's *Rickett's Point* where it is claimed that 'Conder outdistanced Nerli in subtlety of means and *finesse* of touch'. The charming motif of the child with the bucket in Conder's *Rickett's Point*, 1890 (National Gallery of Victoria) reminds one of Robin Boyd's felicitous observation (in *Australia's Home*, Melbourne University Press, 1952, p. 49) that 'Childhood was largely an outdoor state, even when cities developed and playing paddocks were overgrown with fences ... The infant left the pram earlier than his European contemporary'. William Moore, in his *The Story of Australian Art* (Angus and Robertson, 1934, facsimile print 1980, p. 71.

22 William Moore has Mentone Beach as a central meeting point in the annals of the Heidelberg School, *The Story of Australian Art*, p. 71. As early as the summer of 1886, McCubbin and Roberts were renting a cottage at Mentone, and on p. 71 in *Story of Australian Art*, there is a description of how

> One Sunday morning, Roberts found Streeton out on the wet rocks, doing a free sketch of shore and sea ... and we asked him to join the party ... On Sundays we took a billy and chops and tomatoes down to a beautiful little bay which was full of fossils, where we camped for the day. We returned home during evening through groves of exquisite tea-trees, the sea serene, the cliffs at Sandringham flushed with an afterglow.

23 I wrote of the Conder/Arthur Boyd sympathy in my 'The extremes of Arthur Boyd' *Dissent* Spring 1964, vol. 4, no. 3 p. 2, developing 'the sense of recall and tradition' so fundamental of Arthur Boyd's work: 'Arthur Boyd's art presents two extremes. He started as one of the most harmonious of landscape painters, almost as untroubled in his vision of the fertile wheat country as Arthur Streeton ...' His *Mentone Pier* of 1957–8 'is a picture of such a pier as you find shells under in your childhood, it is a picture of sea gulls and children and the remembered sunshine of Charles Conder'.

24 For the sites, see again Helen Topliss *The Artists' Camps* and the letters in *Smike to Bulldog. Letters from Sir Arthur Streeton to Tom Roberts*, p. 6.

25 See Helen Topliss *Tom Roberts A Catalogue Raisonné* p. 92, and note p. 12: '[*The Artists' Camp*] is significant in that it expresses the newly found familiarity with this particular spot at Houston's farm, described by Roberts in a letter to his wife-to-be, Lillie Williamson ... An autobiographical picture, *The Artists' Camp* represents the artist as "pioneer", extending the territory of local suburban spots such as Gardiner's Creek near Hawthorn (or Studley Park above the Yarra River, which was often painted by artists, including Roberts, in the 1870s) ... out to Houston's farm at Box Hill. It would seem that at this place Roberts and his friends

Visual Victoria 137

had preceded contemporary photographers in choosing a landscape beyond the suburbs as an ideal subject.'

26 The tent cities of the goldfields were intimately known to von Guérard: see Marjorie Tipping in her readable *An Artist of the Goldfields, The Diary of Eugene von Guérard*. The Ballarat Fine Art Gallery holds *Old Ballarat, as it was in the Summer of 1853 to 54* (painted in 1884) and *Ballarat Flat, View from Golden Point and Flat*, 1854. Von Guérard carefully records the acquisition of his own tent: 'With some difficulty I found the necessary canvas in a store. The making, and constructing the framework, has taken more time and trouble than I had foreseen, but is quite successful. The sense of freedom this gives me is wonderful . . .' (Tipping *An Artist of the Goldfields*, p. 42.) He draws 'My tent on Black Hill', illustrated on p. 59. That the artist's tent is close indeed, both formally and in its connotations, to the settler's tent, see the publication of Arthur Streeton's *Settler's Camp (Tent)*, exhibited at the National Gallery of Victoria in 1888, in an article by Geoff Maslen, 'The Streeton Boom' *The Age* 6 July 1885, 'The Saturday Extra', p. 12. See also June Clark and Bridget Whitelaw, *Golden Summers, Heidelberg and Beyond* National Gallery of Victoria, 1985, pp. 73-74.

The tent remains a popular architectural form; see Gerard McDonnel's 'The tent form a revival' *Architecture in Australia* vol. 50, 1, March 1961, p. 56A. (I am grateful to Judy Trimble for this reference).

27 Sid Nolan's *Tent*, 1940, is illustrated in Maie Casey, 'A tribute to Sidney Nolan', *Art and Australia* vol. 5, 2, 1967, p. 434.

28 For the Lilydale camp see Mary Eagle and Jan Minchin *The George Bell School Students Friends Influences*, Deutsher, Resolution Press, Sydney Melbourne, 1985; p. 139 illustrates Ian Armstrong's *From the Block Lilydale* c. 1946-8 (the hut replaces the tent) and on p. 145 there is a photograph of the 'First camp at Lilydale', 1946.

See also Jenepher Duncan *School Ties, Ian Armstrong, Russell Drysdale, Peter Purves-Smith, Harry Rosengrave, Fred Williams*, Monash University Gallery, 1985. No doubt Ian Turner and Stephen Murray-Smith, with artists Cliff Pugh and Fred Williams, were not unmindful of the ramifications of their 1975 'Artists' camp' at Erith Island in Bass Strait. See Ian Turner 'Artist's Camp, Erith Island: March 1974', *Overland* 60, Autumn 1975, pp. 41-55.

For these artists' allegories see Patrick McCaughey 'The art in extremis: Arthur Boyd 1972-73', *Australian Art and Architecture Essays Presented to Bernard Smith* (ed. A. Bradley and T. Smith), Oxford University Press, Melbourne, 1980, pp. 210-220.

29 For Ti Parks, see Ken Scarlett *Australian Sculptors*, Melbourne, Nelson. and Margaret Plant *Irreverent Sculpture*, Monash University Gallery, 1980, pp. 504-10; 1985, pp. 60-66

30 Richard Haese and June Helmer *Yosl Bergner: A Retrospective Exhibition*, Banyule Gallery, National Gallery of Victoria, 1985

31 See Bernice Murphy, Tony Trembath, Project 45, Art Gallery of NSW 1985.

32 For the latter, see Nancy Underhill 'The Portrait in nineteenth century portraiture' and Tom Roberts', 'Smike Streeton age 24: a friendship portrait', *Australian Journal of Art*, vol. IV, 1984, pp. 65-84.

33 Arthur Boyd *Recent Work*, October-November 1983, Fischer Fine Art, London, p. 8.

34 I am not endorsing the view that Williams 'begins where Roberts left off' (see note 7) but rather suggesting that Williams deliberately painted in tandem with Roberts, staking the modernity of his own practice, while declaring its continuity with the past. As a horseback Roberts' view, I have in mind *A Mountain Muster*, 1897–8. In the Lysterfield paintings, Williams introduced orbital and aerial views, extended in You Yang paintings; see McCaughey *Fred Williams*, ch. 5, pp. 50 ff.

Von Guérard painted in the Werribee area and the You Yangs; Danila Vassilieff, when teaching at Geelong Grammar in 1939, painted in the area; sculptor John Davis declares the You Yangs to be one of his most important sites.

35 D. M. Meldrum *The Science of Appearances as Formulated and Sought by Max Meldrum*, ed. Russel R. Foreman, Sydney: Shepherd Press, 1950

36 A pupil of Max Meldrum, Clarice Beckett nevertheless belongs to the history of emergent Melbourne modernism, for the moving simplicity of her painting. In fact the circle of Melbourne artists and intellectuals in which she moved has been claimed to be 'as varied creatively and as enterprising in spirit as the renowned Bloomsbury group in London, but had the misfortune to be ribbon-sandwiched between two world wars and a depression, coupled with a definite cultural disadvantage of remoteness from Europe' (Rosalind Hollinrake *Clarice Beckett, the Artist and her Circle*, Melbourne: Macmillan, 1979, p. 7.) For her painting expeditions, most of which were along the Beach Road and Dalgetty Road in Beaumaris, she had a handcart constructed for her painting materials (see photograph, p. 15). Her paintings are small-scaled, summary and undetailed, high and delicate in colour, and she paints the piers, bay roads, the children paddling, the bathing boxes of Beaumaris.

As art critic for the *Argus*, Street responded to her Athenaeum Gallery exhibition in 1931, with a pertinent tribute to a tradition that he had himself in part founded, quoted in Hollinrake, p. 29, 'Beaumaris Bay revealed':

> Though I had biked, hiked and motored along Beach Road round Beaumaris bay a hundred or more times I did not fully realise the beauty of the place until I looked at Miss Clarice Becketts' exhibitions of oil paintings ... today ... she has courageously brought the boxes, pumps and ples, as well as motor cars into the picture, and lo! we see the sun loves to play around them. So I really saw Beaumaris for the first time.

37 Maie Casey 'George Bell in Bourke Street', *Art and Australia* vol. 4, no. 2, September, 1966, pp. 120–124.

See again Eagle and Minchin *The George Bell School*, and Haese *Rebels and Precursors*, especially ch. 1, 'Reaction and Progress, a cultural crisis and problems of orientation in the 1930s', p. 1 ff.

38 See Gavin Fry *Adrian Lawlor: A Portrait*, Heide Park and Art Gallery, 1983, and Haese *Rebels and Precursors*, ch. 2, 'Democracy and Modernism, the Contemporary Art Society and the popular point 1939–1942', p. 61 ff.

39 Barrett Reid 'Background and foreground, some notes on Heide Park and Art Gallery and its origins', *Heide Park and Art Gallery*, 1981, pp. 43–51

40 See Charles Merewether *Art and Social Committment*, Art Gallery of New South Wales, 1984, foreward by Bernard Smith.

41 See Felicity St John Moore *Vassilieff and his Art*, Melbourne: Oxford University Press, 1982
42 *Yosi Bergner, A Retrospective Exhibition*, Banyule Gallery, National Gallery of Victoria, 1985
43 James Mollison and Nicholas Bonham *Albert Tucker*, Australian National Gallery, Macmillan, 1982, pp. 37–38
44 See Max Harris 'Nolan at St Kilda', *Art and Australia* vol. 5, no. 2, September 1967, p. 437: 'the ferris wheel rises like a giant above the houses, the brown bodies arrange themselves in a giddy pattern around the swimming pool, the little girls hold hands.'
Graham McInnes' parallel description of St Kilda from *The Road to Gundagai* is quoted in Geoffrey Dutton, *Sun, Sea, Surf and Sand—the Myth of the Beach*, Melbourne: Oxford University Press, 1985, beside illustrations of 1940s paintings of Boyd, Nolan and Tucker, p. 51 ff.
45 For the Wimmera landscapes, see note 3.
46 Albert Tucker *Faces I have Met*, Melbourne: Tolarno Gallery, 1985
47 Bernard Smith *Place, Taste and Tradition*, Sydney: Ure Smith, 1945. Cf. Humphrey McQueen *The Black Swan of Trespass, The emergence of Modernist painting in Australia to 1944*, Sydney, Alternative Publishers, 1979, p. 73: 'Bernard Smith was the most articulate and best informed proponent for social realistic art during the 1940s. His most substantial contribution, *Place, Taste and Tradition*, is lively, committed and still the single most important contribution to Australian art criticism and history'.
48 The manifesto is republished in *The Antipodean Manifesto, Essays in Art and History*, Melbourne, Oxford University Press, 1976, pp. 165–67. A hindsight view of the 'affair' is offered in Bernard Smith 'The truth about the antipodeans', *Praxis M#8, the Western Australian Journal of Art*, Autumn 1985, pp. 4–9.
49 Franz Philipp gives the background of the Boyd and a'Beckett dynasty in ch. 1, 'Family Background. Early landscapes' in *Arthur Boyd*. He describes 'Open Country', pp. 21–22:

> The setting was hardly middle class suburbia—neither materially nor in its mental climate—but somewhat bohemian and eccentric. The old rambling house with its overgrown garden (in which the father's pottery was later to be joined by the studios of Arthur and his brother-in-law John Perceval) sheltered an artist's family which tended to overflow into an artists' colony ... My own memories of the Murrumbeena household in the early forties, and those of other friends of the younger Boyds, intimate a spiritual climate in which art and religion were indeed very close to each other, merging in a religiosity of a mystic kind which could perhaps be described as Blakean.

Peter Herbst, in response to Richard Haese's *Rebels and Precursors*, offers a corrective primary view of the 'circles' of the 'forties', emphasising that 'the stance at Murrumbeena was quite different from that at Heidelberg, and it is an error to classify the Boyds and Percevals with the Angry Penguins, even if an inner and outer sequence are distinguished' ... 'We cannot accept the image of Murrumbeena as a dissident colony of Heide', Peter Herbst *The Boxer Collection, Modernism, Murrumbeena and Angry Penguins*, Canberra, 1981, p. 4.
For a recent plea for preservation of the artists' country, see *The Age* 24 May 1985, p. 3:

Artist (Guy Boyd) joins plea to save the living landscape ... a 90-year-old park, which inspired members of the artistic Boyd families, could be subdivided for houses by the Metropolitan Transit Authority ... Mr Boyd said a stand of blue-gums in the park had been the subject of at least two oil paintings by his brother, Arthur. The trees and wild grasses also featured in the work of such close family friends as the painter John Perceval and potters Neil Douglas and Carl Cooper.

For Robin Boyd's studio for Arthur Boyd, see *Architect* November–December 1971, vol. 3, no. 17, p. 5 ... 'In the 1920s and 1930s they [the family of Penleigh Boyd] spent time with their cousins at Open Country, Wahroonga Cres., Murrumbeena ... Arthur wanted a studio and asked his student cousin to help. This yellow Box Brownie snap (illustrated) [is] inscribed "first ever—1938" ... It could be a minor Loos or Behrens ... a fitting first in fibrolite'. Illustrated also in Richard Haese *Rebels and Precursors*, p. 235.

For the Murrumbeena pottery, see Geoffrey Edwards *The Painter as Potter, decorated ceramics of the Murrumbeena Circle*, National Gallery of Victoria, 1983, esp. Peter Herbst 'The Arthur Merric Boyd Pottery at Murrumbeena', pp. 7–8

50 See *Sidney Nolan's Ned Kelly, the Ned Kelly paintings in the Australian National Gallery and a selection of the artist's sketches*, Elwyn Lynn's story of the paintings with Sir Sidney Nolan's comments, Canberra: Australian National Gallery, 1985

51 For a well-illustrated and evocative account of the residents of the Eltham Shire (mentioning Withers, Jock Frater, Percy Leason, Max Meldrum, Justus Jorgensen, Neil Douglas, Clifton Pugh, et al) see Alan Marshall *Pioneers and Painters, One Hundred Years of Eltham and its Shire*, Melbourne: Nelson, 1971, esp. Ch. 19, 'Early painters', ch. 20, 'Painters today', ch. 21, 'Warrandyte painters and potters', pp. 111 ff.

In 1970 the artists' cricket matches, to be a particularly 1970s tradition, began at George Baldessin's property at St Andrews, and then moved to the St Andrews oval. Fred Williams was a leading participant. A photograph of Roger Kemp with George Baldessin signing the cricket bat appears in the catalogue: Robert Lindsay and Memory Jockisch Holloway, *George Baldessin: Sculpture and Etchings*, National Gallery of Victoria, 1983, p. 19.

William Moore remembered Warrandyte as 'a sleepy hollow with a winding road, two pubs, and an old wooden bridge spanning the Yarra' (*The Story of Australian Art*, p. 81). A seductive view by Clara Southern at Warrandyte, 'Blythe Bank', is now in private collection, Melbourne. The painting is not unlike McCubbin's *Artist Studio, Macedon* (University of Queensland), rustic and picturesque, protected by trees.

Harold Herbert and Louis McCubbin painted regularly in Warrandyte. Adrian Lawlor (see below) had his house Broom Warren completely destroyed by fire (together with his paintings) on 'Black Friday', January 1939, and rebuilt an ultra-modernist dwelling, described as 'the most be-photographed house in Australia' (Gavin Fry *Adrian Lawlor: a Portrait* p. 34).

In 1939 Janet and Clive Neild established a progressive school at Koornyong, with Danila Vassilieff as art master. In 1940 Vassilieff commenced building Stonygrad on the bank of the Yarra opposite the school, blasting into the river rock. Stonygrad was photographed at the time by Albert Tucker (see Felicity St John Moore *Vassilieff and his Art*, Melbourne: Oxford University Press, 1982, pp. 52, 68, 70). The circle of artists who visited is listed, pp. 58-59—Nolan, Tucker, Joy Hester, Bergner, the Boyds. In fact it might be said that Stonygard bridged the two 'circles' of Murrumbeena and Heide (described below). In 1953 painter and printmaker Grahame King returned to Melbourne with his German born wife, Inge, and they built in Warrandyte. The slope of the bush land accommodates many of Inge King's large outdoor sculptures.

52 For Justus Jorgensen's elaborate and influential folly at Montsalvat near Eltham, and an evoction of the circle, see Rosalind Hollinrake's study *Clarice Beckett, the Artist and her Circle*, with attention to the Meldrum and Jorgensen group.

See also Gary Catalano *An Intimate Australia, the landscape and recent Australian Art*, Sydney: Hale and Iremonger, 1985, ch. 5, 'Politics in the Garden', p. 84, including the mud brick architecture of Alistair Knox.

Cliff Pugh's Dunmoochin near Eltham forms a chapter in Traudi Allen *Clifton Pugh, Patterns of a Lifetime, a Biography*, Melbourne: Nelson, 1981, p. 159 ff.

53 See indexed entries Ken Scarlett *Australian Sculptors*, Nelson, 1980; Graeme Sturgeon *The Development of Australian Sculpture 1788-1975*, London: Thames & Hudson, 1978, p. 138 ff; Margaret Plant *Centre Five at Heide*, Heide Park and Art Gallery, 1984.

54 Brief histories of these galleries are sketched in Alan McCulloch *Encyclopedia of Australian Art* Melbourne: Hutchinson, 1984, and Max Germaine *Artists and Galleries of Australia and New Zealand*, Melbourne Lansdowne, 1984.

55 See Richard Haese 'The Heide Park and Art Gallery: an introduction to the core collection' in *Heide Park and Art Gallery*, p. 8 ff.

56 I have described something of this activity in 'Melbourne Print-makers' *Art Bulletin of Victoria* 1973/4, pp. 27-34

57 Robin Boyd *The Australian Ugliness*, Melbourne, Cheshire, 1960, and *Artificial Australia*, Sydney, Australian Broadcasting Commission, 1969

58 *Portrait of Barry Humphries as Edna Everage* in Ronald Millar *John Brack* Melbourne, Lansdowne, 1971, pp. 25 and 87; for Barry Humphries as 'artist', see Margaret Plant *Irreverent Sculpture*, p. 8

59 *Roger Kemp Cycles and Directions, 1935-1975*, int. Patrick McCaughey, Melbourne, 1979-80

60 For these artists see Gary Catalano *The Years of Hope, Australian Art and Criticism, 1959-1968*, Melbourne, Oxford University Press, 1981.

61 *A Melbourne Mood, Cool Contemporary Art*, Australian National Gallery, Canberra, 1983, Monash University Gallery, 1984

62 A Jenny Watson house is used as illustration of 'The Prosperous Years' in Tony Dingle *The Victorians: Settling*, Melbourne, Fairfax, Syme and Weldon, 1984, p. 235.

63 For the Mildura 'triennials', see Graeme Sturgeon *Sculpture at Mildura, the story of the Mildura Sculpture Triennial, 1961-1982*, Mildura City Council, 1985.

64 On that particular 'sculpture' and the place-orientation of the work of John

142   Victoria's Heritage

Davis, see Gary Catalano *An intimate Australia, the Landscape and Recent Australian Art*, p. 68 ff.

Davis' Mildura tree piece of 1973, using a group of trees on the site; the Hattah Lake installation, May 1976, using twigs, sand, sedimentary deposits; an Oven River installation, September 1976, in a mia-mia effect of rocks, branches, twigs and grass, and a Solar Piece, done in the You Yangs in November 1977 are illustrated in the catalogue of the Venice Biennale 1978: *From Nature to Art, from Art to Nature*, p. 6 ff.

65   Paul Taylor 'Australian "New Wave" and the "Second Degree" ' *Art and Text*, Autumn 1981, pp. 33–38

66   *Popism*, curated and introduced by Paul Taylor, National Gallery of Victoria, 1982

67   For example, *Eureka*, London, 1982; *Biennale*, Venice, 1982; *Australian Visions*, New York, 1984. Booth's *Painting*, 1982, was used for the cover of *Recent Australian Painting: A Survey, 1970–1983*, Ron Radford, Art Gallery of South Australia, 1983.

68   These artists 'graduated' from Fitzroy to Toorak in 1985, for the exhibition 'Raw Reality'; the artists—Wayne Eager, Sarah Faulkner, Andrew Ferguson, Peter Ferguson, Pasquale Giardino, Karen Hayman, Mark Howson, David Larwill, Karl Morkel, Mike Nichols, Jill Noble, Mark Schaller, Judi Singleton.

69   For the Pilbara landscapes, Patrick McCaughey *Fred Williams The Pilbara Series, 1979–1981*, Melbourne, CRA, 1983, and the Kew Billabong paintings in McCaughey *Fred Williams*, pp. 254–87.

70   Jan Senbergs now lives and has his studio in the area. For Liardet's watercolours of early Melbourne, see *Liardet's Water-colours of Early Melbourne*, introduction and captions by Susan Adams, ed. Weston Bate, Melbourne University Press and Library Council of Victoria, 1972. Pl. 33 is 'Liardet's beach and hotel in their heyday', pp. 80–81. See also pl. 32, 'Surveyor Darke's Camp, Sandridge', pp. 78–79. For Senbergs, see Jenny Zimmer 'Jan Senbergs: the port pictures' *Aspect Art and Literature* 25, 1982, p. 8 ff, and 'Jan Senbergs: history and painter. The Port Melbourne and Mt. Lyell series 1980–1983', *Art and Australia*, vol. 22, no. 2, Summer 1984, pp. 206 ff.

71   For the William Strutt paintings of Burke and Wills, see Heather Curnow 'William Strutt: some problems of a colonial history painter in the nineteenth century' in *Australian Art and Architecture, Essays Presented to Bernard Smith*, ed. A. Bradley and T. Smith, Melbourne, Oxford University Press, 1980, p. 36 ff.

Note p. 36: 'as well as Strutt, contemporary artists who painted Burke and Wills subjects included Nicholas Chevalier, S. T. Gill, H. J. Johnstone and H. L. van den Houten'. See also Rudiger Joppien 'The Iconography of the Burke and Wills expedition in Australian art' in *Readings in Australian Arts: papers from the 1976 Exeter symposium*, ed. Peter Quartermaine, University of Exeter, 1978, pp. 49–61.

72   For Charles Summers see Ken Scarlett *Australian Sculptors*, and Graeme Sturgeon *The Development of Australian Sculpture*, pp. 28–29.

73   Geoffrey Dutton 'Sidney Nolan's Burke and Wills series' *Art and Australia*, vol. 5, no. 2, September 1967, pp. 455–59; and (passim) Elwyn Lynn *Sidney Nolan—Australia*, Sydney: Bay Books, 1979

74 On the theme of lost children, see Heather Curnow *William Strutt*, Australian Gallery Directors Council, 1981 pp. 40-41; Strutt's 'Little Wanders, or the Lost Track' was his first exhibited painting in the Royal Academy London. For McCubbin's Lost Children pictures, see Ann Galbally *Frederick McCubbin*, Melbourne, Hutchinson, 1981, which also illustrates popular press rendering of the theme on pp. 75-80; for the 1907 Lost Boy, see p. 114. (McCubbin's *Found*, 1893, should also be mentioned, ibid. p. 89.)

75 William Strutt's painting, *Black Thursday, Feb. 6th, 1851*, was painted in 1864 after his return to England. He described it as his *magnum opus*, observing that 'My large picture of "Black Thursday", a dramatic Australian subject, occupied me nearly three years to accomplish' (Heather Curnow *William Strutt*, p. 46). The painting is now in the collection of the State Library, Victoria.

Von Guérard's *Bushfire between Mount Elephant and Timboon, March 1857* is in the Ballarat Fine Art Gallery. (Timboon is now called Camperdown.)

76 Fred Williams consistently confronted the bushfire and its aftermath: in 1963, the fires in the You Yangs; in 1976, his Bushfire Diptych. In 1968, fires threatened his home at Upwey—a beautiful series of gouaches studied the burnt ferns regenerating: McCaughey *Fred Williams*, 'The Fire and its Aftermath', pp. 200-206.

77 See Jocelyn Gray 'A New Vision: Louis Buvelot's Press in the 1870s', p. 20.

78 Quoted *The Dictionary of Australian Quotations*, ed. Stephen Murray-Smith, Melbourne: Heinemann, 1984, p. 125. Note also, 'I'm not an Australian, I'm a Victorian', *ibid.*, p. 125

For local pie ratings and pie sociology, see Brendan Moloney 'Dog's eye "n" dead 'orse' *The Age Weekender* 13 September 1985.

8

Against the mainstream: *the inclusive tendency in Victoria's architecture, 1890–1984*

CONRAD HAMANN

The twentieth-century architecture of ex-colonies, such as Australia and the United States, has been scoured for distinguishing characteristics—at a national level. This had generally meant that characteristic styles of a particular region, such as the Georgian homestead of New South Wales, have been made to stand for the *real* Australian architecture. The *real* Australian society was seen as living there. In the 1880s the Puritan houses of Massachusetts were portrayed as the genuine America, in a similar way.[1] In both cases, the assessment was vindicated by waves of new building, each based on these assumptions. There were clear enough regional modes beyond these, such as the Queensland stump house or the stone-based architecture of South Australia, which are accepted because they present conspicuous and unaffected adaptations to climate, materials or structure.

The more complex urban architecture of ex-colonies, though, has always sat uneasily in such pictures. In the twentieth century's long-held view, architecture had to be the guileless and direct outcome of responses to technology, shelter and circulation. Too often the buildings of a Philadelphia, a Boston, or a Melbourne were dismissed as 'copies' of overseas forms, 'awkward misunderstandings', or 'pretentions'. It was only through the appearance of major architects from these hybrid cultures—H. H. Richardson from Boston, Louis Kahn and Robert Venturi from Philadelphia, Bernard Maybeck from San Francisco, that attention has been directed to their regional contexts and background. Since then, America has seen the increased study of particular architectural traditions, which in turn contributed to a wider national mode.[2] In Australia such studies have been slow to emerge, at least in areas where the conspicuous regional variations of the nineteenth century have been blurred by the homogenising tendency of twentieth-century architecture. This essay considers particular contributions from one particular Australian region, Victoria.

Recent research has highlighted contributions by Victoria's architects and builders, such as their experiments in new techniques with reinforced concrete at the turn of this century, and Victoria's development of brick-veneer construction during the 1920s.[3] Less well studied, however, is a distinctive approach to ideas and forms in architecture, planning, urban and suburban references, structure and materials. This forms a thread running through Victoria's twentieth-century architecture. At times many architects are involved; at other points, only one or two.

If this approach can be summed up, it may be said to involve a general aim in dealing with culture and society, and to have particular results in architecture. Broadly speaking, numbers of Victoria's architects and builders have expressed in architecture the several societies and contexts with which they deal: the rural, the suburban, the urban. The prevailing Australian tendency has been to use specialised building types to address the country and the city, with suburbs regarded as an unfortunate area in between. In contrast, the Victorian approach has been to develop a common currency of materials, structure, scale, force, animation, reference, compression, and monumentality that could be applied to all three areas. This breadth of involvement precluded an architecture of containment, pure form, and homogeneity. In specific examples, this particular architecture in Victoria tends to be composite and mixed, often with highly disparate elements. A variety of forms or spaces will often occur in an almost narrative sequence, in plans or on the surface of buildings. Static spaces and forms are invariably challenged or mixed with elements which, in architectural terms, embody animation or movement. Architectural gestures are built up in a particular way, only to be suddenly interrupted or 'debunked'. The architects have tended to move toward a common system, but to veer away from the expression, of 'system' at the same time. They have generally avoided, for example, the extreme repetition of parts which characterise the image of mass production in modern architecture. They have also tended to avoid the systems embodied in classical and renaissance architecture, and the system alluded to in modern Mannerism, where rules are broken and parts manipulated; the sense of the rules remains, but the architecture resembles a game.[4]

The first point where Victoria's new approach emerges clearly is in the recasting of architecture that came in Australia's Federation period. This phase, which extends from the later 1880s till about 1914, involved a variety of building types but represents a broad agreement on two principles. First, buildings had to be true to the age they were in, and had to discard the 'falsity' of facades and ornament that was not related to structure. Second, Australia's buildings had to say, more clearly, something of the society, climate and surroundings they were in. These two concerns have sources that had a roughly equal influence around Australia: the Gothic Revival and the Arts and Crafts movements, in Britain primarily, and the national sentiment and constitutional conventions leading up to Federation.[5] Beyond this point, though, crucial regional differences begin to show very early.

In Melbourne, this mood of change brought an upsurge of architectural discussion and debate and contributions from younger architects and students including Wilson Dobbs, A. B. Rieusset and Harold Desbrowe-Annear. Their arguments and papers came in a crowded and collective atmosphere, such as in the Architectural and Engineering Association's meetings in Parer's Crystal Cafe. In contrast, New South Wales was having its forum for debate and discussion torn apart, mainly through John Horbury Hunt's bitter quarrels with others of the Institute of Architects of New South Wales. These conflicts dealt Sydney's architectural criticism and debate a blow from which they have never really recovered. The later writing from New South Wales—that of John Sulman, Hardy Wilson, and Leslie Wilkinson—has a strongly private flavour to it, and this continued into the 1950s and 1960s, when reluctance to discuss buildings became dominant, and when, for many, architecture became the basis for private and individual views of the world.[6]

Differences, too, showed in what architects of this period chose to attack. In Brisbane and Sydney, particularly, critics emphasised how architecture had to fight rawness and crudity in the surroundings, and how their response had to be *specialised*. Their response prefigured the two specialising emphases of Australia's 'mainstream' architecture. They prescribed country homestead forms for both country *and* suburbs, and urged that the architecture of Italian cities, civilised and ingenuous at once, be adopted in urban settings. They also placed far more importance on an architecture which could escape the transience of 'fashion', as they believed themselves above fashion.[7] This too, carried deeply into Australia's later architectural thinking.

In contrast, Victoria's architectural reformers stressed different things. They seem to have been driven away from the Renaissance, which surrounded them in Melbourne, Bendigo or any number of towns. Against such 'fat' and 'ornamental splatterings' they tried to work out an architecture which would be equally applicable in country, suburb and city, a unifying form, inevitably composite and complex in itself. This becomes apparent from the writing of Desbrowe-Annear, Walter Butler, and Wilson Dobbs, particularly Dobbs' *Rise and Growth of Australasian Architecture*, published in 1891. Applying Darwinian models to Australian problems, Dobbs stressed synthesis and fusion constantly. He wanted an architecture which was at once answerable to the city and the homestead, which could draw together a range of approaches from the country homestead to the sophisticated new 'Free' architecture of Norman Shaw in Britain or H. H. Richardson in America; to 'the Great Pre-Raphaelite Movement', as he called it, seen in the Crystal Palace, where industrial civilisation would be reconciled with architecture. Butler and Desbrowe-Annear place a similar emphasis on fusion, and likewise, stress the role of industry and engineering in future design.[8] By comparison, such themes appear sporadically in other states after 1900. In New South Wales and Queensland, George Sydney Jones and Robin Dods held similar views, but only became prominent much later. After about 1907, George Taylor of the Sydney magazine *Building* showed great interest in concrete and tower building construction, but primarily because it was an emblem of economic dynamism and the aggressive entrepreneur. This view, too, would become a strong influence in the Australian 'mainstream' later on.

Victoria, therefore, showed distinctive tendencies even as Australia's pattern of early architectural reform was being worked out. Victoria's architectual criticism and debate emphasised synthesis and fusion, rather than the selection of a range of existing prototypes. This shows quite quickly in Melbourne work of the 1890s, such as the 1894 Post Office in South Yarra, by A. J. McDonald and J. T. Kelleher. Dobbs was an obvious influence, for all three were in the Victorian Colonial Architect's office. This building combines London townhouse forms by Norman Shaw with round arches and corner towers from the 'American Romanesque' of Henry Hobson Richardson. This fusion and 'collision' of sources was quite radical. But interestingly, the building has an additional element: a tense, even febrile character in its line, verticality, and sense of movement. McDonald and Kelleher had sensed how perimeter and corner towers, built of small-scale materials such as brick, could express movement and animation in architectural terms, and this animation is crucial to the way the building 'declaims' on its corner site. It gestures at the street and the railway junction next to it. It sits on its standard Melbourne block not with repose, but with marked restlessness, pressing against the boundaries, with its sense of movement generated in part from the restricted site.

The South Yarra Post Office was a public building, but its forms already show approaches and details that were being worked out in housing. Alfred Dunn's houses on the Irving estate in Toorak (c. 1890) press out towards their site boundaries in a similar way. They are intended to address the street and their neighbours, and they introduce into the suburb a device for generating a streetscape of collective form. Dunn combines this with large hipped roofs, restating separateness by reference to the Australian homestead. The result is composite. The hipped roof form of the homestead is no longer a restated prototype; it is broken up by wings and window bays. This disruption, this restlessness of form, in turn derives from a desire to express externally a new plan, dominated by a central hall, from which surrounding rooms seem displaced, radially. Similar combinations of form, part urban and part rural, occur in work by other Melbourne architects after 1890. These include Arthur Fisher, Walter Butler, Beverley Ussher and Christopher Cowper.[9] In most cases the actual setting was the Melbourne suburb, a meeting point between city and country, opposing 'Australias'. In the process, though, the suburb becomes more than incidental. It is clearly viewed as a third Australia, as valid in its way as the other two, and celebrated in the new Federation house form.

These tendencies in Victoria's house design find dramatic expression in the single-storey houses of Beverley Ussher. Ussher wrote several articles on the question of a regional architecture, and of appropriate urban planning. He became so identified with the Federation house that Martin Boyd later credited him with its invention. In Travancore

Beverley Ussher and Henry Kemp, 'Travancore', John Cupples' house, Riversdale Road, Camberwell, 1899–1900. (Adrian Featherston)

of 1899–1900 for John Cupples, Ussher brings all the concerns and elements of Federation housing together in memorable form.

Ussher's work has a strong sense of outward displacement and tension of mass against site boundaries. In this his work is similar to designs by Dunn or Fisher, but he reworked this in several new ways. Ussher was interested in fusing the spaces of living, dining and hall areas in a single space, in a way that resembled the modern open plan. Following the Arts and Crafts precept that exterior must express interior, he focussed these spaces in one corner of his plans, and expressed them externally with a series of mobile, flowing perimeter elements: corner bays, towers, winding and turning verandahs. These elements are geared to 'greet' visitors approaching his houses. Paths would lead in from the gate towards a corner tower, then swing round towards another projecting mass, such as a wing, then turn again towards the front door area. The twisting front path acted like the drive on a large estate that introduces visitors to vistas of tall trees and a wide landscape. But, in response to the suburb and the typical Melbourne site, the vistas are now suburban fences and rose bushes. In this sequence, corner and perimeter masses give a sense of physical accompaniment to movement outside these houses. In this way, country landscape, and the house in landscape, is compressed to fit the dimensions of an ordinary suburban site. The general Australian tendency would be to make the suburban site as easily in this setting as possible to keep its plan square, to keep site boundaries clearly away. Not so Ussher; he positively delights in this sense of compression, of accommodation, of compromise forced by Melbourne's urban and suburban surroundings and site limits.

In Travancore the homestead roof remains, its hipped upper level now just visible behind projecting wings and dormers. Following the homestead, too, Ussher treated the verandah as integral, flowing out of the roof. From there, however, the house was primarily concerned with responses to its corner site, and to movement and activity in the streets around. These elements combined urban and suburban images and activity, and Ussher's responses were based on a sense of movement and animation. This can be seen in the dormer, in the perimeter, the two gabled wings which framed the composition and in the corner tower with its rhetorical conical roof extension. This lacked any lookout and was mainly intended to address the street corner and dramatise the verandah's turn from north to east. This perimeter activity, making urban and suburban links, shrouds and changes the original homestead prototype. The sense of country origin was still there, but at its edges the house now had a vigorous, animated group of frames and masses, with a strength now almost sufficient for inner city locations. Then, as Ussher realised that this house risked losing its visual coherence, he thickened the encircling timber elements: the verandah posts, the valences. With a new large scale, these gained a particular sense of linking tension, of timber 'sinew'. This sinew recurs constantly in Victoria's design after 1900, and there, as with Ussher's houses, it becomes a linking and unifying device for a composite architecture. It is seen in buildings which often have several major references and meanings, and there is, generally, some fusion made between three societies: urban, suburban and rural.

Ussher died in 1907, but for some time the themes of his work flavour the architecture of his former partners, Walter Butler and Henry Kemp. Ussher also seems to affect Harold Desbrowe-Annear and Robert Haddon, whose designs have been seen as early manifesta-

Harold Desbrowe–Annear, House, The Eyrie, Eaglemont, c. 1903. (Adrian Featherston)

tions of a clearly modern architecture.[10] A particular case is the group of three houses which Annear designed at the Eyrie, Eaglemont, between 1899 and 1903.

Like Ussher, Annear had a general desire to develop an Australian architecture, but the way he intended this, by use of climate, landscape and social references[11], also acted to give his work a strong link with Victoria's surroundings and design themes. As with Ussher, Annear retained elements of the homestead form, using large and spreading roof masses which flow over into verandahs. The L-shaped spine, which framed and ordered Ussher's plans, resurfaced in Annear's, to govern the now very open and continuous spaces of his living and dining rooms, halls and breakfast areas.

On the exteriors of these houses, Annear extends the diagonal and rotational themes of Federation architecture. This is particularly so at 38 and 34 the Eyrie. The verandahs are swung round at 45 degrees against the 'core' of each house. No longer is the verandah a harmonious perimeter envelope; it is now broken up by diagonal intrusions of inner rooms. Annear was also answering a particular question raised in Victoria's discussion of new architecture, which had not been so prominent in other Australian colonies or states.

This was how to interrupt and limit the verandah, so that warming sun and light could enter houses at important points, and compensate for Victoria's colder climate.

This arrangement of movement and collision allows Annear to split up the outer layers of his houses, to create particular places. Stairs or bedroom areas intersect and divide the verandahs. This creates 'private' verandahs for sitting and relaxing, and public verandahs or expanded entry porches. In each case the verandah is split by a room or space with an opposing theme or pattern of circulation: the privacy of a bedroom in one house, the vertical circulation of a stair hall in another.

This opposition of mass and perimeter is carried down to the smallest details. The 'cores' of his houses are planked and roughcast in panels. The dominant theme is of faceted or rigid surfacing, which changes angles in stiff and jerky stages. The roofs, still red-tiled but lightened dramatically, seem almost to ride on top of the movements suggested in the masses and framework underneath them. A clear sense of animation is apparent again, and this now seems powered by certain elements, in a way that extends Ussher's encircling timber 'sinew'. Something of this is expressed in the brackets, unceremonious and sharply angled wooden struts, that support bays or roof projections at points where exterior walls change direction. This 'sinew' also marks the sweep and curve of the balustrades and valences, which tauten noticeably near points where they join posts or wings.

These components are Art Nouveau, but have a push and muscularity that is distinctive when seen against Art Nouveau elsewhere, such as the stylised rectangles of Scots or Austrian design, or the thin, unfolding tendrils of West European Art Nouveau, worked in metal or lines of paint. Annear's response is to local materials, a particularly Melbourne usage of rather thick verandah timber. He also responds to the scale and line of the large trees round each of his Eyrie houses. He restates this 'sinew' inside too, in the taut line and brackets of chimney pieces, that grow as episodes from the panelled dadoes round each wall. In this case Annear uses timber sinew to express metamorphosis and fusion between one form and another.

Annear was hard put to carry this theme of movement much further. His Toorak and South Yarra houses of 1918–20, show an extreme simplification of external form, with almost flat roofs and smooth stuccoed walls. Annear's earlier themes are kept inside, as with the circular sequence of rooms in Broceliande, 1918, or they appear in small details, such as the sharply angular brackets on Inglesby, 1919. Both houses prefigured Australia's most progressive architecture of 1935–50, but have, unfortunately, been demolished.[12]

Aspects, but not all, of this general pattern of reform could be found in other states fairly easily—until about 1920. By that time a new 'mainstream' Australian architecture was beginning to emerge. While

Victorians such as Ussher, Dobbs or Annear made distinctive contributions to Federation architecture, architects such as G. H. M Addison in Queensland, or John Sulman in New South Wales, had a great influence on bringing its overall forms together. But it is also true that around Australia many leading proponents of Federation architecture were Victorians who had left Melbourne during the depression of the early 1890s. These included Howard Joseland in Sydney, G. D. Payne in Brisbane, Allan Walker in Hobart, and Hillson Beasley, A. B. Rieusset, George Lavater and others who settled in Western Australia. Most of these had participated in the formative phase of Federation architecture, between 1885 and 1891.[13]

Clear regional approaches also characterised Federation architecture outside Victoria. Architects and builders in South Australia, Western Australian and Queensland all gave the encircling homestead roof more prominence in their hotter climates. As a result their houses had a squarer outline. They also tended to subordinate the animated perimeter elements that pervaded Victoria's architecture and speculative building after Ussher's example, though angled bay windows were widespread in Queensland. Tasmanian architecture was widely influenced by Victoria around 1900, though this influence was supplanted by more directly British forms after about 1905. Fusions between American Romanesque and British modes were widespread on Sydney's North Shore, but concentrated more on topographical resemblances than on linkages with surrounding streets. Sydney's closest equivalents to the Victorian's experiments were in the flatter western suburbs, as with the radial and butterfly-plan houses of George Sydney Jones, or the compressed estates of Howard's Haberfield houses.[14] Outside Victoria, though, attempts to develop a unified architecture that could relate to country, suburbs and city were sporadic. Suburbs were, in many ways, treated differently outside Melbourne, and other states and cities showed a greater preference for using Italianate and Renaissance designs for larger and more urban buildings. They continued that preference for specialist prototypes that had marked New South Wales' proposals for architectural reform in the late 1880s.

By 1914, what links there were between states that were based in Federation architecture had begun to break down. Inclusive architecture became far less conspicuous outside Victoria, and a different Australian 'mainstream' began falling into place. The first clear evidence of this was in a concerted attempt to end Australian isolation and re-establish strong links with great European civilisations —Britain, particularly. This mood was widespread in Australia after Federation. In large city buildings it showed in the soaring popularity of 'English Renaissance' after about 1903. This was a system of surface treatment and detailing which derived from the buildings of Inigo Jones, Christopher Wren, Nicholas Hawksmoor and others, and had gained favour in Britain as an expression of national identity. In

Australia it provided a clear link with the 'hub of Empire'. It seemed up-to-date and had a massivity that satisfied traditional notions of urban monumentality.[15]

Brisbane and Sydney were the real foci of this development in Australia. Both cities had extensive city building between about 1907 and 1914, a time when inner Melbourne was still overbuilt after the 1880s boom. In Sydney examples were influenced by Walter Vernon and his huge State Government architect's office, and taken up by several large firms re-organising themselves on twentieth-century corporate lines after United States models. In Queensland, A. B. Brady's government architects, together with private firms such as Hall and Dods, or Chambers and Powell, all took up the new Renaissance with great skill. Such Brisbane and Sydney designs dominated Melbourne's AMP Insurance offices competition of 1903, providing the first of many modern incursions into Melbourne's commercial buildings, something that had been a traditional preserve of Victoria's architects.

Victoria's architects were quick to become involved. Two strong essays in this mode came with Fawcett and Ashworth's Flinders Street Station, completed in 1909, and Oakden and Ballantyne's Dalgety building of 1913 in Collins Street. Both were typical of Victoria's tendency towards amalgams. They linked 'English Renaissance' with 'American Romanesque'. Bates, Peebles and Smart used the new Renaissance in their fine Bourke Street facades for Buckley's department store (c. 1913), and their reading room for the State Library of Victoria. This was briefly the largest reinforced concrete dome in the world. It also alluded to Basevi and Smirke's British Museum dome, in a way that recalled Melbourne's nineteenth-century urbanism. These Melbourne buildings were now among the last manifestations of strongly collective urbanism typical of Melbourne in the nineteenth century. In contrast, the modern approach was to conceive buildings more and more in isolation, independently of physical context.[16] This marks many Sydney and Brisbane city buildings, which had by now acquired the bulk, structure and fittings of the modern skyscraper beneath their English Renaissance ornament. The Melbourne examples, significantly, show a continued interest in controlling and addressing streets and surroundings, but Victoria now lacked critical leadership in large urban buildings.

Even in Melbourne work, the large building became treated more as an isolated object, a device to focus on a distant metropolis. Beyond that, though, Australia generally became drained of a sense of clear and autonomous urban direction. The desired 'metropolis' imagery shifts in the teens and twenties of the century, from the political metropolis of London to New York, the metropolis of cultural vibrancy and *laissez-faire*. There it remained till the late 1970s, until the financial metropolis of the American South and West, the mirror-glass towers and atria of

Atlanta, Dallas, Houston or Tulsa, claimed corporate attention around Australia. By 1920 Australia's inner cities, Melbourne included, had become part of a new mainstream. In this mainstream, central business districts became receptacles for a range of 'international' metropolitan imagery, carefully reproduced but wandering and capricious in its selection, and with a decreasing regard for existing urbanism and context. Not surprisingly, writing that characterised the new mainstream centred on the considerable technical difficulties of new city building, and on details of their structure and services. This emphasis was largely at the expense of broader architectural and urban considerations. This sustained that specialising tendency seen in the division of building forms according to location. General discussions of urbanism, composition, and the expression of architectural meaning were now increasingly treated as separate considerations, and they continue to take a diminishing role as Australia's selection of ready-made prototypes continues.

This can be seen in housing, too. The Australian bungalow, in the early twentieth century, began as an amalgam of Federation design and later Arts-and-Crafts free style, as practised in Britain. Then, as films presented Los Angeles as a desirable metropolis for housing and suburban systems, the bungalow was given details, from Pasadena and Alameda, and sold as 'Californian'. Australian examples of 'the Californian Bungalow' looked quite different from Pasadena houses, and have acquired state-by-state differences in materials, weight, outline, roof massing. But these differences are either accidental or the result of pragmatic adjustments to materials or climate, rather than through any strongly developed, comprehensive vision of architecture.

It would, however, be wrong to assume that the Australian mainstream lacked any basis in ideas. On the contrary, an ideology emerges in Australian architecture around 1920, and has dominated Australian architects, many Victorians included, ever since. This ideology rose out of Colonial Revivalism in New South Wales. That interest was apparent in Sulman's nomination of suitable prototypes for an 'Australian Style' and recurs in a large number of buildings and in articles on architecture.

The mainstream argument went this way: Australian cities were corrupt and barbarous; the real Australia must be in 'the landscape'. Architecture must therefore be centred on the landscape and the house, particularly the Georgian homestead, was the principal intermediary between Australians and their landscape. From there, architecture had two options: either to blend with the landscape, or present a counterfoil to it. If the latter, delicacy of Australian foliage and light demanded that the form be simple, prismatic, and pure. This idea has origins in the English picturesque, but denied picturesque qualities in the composition of buildings themselves. If, by any misfortune, a building had to be designed in an urban setting, the appropriate response was a pure block form as both confrontation and example. The homestead or a selected prototype from overseas was the usual source. If more than one building was involved, a Mediterranean village was seen as the best solution. Such buildings were, after all, prismatic white forms in direct confrontation with land or seascape.

In Sydney, this view was put potently by Hardy Wilson and Leslie Wilkinson, then later by George Beiers and Morton Herman. But interestingly, it was three Victorians—Martin Boyd, Robin Boyd and J. M. Freeland—who made this view an instrument by which new Australian architecture could be judged and screened. This can be seen in Martin Boyd's articles in *The British Australian and New Zealander*, Robin Boyd's articles in *The Age* and many architecture journals, his *Australia's Home*, *The Australian Ugliness*, *The New Architecture* and *Artificial Australia*, as well as J. M. Freeland's *Architecture in Australia*.[17] All grafted extra themes and developments onto the original Neo-Georgian vision. Australian architecture was seen as beginning with a Georgian 'Eden', descending into a nineteenth-century chaos of pretension and debauched taste. A prime duty of modern architecture was the restoration of Georgian propriety, purity of form and an instinctive good taste that would be shared by all Australians. Planning would involve constant simplification, and the centring of space and form around the expression of a single dominant idea, existing within the brief and revealed through design. Favoured movements were those whose work promised directness and Georgian values. Particularly influential were various arguments of 1962–68, for a 'Sydney School'. Favoured architects were those who seemed in conflict with an 'inherently Australian' pettiness and conservatism. Hardy Wilson had already cast himself in this role. Robin Boyd and Max Freeland added Francis Greenway, Colonel Light, Walter Burley Griffin and Harry Seidler. There is considerable evidence that Boyd saw himself in that role.[18]

In most cases, these favoured movements were found outside Victoria, and, with the exception of Griffin, so were the favoured architects. This movement shows a distinct unease in dealing with Victoria's twentieth-century architects and themes. Griffin's semi-rural idyll at Castlecrag was clearly preferred to his inner-city buildings in Melbourne; Roy Grounds was alright as long as his work seemed simple, but large portions of his career seem skated over. Frederick Romberg had a European background and experience rivalling Seidler's, but produced buildings that were 'complicated', 'jumpy', and 'heavy'. More recently, Melbourne architects' exploration of suburban forms has been seen as 'strident chauvinism'.[19]

A resumé of all this work was described in Perth as being essentially 'Victoria', and there lies the clue. The pursuit of an inclusive, composite architecture, that denied homogeneity and sought to span city, suburb and country, continued in Victoria, alongside the mainstream and all its works.

The urban architecture of Walter Burley Griffin shows this. Griffin had a number of clients for urban work in Melbourne, where his work in Sydney, Queensland and South Australia was for outer suburban work or in large country towns. Here, Griffin's designs were long presented as those of a poor person's Frank Lloyd Wright, much too heavy and complex to bear sustained comparison with the Master.[20] But Griffin pursued this course by intention, and urban work in Melbourne was crucial to his Australian development. Donald Johnson has commented on Griffin's affinities with Louis Sullivan and Richardson rather than Wright, and to those influences might be added Harvey Ellis and several other American architects from the late nineteenth century.[21] What they all have in common is a fascination with radical opposites, of architecture based in contradiction, and the projection of unity in diversity. Ellis and Richardson achieved this by the opposition of metamorphosis and rotary movement within massive stone solids, and by the projection of this tension in exteriors, a muscularity which, as one critic put it, gave their architecture a strength sufficient for the industrial American city. In Sullivan's case, grid structure and earthen materials, steel and terra-cotta, are seen as having life in an organic sense. Sullivan also expresses this by external contradiction, the movement of floral ornament on grid facades.[22]

With this background, Griffin's sensibility clearly originates in

Philip Hudson and J. H. Wardrop, Shrine of Remembrance, St Kilda Road, Melbourne, 1922–34.

American precedents, and his contribution to Victoria's inclusive architecture is largely fortuitous, stemming from his Canberra commission. But in Melbourne he received a long series of complex inner-city jobs. On his own terms he used these to push many of the implications of Richardson, Sullivan and Ellis further, in a way that has not been parallelled elsewhere in Australia or the United States.

In the Capital Theatre, (1921–24), Griffin established a wandering, spiral circulation path between Swanston Street and cinema auditorium, surrounded by a massive steel-and-concrete structure. Griffin represented the entry as progress into a cave, winding and twisting against the frame of the office building overhead. The auditorium sustained the cave theme further, in an immense assertion of place, of final arrival. As Griffin saw the pattern of circulation, the materials and the structure as embodiments of nature's diversity, he used his signature images of rock crystal, sprouting like flowers around points of light on the way in, enveloping the audience in the cinema itself. Crystals showed again on the window tracery outside, and pushed outward towards the street, through balconies and awnings on the

Walter Burley Griffin, Auditorium, Capitol Cinema, Swanston Street, Melbourne, 1921–4 (altered). (Adrian Featherston)

facade. These linked urban life outside with the 'life' of materials and structure within. Then, in opposition, Griffin dominates the facade with massive piers, restating the grid and, at the same time, echoing the thick pilasters of Joseph Reed's Town Hall opposite.

In this tension of opposites and the use of crystalline detail, Griffin was employing themes shown earlier in the Australia Cafe of Collins Street (1915) or Newman College at the University of Melbourne (1915-17). Newman College, in particular, drew together Romanesque, Byzantine, Gothic, Renaissance and Ancient Roman forms, using the dining-room as a meeting point, the site of a controlled impact between the south-and west-facing residential wings.[23] The theme of fusion, and Griffins expression of this in imagery of crystal growth, continued in his 1921 proposal to roof the Jolimont railway yards, a crystalline ziggurat form which parallels the glittering Stadtkrone being developed by Expressionist architects in Germany.[24] Leonard House, of 1924-26, resembled in some ways the glass-walled tower that Wright had longed to build in America. But again Griffin's architecture emphasises contradiction. The concrete interior is resolved into crystal, pushed out through the glass facade towards Elizabeth Street and the city movement around it; in a related way the Mary Williams flats project in Toorak, of 1927, set massive block forms against circular layouts of window mullions which swung round and through them. The opposition of solid square and rotation, and Griffin's use of these in gesturing movement against the converging suburban streets outside, shows that at this point he was paralleling the themes of Victoria's Federation architecture. The forms were applicable to country, suburb or city. The design showed a concern with the streets around it and the movement of the suburb.

Such work is a clear development of Griffin's American public buildings, such as the Stinson Memorial Library or the Fox store and flats in Chicago.[25] In comparison his Australia Picture Palace of 1915-17 in Sydney, now demolished, lacked the same eloquence. His magnificent and now ruined Pyrmont incinerator, at the edge of Sydney's inner-city area, was really a building in the landscape rather than an urban creation. The same emphasis dominated Griffin's other council incinerators and the houses at Castlecrag, though interestingly, many of these reiterate his Melbourne explorations of 1915 onwards. Many have a tension of movement within and against massive solid, expressed in crystalline detail. The Castlecrag houses were later seen as serving the Australian ideal of 'houses in the landscape', though they were actually tied together by a system of parks and community foci, such as a Greek theatre. Most of these were neglected, or later fenced off, ironically by those who took the 'house in the landscape' as Castlecrag's main ideal.

Victoria therefore provided a focus for Griffin's experiments with inclusive architecture. It was also the location of a Griffin 'school':

Edward Billson, Roy Lippincott, Les Grant, J. F. W. Ballantyne.[26] Outside Victoria, Griffin and his office worked more in isolation, and it is not hard to see why. The mainstream Australian view of architecture had now been clarified. Even Victoria's contemporary experiments with Greek Revivalism, Art Deco, the Bungalow, Spanish Mission and Colonial Revivalism show little difference in aims and sensibility from those in other states or elsewhere. Even the State cinema of 1929, a Saracenic fantasy that seemed to breathe back something of Marvellous Melbourne, was designed in the United States, and was ultimately yet another expression of Los Angeles as a metropolis for dead-level culture.[27] A possible exception to this pattern was Marcus Barlow's Manchester Unity building of 1932. Its tower and detail emulate the metropolis of dynamism, having as a source the Chicago Tribune tower of 1921. But this image is combined with two lengthy facades that frame and complement Swanston and Collins streets.[28] With these elements, the corner tower creates a diagonal emphasis that links the building firmly with the street outside Manchester Unity and recalls Melbourne's nineteenth-century buildings in the way it celebrates Melbourne's urban grid, yet tries to break free from it.

Victoria's progressive architecture of the 1930s has been traditionally linked with Australia's mainstream, and with the broader mainstream of International Modern architecture. But in these years Victoria's 'new architecture' seems to reassert its pluralist, inclusive tendency—in a new form, and more widely. The contained, skin-like forms of Walter Gropius' Bauhaus were much admired, but in Victoria they occur in constant combination with other sources and themes.[29]

Edward Billson's Sanitarium factory of 1936-37 in Warburton has a Bauhaus-like massing of thin-skinned brick boxes. These are, however, combined with a legacy of Griffin: movement against the cube. In this case it is a series of spreading lines, generated from around the entry door, which seem to grow outward like the trunk and branches of a tree, co-ordinating the elevations. The work of other architects in Victoria complements this. In many cases the originally contained and Platonic Bauhaus forms are combined with a quite different animation and layering of mass, and are projected as echoes of city life and streets.

A leading early example of this was Mac Robertson Girls' High School in South Melbourne (1933-35) by Norman Seabrook and Allan Fildes. Their school was at once an expansion of a villa form into Albert Park, yet the advance and recession of its forms, the stepping of its walls with its general sense of animated line and movement responded to the mass movement of the city: of pupils, cars, and pedestrians at its busy corner site.

Billson, Seabrook and Fildes all use forms from Willem Marinus Dudok's architecture in Holland. Dudok was subsequently written out of the histories and criticism that marked architecture's mainstream overseas, possibly because of his continued emphasis on brickwork, mass and urban monumentality. These factors probably influenced Dudok's prominence as a Victorian influence, though he also affected architects outside Victoria, such as Frank Heath in Brisbane and Harry Rembert in New South Wales.[30] Heath's work was much later, and Rembert's is linked to rather classical symmetry and articulation of individual forms. In contrast, work by Victorians combines this with a curious revisiting of Federation themes: projection towards the street, elevations where individual parts are presented as episodes or occurrences, narrative and metamorphosis in each exterior. This is certainly true of Billson, Seabrook and Fildes, and can be seen also where Dudok's influence is less pervasive. Examples are the designs of Geoffrey Mewton, Roy Grounds and Frederick Romberg.

Work by these architects is pervaded by amalgamation and agglomeration of varied modern forms, and, in Grounds's and Romberg's buildings, an increasing emphasis on earlier Melbourne architecture of the inner suburbs. Mewton's Stooke house was voted by the Victorian Institute of Architects as the best house to be built in Victoria during the first 35 years of the century.[31] It showed the resurgent tendency towards amalgamated influence, with its white-painted, broadly winged massing, moving against the limitations of its suburban site. It had the line and weight of Dudok's monumental town buildings, and its T-form planning is similar to American architecture of the 1920s. The amalgam was distinctive enough, and emulated sufficiently, for Robin Boyd to describe this combination of wing emphasis and white colour as a new 'Victorian Type'.[32]

Roy Grounds, who shared an office with Mewton, gave a similar emphasis to amalgam, with a strong traditional sense which derived initially from the Colonial Revival[33]: the soft textures, the wall as a foil for light and shadows, and the homestead, for a time, as the focus. But the collective character of his forms, where wings grew everywhere and seemed added on as if over time, often gives his houses and flats the character of small towns. Lyncroft (1934) at Shoreham illustrates this. Its forms suggest all manner of traditional buildings: homesteads, a manor house, shops, pubs, sheds. Town and homestead forms are brought together in a single building, and this hints at a renewed attempt at architecture which, with common elements, could embrace the several Australias.

Lyncroft's spreading wing plan rises and falls in response to site contours, and the house seems linked to its landscape in a way reminiscent of Frank Lloyd Wright's Prairie houses. But the wing plan is also a new way of organising superimposition, collision, 'episodes' in exterior architecture. Grounds repeats this in various settings, notably in a rebuilt homestead at Chateau Tahbilk (1935) and in the outer suburban house for Joan Rosanove at Frankston (now demolished). But the full implications of his approach for Victoria's inclusive architecture come with the Quamby flats of 1941 in Toorak.

Quamby was a group of six flats on a tight, craggy, and steeply sloping site overlooking the Yarra. Grounds grouped the flats in three masses, coordinating them with a series of lines drawn from a point in the turning circle of Glover Court, where the flats were entered. Near the entry, the flats have a linear and planar emphasis fairly characteristic of new European architecture. But the flats soon take on a sense of movement and increased weight in detail, as they spread out to take in the northern sun. Lyncroft's ambiguity and variety in form and reference returns, seen this time in the changing function of the plank access ways. These change and merge function from one point to another, turning from entrance path to steps, to balcony, to verandah, to sun deck. This again has the tension and strength, in its timber materials, to act as a sinew, which in this case works to bind the spreading masses together. Circulation and perimeter structure combine in this linkage, and, as with Annear's houses one senses a tension between this outer frame layer and a brick core. The suggestion of the homestead, of core and perimeter frame, is there but, as with Annear's architecture, the homestead is not treated as a pure prototype to be dropped into the suburb. The homestead is instead presented as a source of tension, of argument between core and perimeter, which can, in turn, be the expression and orchestration of variety and change from one part of the building to another. The extent of this change is clear when looking back at Quamby from the north side. Here it is a series of quite solid masses, grouped round the hillside like a small town. The proportions, the wing walls and balustrades now resemble verandahs and facades of inner suburban housing, particularly terraces. The homestead, the town, the inner suburb, elements of the various Australias and of Victoria's varied society, were drawn together in a single building.

By that time a number of other Melbourne flats had been designed by Frederick Romberg. Romberg won a scholarship from the Swiss Technical Institute in Zurich, and visited Melbourne on his way to Japan. He ended up staying in Melbourne.[34] His early Newburn flats, of 1939–41, were in a white painted concrete building in South Melbourne, possibly the first city building in Australia to have surfaces entirely of raw concrete, straight off the form work and left unplastered. This was a favourite Swiss treatment. Newburn also recalled the long white Siedlung flats of Germany in the 1920s, such as Walter Gropius' Siemenstadt.[35] But Romberg broke up the facade into steps, giving individuality and privacy to each of the flats. This also gave Newburn a sense of animation set against both the tight verticality of its mass (drawn up to save as much garden as possible) and the limitations of the site, which in size and shape is not much different from a large suburban lot. It is an urban form, resilient and powerful, with a front end swung round to engage the street outside, on an allotment of suburban character. Newburn's rippling concrete gave it a distinct sense of muscularity; the variety of its forms made it a clearly compressive architecture.

The Stanhill flats, of 1943–51, were on a similar site four doors away. They make the inclusive tendency in Romberg's architecture even more apparent. By this time Romberg was expressing a clear interest in Melbourne regional forms, most particularly those of terrace housing in inner-suburban, inner-city areas. The proportions of terrace railings and balustrades are suggested in the frame of Stanhill's south side. The sense is heightened because Romberg steps the flats back partly to answer height regulations, partly to avoid repetition. His interest was, again, in establishing the 'territory' of each dweller and flat, while at the same time suggesting that Stanhill formed a community. Therefore Stanhill was split up into a series of wings, with their masses connected by a series of stairs and walkways, as at Quamby. These seem to link Stanhill's wings. It is as if several individual parts have come together by agreement. This variation in a single building is often quite extreme, as in the glass and frame treatment of the west and south sides, and the flowing, sculpted character of the north side, more massive and protective against the northern sun. The concrete, again off the form and rippling, seems to register the stress of this difficult unity.

A related amalgam, again working towards an architecture that could

Frederick Romberg, 'Stanhill Flats', Queens Road, South Melbourne, 1943–51. (Adrian Featherston)

address the several Australias, came with Romberg's Hilstan flats of 1945-51 in the Melbourne suburb of Brighton.[36] A long Siedlung block formed the spine, wings projected out, reading (from the street) like a succession of free-standing houses. At the front of each wing, Romberg restated the wing walls and balustrades of terrace housing, with each verandah pair as a fragment or episode, from a row of terraces seemingly pulled apart. At the south corner, Hilstan's central spine swept round, in a curve, its scale blown up by a large window grouping divided with a cruciform frame. The movement, the scale, were of the city, complementing the sweep of cars at the intersection, yet acting like an encircling arm to protect the gardens and wings on Hilstan's north side. Ironically, the road and intersection, which Hilstan responded to, devoured it in a road widening programme of 1979.

Romberg's early flats were built over long periods, being almost emblems of wartime and post-war austerity. Both these restrictions affected the inclusive tendency of Victoria's architecture, and impelled Victoria's architects towards the mainstream again. Civilian building was virtually halted between 1942 and mid-1945, and even in peacetime larger buildings were curtailed from late 1945 till about 1954. Post-war austerity made even the building of houses difficult, and made clients less willing to use architects. Robin Boyd, who had great hopes for radical change in Victoria's architecture, later remarked that its architects 'were beaten before they started'. In this atmosphere the Australian city, and Melbourne in particular, was seen as the embodiment of complacency, conservatism and overpowering visual chaos. This was a principal theme in Boyd's *Australia's Home* of 1952, and the main argument of *The Australian Ugliness*, 1960.[37]

As an alternative, architects increasingly aligned themselves with a developing mainstream in Europe and America. There, many architects, critics and historians drew together several strains of modern architecture into a single set of principles and concerns, a convergence, a 'common will'. This stressed universality of architectural form, with necessary concessions to materials and climate. The building was to be treated as a free-standing sculpture, with design focussed on its internal circulation and services rather than on creating defined place or acknowledging surroundings. Imagery and representation were directed at structure and technological achievement, based on an assumption that twentieth-century life had a single pre-eminent characteristic: industrialisation. References to context and history were mostly condemned as cowardice, 'regression' or betrayals as if in defence of a revolution. But at the same time this general approach of c. 1940-60 rubbed the corners off Europe's earlier architectural movements, particularly the energy and political commitment of Russian Constructivist architecture. In Australia, as overseas, its architects now generally spoke of a need to change and reform society, but their calls centred increasingly on a need for visual harmony and 'order', 'good taste', and the conquest of 'vulgarity', elements which gave the political and social direction of this architectured a distinct ambivalence.[38]

Evidence of this shared outlook were clear by the late 'forties. Boyd urged Australia's architects to join 'the new International'. Romberg's buildings were criticised for their visual and thematic complexity.[39] Evidence of a renewed specialisation of building forms appeared, with a move towards light, skeletal, or thinly surfaced buildings in inner-suburban or city areas, and a concentration on the free-standing house in landscape for domestic design.

Logically, the main target was the suburb, the territory that the spec builders had won in the late 'forties. Robin Boyd's war on Melbourne suburbs led an Australia-wide reaction. This reaction involved several approaches, all of which led away from that mixture of country, suburban and city forms which marked Victoria's inclusive tendency. Houses of 'the new International', particularly the Sydney designs of the newly arrived Harry Seidler, were emulated throughout Australia and, whatever Seidler's original intentions, were seen as a union of new structure and form with Colonial Revival ethics.[40] But unlike Grounds' earlier work, which had moved in this direction, the houses of Seidler and his numerous emulators were tight, contained, box forms, now hoisted off the ground, poised and insectile. The imagery of these buildings avoided any sense of a middle ground, and avoided that particular energy and monumentalism suitable for city building. They were essentially one of two specialised building types, with the country and the landscape at one extreme, and the tall glass office tower as the other.

At its most regionalist, Victoria's work tended to use elements found elsewhere in the country, though in some cases the precedents were forms and planning used by earlier architects in Victoria. A case in point is the widespread appearance of Grounds' detailing and overall form in housing in bush areas at Melbourne's fringe: Eltham, Warrandyte, Beaumaris and the Mornington Peninsula. Such work was quickly extended to use plainly rough and ad hoc materials, particularly the use of mud brick. Encouraged by *Home Beautiful*'s 'Operation Periwinkle' articles during the late 1940s, this became a continuing movement in Victoria's architecture, of which the designs of Alistair Knox became best known.[41]

In large buildings, Victoria shared precedent with the rest of Australia, in developing the glass-walled towers sometimes referred to as 'corporate international style.' As with Boyd's championing of a move to the mainstream, this direction was also, interestingly, dominated by Victorian firms, particularly Bates, Smart and McCutcheon, Stephenson and Turner, and Yuncken, Freeman, Griffiths and Simpson. From the early 'fifties their work employed the glass-walled architecture of Mies, or Skidmore, Owings and Merrill, based in Chicago.[42]

Reaction against this general approach is often seen as a recent

Gregory Burgess, 'Hackford House', Traralgon, 1981–2. (courtesy Gregory Burgess)

phenomenon, but in Victoria it was well under way by the late 1950s. Robin Boyd complained at one point that 'the glass box' had become 'the deadly constant of modern architecture'.[43] In *The Australian Ugliness* he reasserted his support for this form, but by then he sought to link it more thoroughly with the city and the demands of urban settings. His Domain Park flats in South Yarra (1960–62) were an attempt to put this into effect. He piled up a large number of people in a tower, which was linked to the amenities of Melbourne by a walk through parkland.[44] This was the earliest point where he clearly sought a relationship between new architecture and 'existing' Melbourne, rather than a Melbourne whose building types had been radically transformed. Domain Park's rearing lift towers gave it an animation and gesture towards the city that was quite different from the hovering glazed towers more frequently designed for Melbourne at that time. They also reflect strong influence from contemporary Japanese architecture and the work of Louis Kahn, an American architect who was concerned with restoring an urban strength and monumentality to urban architecture.[45]

Boyd was now linked in a partnership with Roy Grounds and Frederick Romberg. From 1957 the three worked on several new buildings at Ormond College in Parkville, sited around a Gothic Revival building by Joseph Reed. Rather than employing large slabs, or lurching to the other extreme with homestead forms, Grounds, Romberg and Boyd drew on middle- and late-nineteeth century buildings—garden follies and summerhouses—so that the original Reed buildings would not be disturbed by direct additions. In so doing, the trio departed from the Neo-Georgian, virtually the only historical reference permissible at that time. Their earlier extensions, such as the Master's and Vice-Master's lodges, have a planarity still typical of the post-war period, but the Picken Court dormitories (1961) and the Library (1964) take on a sense of movement and musculature. This recalls Romberg's work of the 'forties, but in a more compact form, with faceted shapes which also drew from polygonal towers and bays on the older Ormond buildings. This work again gave promise of an architecture that could respond equally to urban and 'landscape' locations, in a way that moves towards re-establishing Victoria's inclusive approach in architecture. The new Ormond domitories bring back an architecture of movement and of rotation. There is activity in masses at the perimeter of a core.[46]

Grounds left this partnership to tackle the Victorian Arts Centre on his own. With its National Gallery building of 1960–68, Grounds returned to a Palazzo form seen in many of Melbourne's middle- and late-nineteenth-century buildings. J. J. Clark's Old Treasury and Mint are examples. Grounds observed that he had been asked for a protective 'jewel box'. In the gallery design he generated a tension between solid mass and lighter structural elements: roof trusses, columns, ceiling frames, cornice and window details. This hinted, in some ways, at Ussher and Annear's recasting of the traditionally reposeful core and verandah periphery in homesteads. But Grounds was not ultimately successful here. He was still committed to a minimal lightness in these structural elements, so crucial to the buildings meaning. The dead weight of the gallery's huge walls overwhelmed them. Grounds sensed the monumentality in his task, and at that point too, his Neo-Classical design training returned from the 'twenties. This can be seen in the spaces that were often closed and defined, but frequently unsympathetic to what they held. The problem seemed to be the rigidity and stasis of classically organised space and mass, and the way it dwarfed and froze humanistic movement and animated gesture. A similar imbalance marks the contemporary classicism now widespread in Melbourne, which has anyway remained very close to prototypes in American and European magazines.[47] Only by violent fragmentation, or debunking of otherwise strong, contained forms, does both animation and the means to an architecture of broader reference seem to return. Recent examples are Ian McDougall's Kensington community centre (1981–83) or Des Smith's Faigan house at Heathmont (1982–83).[48] These buildings, in their wide breadth of dealing, manage a combination of forms that is applicable to city, suburban and even country settings and circumstance.

Victoria's early departures from mainstream post-war design were also seen in a group of architects who placed great emphasis on expressing taut, animated structure. Most of them admired Seidler's work in Sydney, but moved away from his emphasis on perforated box forms. Though hovering, these had been essentially static in outline and mostly avoided perimeter activity. Peter McIntyre, in particular, began framing or surrounding box forms with light structure and screens, hinting at enveloping foliage. The tree-like suggestion of some of these details, and they way they often hit or encircle core masses at a diagonal, recalls Annear's use of perimeter structure as a means to layer the surface of houses—to gesture at street and surroundings and to give a variety of spaces strong definition. This is seen particularly with the McCartney house of 1957, and McIntyre's own house in Kew (1954).[49] This was suspended on a pylon amongst trees by the Yarra, hovering amongst them like a flower, but directed outward towards Richmond and the city.

This architecture could work urbanistically: this was shown with the Olympic Pool of 1956, where McIntyre collaborated with Kevin Borland, John and Phyllis Murphy, and the engineer Bill Irwin. Here the structure, taut and tense, was scaled up to a level where the building could answer the movement of crowds and cars outside. It could face both the Botanical Gardens behind it, and the city to its north-west, on equal terms. Its strength was in the musculature of its structure. Derived from housing, it had been scaled up. Its form was applicable to country, suburbs or city. In 1982, the addition of huge areas of glass, opaque sheeting and external pipes obscured most of these characteristics.

There was an unceremonious, ad hoc aspect of this movement at times. It made cheerful use of a scratchy array of light materials and improvised techniques that recalled Annear's debunking of grand architectural gestures. In many instances this allowed not only structural representation, but rather ironic references to 'pretension' and austerity, as in one of Boyd's forays into this approach, the 1952 shop and house for William Wood at Jordanville. These used an Italian wartime technique where concrete was sprayed over chicken wire, drooping between paraboloid hoops. They made a sardonic allusion to their suburban context, echoing the Nissen huts of a migrant hostel nearby.[50]

Kevin Borland, who also used this sprayed concrete technique, would also build up the idea of a pure form only to undermine it in ways that suggested improvisation and sudden adaptations to circumstance. This appears with his McHutchinson house of 1957, but runs through to the Nichol house of 1973 and the Colvin house of 1974, at Eltham and Research respectively.[51] All three have timber structures strung around a core, but Borland's detail is heavier than that around McIntyre's houses, so they read as timber sinew. In Borland's later houses this seems to pull and twist the core of each house. Over each rides a large roof, starting with a great spread. As the Nichol and Colvin houses show, the roof drops in steps, down over brackets and bays and trickles off into long stems that run over casually angled struts into water tanks.

Borland's design is still focussed in bush settings, though his Grossman house in Malvern is a partial adaptation to suburban surroundings. His later design also uses timber 'sinew' internally, to link particular areas of function. These are treated as an unfolding series of events in a way that recalls Annear's use of dadoes and beams. In this case, though, it is rooms which become the 'events'. Often they are treated as buildings or four-sided enclosures within a common space which flows under a common ceiling. This resembles interiors by Ralph Erskine in Sweden or Charles Moore in California,[52] but in Borland's houses there is much more of a sense of these buildings being encountered along a winding path, as in the Nichol or Colvin houses. In that way Borland draws a casual topography, a landscape, into his houses. At the same time each has a collection of room-masses under its roof, expressing a community of form and place within single buildings.

By about 1975, the inclusive tendency among Victoria's architects had been reasserted in various new ways. The pattern continued and spread among architects after that, some of whom took Victoria's

House, Marshall Street, Ivanhoe, c. 1956.

inclusive architecture in yet further directions. Among these were Peter Crone, Cocks and Carmichael, Max May, Norman Day, Daryl Jackson (in his wooden pergola architecture of c. 1975–80), and Graeme Gunn between about 1968 and 1974.[53] Three of these inclusive architects, Gregory Burgess and Edmond and Corrigan, show individual approaches within inclusive architecture. Yet their work is almost a summary, a gathering together of the ideas, concerns and forms which mark this distinctive characteristic of architecture in Victoria.

Annear, Grounds and McIntyre were able to generate forms in their houses that could be applied to city buildings later, with changes in scale. In 1980 Gregory Burgess almost seemed to go the other way. In his competition design for the Stockmans' Hall of Fame at Longreach in Queensland, he broke his plan up into as many buildings and spaces as possible. The building became a town, a collective form rather than a linked, homogeneous mass. It was in part a representation of the city, where a whole series of shapes and forms agreed to come together.

This was followed by the Hackford house of 1981–82 near Traralgon. Here, a series of varied spaces and shapes converge on a point of unity in a central hall and stair. Each room has a specific shape and one senses, in the convergence or redirection of walls, the presence of another distinctive space unseen but neighbouring, in adjacent rooms.[55] Outside this, agreement shows in angled and superimposed room layers, which have a sense of pivoting movement that seems almost generated by the arcs of verandah balustrades. As in Annear, the homestead is not seen as a static form, but rather as a source of tension between forms. The house in this case stands like a person in the surrounding landscape. That sinew of timber structure, that muscularity which parallels the human form, is close to Annear's. Then, when Burgess brings this form back into inner suburbs, as in his Canning Street buildings for the Ministry of Housing (1983–84), a timber and mesh sinew binds the undulations of brick facades together, so they seem compressed, and large surfaces buckle out towards the inner suburban street and corner.

The work of Edmond and Corrigan is perhaps most identified with the suburbs, and they are often seen as the first Australian firm to make the suburbs a source of imagery.[56] Their buildings, though, are recognisable as belonging to Victoria, and this is probably because their work draws from a great range of sources: city, suburb, country. The first example of this approach was actually in the country, with St Colman's Catholic church at Mortlake (1974–76). Rather than being a prototype dropped in from elsewhere, the church reflects specific elements of typical buildings of Victoria. A monumental character can be seen in its large red-brick facade against the main road. The local incursions of Melbourne suburb architecture are taken up in the thickly detailed windows on the church's west side. The homestead can be seen in the verandah on the north side, and the neighbouring pub in the chamfered corner on the east side. The church draws this whole context into its form and this in turn modifies the original church space, which in early sketches was an enveloping oval.

A similar breadth of reference occurs in two later churches, the Church of the Resurrection in Keysborough (1975-77) and the Chapel of St Joseph at Box Hill (1976-78). Suburban housing is drawn on, as are certain monumental buildings from the suburbs, the rearing masses of sports pavilions, for example. This influences their internal planning. St Josephs, with its linked sequence of spaces, Victoria's theme of episode: each space is given a strongly individual character. In the Resurrection church, the nave is protected by a solid south wall, housing toilets and service rooms, and by the chancel, long and spreading. Together they form 'L', against which the nave area, rounded and flowing, sits like the active corner of a Federation house, not directed at the street now, but pointing instead towards the other buildings around the church. These include a parish centre, a hall, a church shop, a large primary school, elderly people's housing, and a child-care building.

This was a complex group, a small town within the suburb and intended to give cohesion to its area. Keysborough is several kilometres from the nearest train or large shopping centre, and the parish

Maggie Edmond and Peter Corrigan, Chapel of St Joseph, Strabane Avenue, Box Hill, 1976-8.

buildings were to provide a focus that would lessen isolation, that pervasive problem of Australia's outer suburbs. The general Australian response would have been to drop in a homestead, or a single homogeneous building. But in these Keysborough designs, Edmond and Corrigan call on the suburb's strengths: its sense of individual place, the quite complex relation of suburban houses to the street, the great range and variety of forms, colours, detailing, and inheritances of life in other places—inner suburbs, the city, the country. Nor are the references centred on the post-war suburb. The elderly people's housing, with its forced perspective, most resembles the long streets of the 1920s suburbs, while its patterned brick, lattices and small front yards recall Melbourne terracing of much earlier periods.

In the school, a curving range of classrooms springs from a more solid mass formed round an entrance. Like Annear's L-plan open areas,

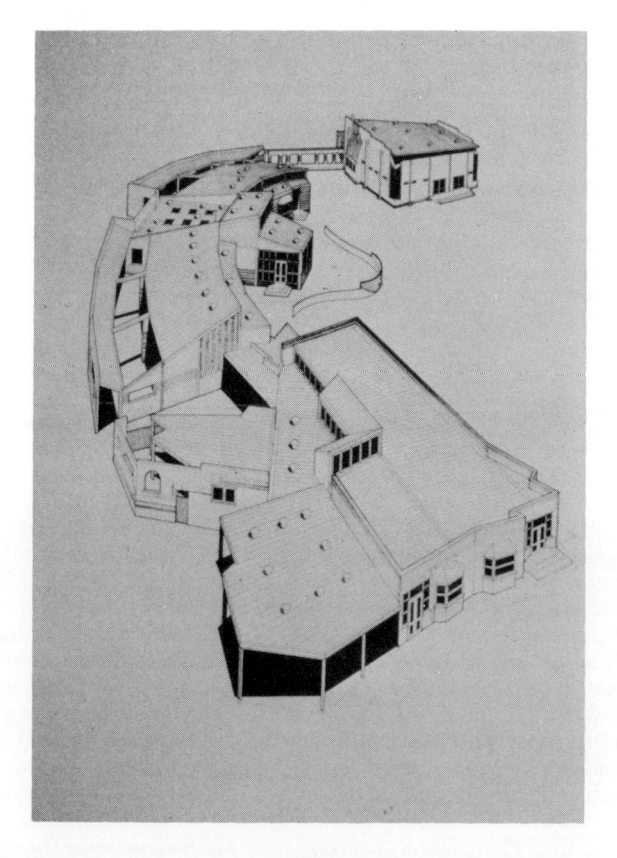

Maggie Edmond and Peter Corrigan, Primary School, Resurrection Parish Centre, Keysborough, 1974–9. (courtesy Edmond and Corrigan)

172 *Victoria's Heritage*

this is almost an inversion of the Federation closed 'L' and animated corner grouping of rooms.[58] From the play areas the north arc of classrooms appears like a terrace of an inner-city street. The scale and sense of enclosure found in inner-suburban schools, with their shelter sheds, are recalled by a long screen. It acts to control sun and to divide play areas of increasing size, so that small spaces and garden plots would surround younger and more cautious children. Then, viewed from the west, the school takes on the spread of a homestead, with bright girders propping up a long screening wall. Now, though, the screen has more weight than a verandah, and is laced with brick striping, almost as in High Victorian Gothic architecture. It is from some angles an isolated form, as houses are in the country. Closer in, the school masses around a long common space, like a Melbourne street. It has the sense of a core, the opposition, layering and gradation of space distinctive to a particular group of buildings, which, in related yet varied ways, have made Victoria's architecture distinctive. It is an architecture of individual parts, connected and animated by a taut sinew. This time it is steel girders. With Romberg, the sinew was in concrete circulation paths; with Annear, the sinew was in timber. In all these cases, it not just building masses that are drawn together; it is three Australias—country, suburb and city. It's this belief in a form that could address all three, in an architecture of animation and complexity, that has become, with a few exceptions, Victoria's. Perhaps it may now become, distinctively, Australia's.

Notes

1   In ex-colonies the development of this attitude had its origins in the late nineteenth century. In Australia, the homestead form is made central to proposals for architectural reform by John Sulman, 'An Australian style', *Australasian Builder and Contractor's News (ABCN)*, 14, 21, 28 May 1887, pp. 3, 23, 40 and by E. Wilson Dobbs, *The Rise and Growth of Australasian Architecture, ABCN* Pamphlet, Sydney, 1892. The homestead is the virtual basis for reforms proposed by the Georgian revival movement, as in the early writing of Martin Boyd as 'Martin Mills' in *The British Australian and New Zealander*, esp. July 1927, pp. 18–19, and writing and drawing by William Hardy Wilson, particularly his *Old Colonial Architecture in New South Wales and Tasmania*, Sydney, 1924, and *The Dawn of a New Civilization*, London, 1929. From there it is dominant both as a prototype and an ideal, particularly in Robin Boyd's *Australia's Home: Its Origins, Builders and Occupiers*, Melbourne, 1952; Boyd's *The Australian Ugliness*, Melbourne, 1960; J. M. Freeland's *Architecture in Australia A History*, Melbourne, 1968. Recent work with this emphasis includes the writing of Philip Cox, Philip Drew's *Leaves of Iron: The Architecture of Glenn Murcutt*, Sydney, 1985, and Rory Spence's 'The Concept of Regionalism Today: Sydney and Melbourne Considered ...', *Transition*, 4, April 1985, pp. 3–17. This development parallels that of the United States, where the

free-standing seventeenth century house was celebrated as an embodiment of 'the older and purer', and eighteenth century successors were admired as ideal forms in the landscape. Vincent Scully, *The Shingle Style and the Stick Style*, New Haven, 1955, 71, esp. pp. 19-53.

2 For such urban traditions in architecture, see esp., Walter Kidney et al., 'Philadelphia Story', *Progressive Architecture*, April 1976, pp. 6-88; Vincent Scully, *American Architecture and Urbanism*, London, 1969, esp. Scully's discussions of a Philadelphia tradition; Richard Longstreth, *The Edge of the World*, Cambridge, Mass, 1983; Mark Peisch, *The Chicago School of Architecture*, New York, 1965; H. Allen Brooks, *The Prairie School: Frank Lloyd Wright and His Midwest Contemporaries*, Toronto, 1972.

3 Noted by Robert Irving (ed.) in *The History and Design of The Australian House*, Melbourne, 1985, pp. 199, 210. A 1915 example was first noted by Neil Clerehan in *The Age*, 27 February 1961. Miles Lewis has pursued research in this area and notes seminal examples in Essendon and Geelong during the 1920s. The Essendon building shows the later formula well developed with boxed eaves, and appears to have been guided in this direction by the 'boxed eaves and mushroom roofs' seen in the colonial revival work of Hardy Wilson and others. Such amalgams were frequently mooted in *The Home* and *Australian Home Beautiful* during the 1920s, and seem influential in the emergence of what is now known as post-war Australian suburban vernacular.

4 This development is the subject of two compilations by Charles Jencks: *Post Modern Classicism* and *Free Style Classicism*, London, 1980 and 1982 respectively, each of which was published as a whole issue of the journal *Architectural Design*, May 1980 and January/February 1982. In Australia, this approach gained prominence with some of the designs submitted for a hypothetical completion of *Engehurst*, in Glebe, NSW, originally designed by John Verge: see *Architecture Australia (AA)*, 69, May 1980, pp. 40-78. For subsequent examples, see esp., *Daryl Jackson, Drawings, Buildings and Photographs*, Melbourne 1984, and Roger Pegrum et al., *Philip Cox*, Canberra, 1984.

The classical and mannerist approaches, with certain parallels in sixteenth century Italian architecture, are now widely used in several Australian cities. While having minor regional inflexions, its forms are largely beyond the scope of this essay. Several commentators, including Harry Seidler, have seized on this particular development and in polemical writing have tried to present it as the sum total of modern inclusive approaches to architecture: Harry Seidler, 'Internationalism' *AA*, 71, September 1982, pp. 58-60, and examples Seidler employs in reply to the author, *ibid.*, 73, June 1984, pp. 68-71. See also Philip Drew, 'Mannerism in contemporary architecture', *Transition*, I, 1, July 1979, pp. 4-10; 'Post-modern: the renewal of style in architecture', *ibid.*, 1, 3, March 1980, pp. 9-16

5 For the question of national identity and architectural reform, and the sources of this interest, see David Saunders, 'Domestic styles of Australia's federation period Queen Anne and the Balcony style', *Architecture in Australia*, 58, August 1969, pp. 655-62. Conrad Hamann, 'Nationalism and reform in Australian architecture 1880-1920', *Historical Studies*, 18, October 1979, pp. 393-411; George Tibbits, 'The so-called Melbourne domestic Queen Anne', *Historic Environment*, II, 2 (1982), pp. 4-44;

174 Victoria's Heritage

Geoffrey Serle, *From Deserts the Prophets Come: The Creative Spirit in Australia, 1788-1972*, Melbourne, 1973, pp. 83-7.

6   Hunt's quarrels with other Sydney architects were an extraordinarily bitter episode, recounted by J. M. Freeland in *The Making of A Profession*, Sydney, 1971, pp. 58-75. The sour and disappointed tone of Sydney's later architectural discussion is reflected particularly in John Sulman's entry on 'Architecture' in the *Australian Encyclopaedia*, Sydney, 1925-6, and Hardy Wilson's assumed role of sensitive exile in a city of barbarism: *The Dawn of a New Civilization*, op. cit. Peter Proudfoot has recently commented on Leslie Wilkinson's approach, which was to deny the necessity of extended debate on architecture altogether, the building was the only document ultimately worth considering. Peter Proudfoot, 'The Development of Architectural Education in Sydney, 1880-1930', *Historical Studies*, 21, October 1984, pp. 197-211.

7   In Sir John Sulman's early writing, mid-nineteenth century architectural movements are presented as a shifting series of fashions and enthusiasms: 'An Australian Style' (n. 1). Sulman's preference for Italian Renaissance precedent stemmed partly from a desire to establish an 'enduring' and substantial architecture. The same wish for a clearly recognisable 'substance' and lineage pervades American architectural discussions at the same time, as in the writing of Henry van Brunt and Ralph Adam Cram in *American Architect* and the (Massachusetts) *Architectural Review*. Both here and in the United States, evidence of architectural 'fashions' was seen as a frivolous marking of time in the pursuit of a genuine national architecture and a symptom of architectural enslavement to older cultures. By c. 1910 'fashion' and 'substance' were very widely used opposites in Australian architectural discussions, generally coupled with exhortations that Australian architects, new in their nationality, keep to the right path and avoid false moves. This epitomised a general move towards conservatism in architectural debate, which persisted through the 1920s and governed early responses to Modernism.

Generally 'fashion' came to be synonymous with something a commentator disliked or wished would go away, and in architecture has been as persistent in the US as in Australia, cf. James Marston Fitch, 'A Funny Thing Happened', *American Institute of Architects, Journal*, 69, January, 1980, pp. 66-68; and Harry Seidler, (n. 4).

8   E. Wilson Dobbs, op. cit.; Walter Butler, 'Modern Architectural Design', *Royal Victorian Institute of Architects, Journal (RVIAJ)*, July–September 1903; Harold Desbrowe Annear, *Building, Engineering and Mining Journal*, 15 February 1902.

9   See esp., Walter Butler and Beverley Ussher, 'Cottage by the Sea', *Building and Engineering Journal* (later the *Building, Engineering and Mining Journal*), 9 January 1892. Arthur Fisher, 'House in Irving Road, Windsor', ibid., 23 August 1890, ff. p. 290. For Ussher, see *ibid.*, 4 December 1897 in particular.

10 Robin Boyd discusses Annear and Haddon as pioneers of architectural modernism in *Australias Home*, op. cit., pp. 160-3, 68-9, 165, 9,. See also Hamann, 'Nationalism and Reform', op. cit., pp. 404-7; Donald L. Johnson, *Australian Architecture 1901-1951, Sources of Modernism*, Sydney, 1980, Ch. 1.

11 Harold Desbrowe Annear, 'The Recognition of Architecture', in S. Ure Smith (ed) *Domestic Architecture in Australia*, Sydney, 1919, pp. 19–24.
12 Progressive, that is, in their resemblance to the plain, rectangular architecture of European modernism. Broceliande and Inglesby are discussed by Boyd in *Victorian Modern*, Melbourne, 1947, pp. 15, 23, and by Geoffrey Woodfall, Harold Desbrowe–Annear: 1866–1933', *Architecture (in) Australia (AA)*, 56, February 1967, pp. 100–108.
13 Architectural migration to Western Australia is noted be Ian Molyneux in his introduction to *Looking Around Perth*, Perth, 1980, p. xvii.
14 Conrad Hamann, 'Forgotten Reformer: the Architecture of George Sydney Jones, 1865–1927', *AA*, 68, October–November 1979, pp. 39–45, 64.
15 Cf. Alastair Service, *Edwardian Architecture: A Handbook to Building Design in Britain, 1890–1914*, London, 1977; Conrad Hamann, *A History of Australian Architecture, Unit 3: 1900–1945*, Melbourne: Educational Media, 1985.
16 This was partly due to the spread of *Beaux Arts* architectural training, both in Technical Colleges and new faculties in Australian universities. Based on the atelier system at the Paris *Ecole des Beaux-Arts*, this training emphasised the rapid design and resolution of buildings around particular problems of space and role. The Beaux-Arts method retained the forms of classical monumentality, but encouraged architects to conceive buildings as isolated objects, independent of their surroundings.
17 see n. 1.
18 Conrad and Chris Hamann, 'Anger and the New Order: Some Aspects of Robin Boyd's Career', *Transition*, September–December 1981, pp. 26–39.
19 Roger Pegrum, in *Architectural Monographs I; Philip Cox*, Canberra, 1984.
20 Robin Boyd, 'Walter Burley Griffin in Victoria', *The Victorian Historical Magazine*, 26, September 1954, pp. 102–115.
21 Donald L. Johnson, *The Architecture of Walter Burley Griffin*, Melbourne, 1977, pp. 26, 103.
22 Louis Sullivan 'The Tall Office Building Artistically Considered', reprinted in *Progressive Architecture*, 38, June 1957, pp. 204–6. As with Sir Nikolaus Pevsner in Britain, Robin Boyd dismissed Sullivan's ornament as irrelevant. Cf. Vincent Scully, 'Louis Sullivan's Architectural Ornament', *Perspecta*, 5, 1959, pp. 73–80.
23 Observations by Ellen Mitchell and Ruth Bulpitt presented in undergraduate essays at Monash University, 1982. See also Karen Burns, 'Walter Burley Griffin, A Complex and Contradictory Architecture', B. A. Honours Thesis, Monash University, 1983.
24 Cf. Griffin's Scheme (Johnson, *Griffin*, p. 113), and the designs in Bruno Taut's *Die Stadtkrone*, Berlin 1919. Cf. Michael Markham, 'Walter Burley Griffin: Order and Expression', *Architect*, 8, May 1984, pp. 8–15.
25 Illustrated by Johnson in *Griffin*, pp. 99, 100.
26 Outlined by Donald Johnson, 'The Griffin School of Australian Architecture', *Art and Australia*, 17, Winter 1980, pp. 374–84, and in his *Australian Architecture*, pp. 113–31.
27 Australia's 1920s tendency towards medians and a 'dead-level' in emotional and intellectual involvement with culture is suggested by Heather Radi's, essay, '1920–1929', in Frank Crowley (ed.), *A New History of Australia*, Melbourne 1974, pp. 357–414, and is reflected in the fate of

Australian theatre and writing in those years by Geoffrey Serle, *From Deserts the Prophets Come*, Ch. 6.

28 Hood and Howells' Chicago Tribune Tower was in contrast a free standing tower on a corner site, escaping Chicago's grid by ignoring its street line and creating a fantasy largely on its own terms. There are several nineteenth century Melbourne precedents for Barlow's particular use of long facades and a corner tower: the General Post Office, the Town Hall, the Federal Hotel, the E. S. and A. bank headquarters, Flinders Street Station. All use strongly accentuated corner masses to generate diagonal forces against the prevailing grid of Melbourne's street plan.

29 Most notably with the Dutch brick architecture of Willem Marinus Dudok, the streamlined architecture of Erich Mendelsohn in Germany and Britain after 1925; the more massive and complex concrete architecture of Alvar Aalto (after c. 1932). See Hamann, *A History of Australian Architecture, Unit 3* (n. 15), and Hamann, 'Frederick Romberg, Architect', in Stephen Jefferies and Leslie Bodi (eds), *The Germans in Victoria*, Melbourne, 1986.

30 See G. P. Webber, 'E.H. Rembert', *AA*, 74, January 1985, pp. 51–8, and the Royal Australian Institute of Architects, *Buildings of Queensland*, Brisbane, 1959, p. 68 esp.

31 'First Prize', *RVIA*, 34, March 1936, p. 19.

32 In *Victorian Modern*: 'The Victorian Type-and the Great Asymmetry', pp. 60–70.

33 See Hamann, *Australian Architecture* (n. 15), section 27, and Roy Grounds, Frederick Romberg, Robin Boyd', in Howard Tanner (ed.) *Architects of Australia*, Melbourne, 1981, pp. 129–39.

34 Hamann, Ibid; 'Early Romberg', *AA*, 66, May 1977, pp. 68–75; 'Frederick Romberg, Architect' (n. 29).

35 Illustrated widely, esp. by Arnold Whittick in *European Architecture in the Twentieth Century*, New York, 1974, Ch. 22; Manfredo Tafuri and Francesco dal Co, *Modern Architecture*, New York, 1979. Ch. 11.

36 Hamann, 'Frederick Romberg, Architect', n. 29, and 'Hilstan', *Architect*, May 1977.

37 *Australia's Home*, n. 1; *The Australian Ugliness*, Melbourne, 1960. The second book pictured Australia's society in retreat from the Australian landscape, indulging in a visual fidgeting or whistling in the dark which Boyd termed 'featurism'. Later chapters of the *Ugliness* set out examples that oppose Victoria's exploration of urbanism. Architecture was to engage the bush directly, where possible, and in cities it was to assume Georgian decorum and anonymity (pp. 107–18 esp.). Discussed by C. and C. Hamann, n. 18, pp. 33–4. Georgian revivalism dominates Australia's architectural history and criticism, as seen in the focal role of homestead and house in writers from Sulman to Spence (n. 1), cf. J. M. Richards' 'The Condition of Architecture and the Principle of Anonymity', in J.L. Martin et al. (eds) *Circle*, London, 1937, pp. 184–90, a representative and influential example of British Neo-Georgianism.

38 This includes Hardy Wilson and Martin Boyd (n. 1), Leslie Wilkinson, and even Harry Seidler's recent 'Internationalism' (n. 4).

39 By Robin Boyd, in *Victorian Modern*, Walter Bunning in *Art in Australia*, and Walter Gerardhin in *Smudges*. See Hamann, 'Frederick Romberg, Architect' (n. 29).

40 Robin Boyd, 'A New Eclecticism', *Architectural Review*, 110, January–March 1951, pp. 151–3, and several of his *Age* articles from that time; J. M. Freeland, *Architecture in Australia* (n. 1).
41 Alistair Knox and Leslie Runting, 'Operation Periwinkle', *Australian Home Beautiful*, 29, February 1950, pp. 30–1, 33, 49; March 1950, pp. 36–7, 44–5, 74–5; April, 1950, pp. 34–5. Alastair Knox, *Living in the Environment*, Melbourne, 1976; *Alternative Housing*, Melbourne, 1980. For an overview of this regionalism in Victoria, see Winsome Callister, 'Melbourne Architecture: A Continuing Regionalism, 1950–1984', B.A. Honours thesis, Monash University, esp. Ch. 2, and articles in preparation. 1985.
42 C.f. Christopher Woodward, *Skidmore, Owings and Merrill*, New York, 1970, or Arthur Drexler, *Ludwig Mies van der Rohe*, New York, 1960. Important prototypes were Skidmore Owings and Merrill's Lever house in New York, 1951–2, and later buildings such as their Crown Zellerbach offices in San Francisco, of 1957–9. Cf. Stephenson and Turner's Lever house in Sydney, completed in 1950s, and Bates, Smart and McCutcheon's curtain-walled offices completed between 1956 and 1963, esp. the M.L.C. insurance building in North Sydney, and, in Victoria, I.C.I. house and the early Monash University buildings.
43 Robin Boyd, 'The Functional Neurosis', *AR*, 119, February 1956, pp. 84–88.
44 Enacting a view of urbanism put forward in *The Australian Ugliness*, in which his Neo-Georgian order for the Australian city was to be a succession of experiences enjoyed on paths of movement between work, home or leisure.
45 See esp. Vincent Scully, *Louis I. Kahn*, New York, 1961; Toshio Nakamura, et al., 'Louis I Kahn', whole issue of *Architecture and Urbanism*, Tokyo, 1983. Kahn is discussed by Boyd at some length in *The Puzzle of Architecture*, Cambridge and Melbourne, 1965. Others of influence included the Japanese Architect Kenzo Tange and his contemporaries, on whom Boyd also wrote and who excited considerable interest: Robin Boyd, *Kenzo Tange*, New York, 1962, and *New Directions in Japanese Architecture*, New York, 1968.
46 See Hamann, 'Frederick Romberg, Architect' (n. 29).
47 C.f. local examples with the new classicism evident in the US, Britain and Japan, particularly, and compiled in by Charles Jencks in three issues of *Architectural Design*, London: 'Post-Modern Classicism', 50, May–June 1980; 'Free-Style Classicism', 52, January–February 1982, and 'Abstract Representation', 53, July-August 1983. Also Paolo Portoghesi, et al. *The Presence of the Past; Architecture 1980*, New York, 1980. C.f. Australian work in recent surveys, such as *UIA. International Architect*, 4, 1984, *AR*, December 1985, *Domus*, July-August 1985.
48 These designs await publication.
49 The McIntyres' own house was published extensively in *Architecture, Architecture and Arts*, and the *Olympic Guide to Melbourne Architecture* (1956) also in work being prepared by Philip Goad for *Transition* magazine.
50 See Neil Clerehan, 'Robin Boyd' whole issue of *Architect*, 17, November–December 1971, pp 5–38. Boyd's laconic references to suburban imagery invite comparison with the inflential American architects Robert Venturi and Denise Scott Brown: *Complexity and Contradiction in Architecture*, New

York, 1966, and *Learning from Las Vegas*, Cambridge, Mass., 1972. Boyd publicly disapproved of Venturi, though Boyd's *Puzzle of Architecture* looked favourably on an architect with similar approaches to Venturi's, Charles Moore.
51 See Conrad Hamann and Jenepher Duncan, 'Seven in the Seventies: An Exhibition', *AA*, 71, February 1982, Conrad Hamann, 'The Return to the City', in Leon Paroissien and Michael Griggs (eds.) *Old Continent New Building*, Sydney, 1983, pp. 33–42, Jennifer Taylor (n. 49).
52 Particularly Moore's *Sea Ranch of 1965* and Gerald Allen's *Charles W. Moore*, Whitney, 1980.
53 See Hamann and Duncan (n. 51).
54 'Australian Stockmans' Hall of Fame and Outback Heritage Centre Competition', *Transition*, 2, March 1981, pp. 26–7 esp.
55 Illustrated on Michael Tawa: 'Gregory Burgess: The Way of Transformation', *Transition*, 4, October 1984, pp. 14–19.
56 Richard Munday, 'Passion in the Suburbs', *AA*, February–March 1977; pp. 52–61; Greg Missingham, 'Edmond and Corrigan: the Australian Architecture', *A + V*, March 1981, pp. 38–72; Peter Corrigan; a Kind of Exposition', *Transition*, 2, March 1981 pp. 14–19; Philip Drew, 'Peter Corrigan', in Muriel Emanuel (ed.) *Contemporary Architects*, London, 1980, pp. 168–9.
57 Office archives, Edmond and Corrigan.
58 Ibid.

9

Drama and music in colonial Melbourne

HAROLD LOVE

I have shamelessly purloined my title from Frank Brewer's *The Drama and Music in New South Wales*, that invaluable compendium published in 1892.[1] Just as shamelessly, I intend to purloin Brewer's method which was to consider drama and music in two separate sections with drama first and music, the more diffuse topic, second. But this is largely a matter of convenience and should not be allowed to conceal the very close links that existed between the two arts over the period when each was establishing itself on a professional basis in Australia. In particular, I would like to stress the extent to which instrumental musicians relied on the employment offered by theatre bands and the enlarged orchestras of opera seasons. This and teaching were the main support of Melbourne's leading players during the colonial period. I will depart from Brewer in treating opera as part of my drama section. Otherwise, I hope that this account can be regarded as a tribute to his, which has no counterpart for Melbourne apart from James Smith's narrative history of the Melbourne stage in the *Cyclopedia of Victoria*.[2]

Drama

Theatre began in Melbourne as a very local and particular activity and in the space of 60 years had become a national industry masterminded from Bourke and Exhibition streets. In some ways this is a very exciting story and in other ways a rather depressing one. The excitement lies in the remarkable achievements of the entrepreneurs—Coppin, Lyster, Darrell, Dampier, Holt, Musgrove and Williamsson—and the best of the pioneer performers; the depressing part lies in the narrowing of the repertory from its point of maximum divergence in the 1860s and the growing subservience in all things theatrical to London and New York reputations. Since there are four distinguishable levels of complexity in the process by which theatre grew from a municipal to a pan-colonial activity, I intend to divide the story into four phases which I will call the phase of the strolling players, the phase of the stock companies, the phase of intercolonial management, and the phase of the national chains. I must warn, however, that the divisions between phase and phase are structural rather than chronological. One way of doing things did not necessarily cease the moment another was introduced, and new conceptions did not necessarily take hold, even on different sides of Bourke Street, at exactly the same time.

The phase of the strolling players

The earliest phase of professional theatre in Australia was signalised more by a sanguine faith in the future benefits of the drama than by much in the way of artistic achievement or civilising influences. The public performance of plays was a development from less formal kinds of entertainment conducted in halls attached to hotels, and when the first actual theatres were put up there was not much change in the behaviour of the patrons.[3] The authorities in Sydney had refused permission for the establishment of a playhouse there until as late as December 1832, when Barnett Levey's first auditorium was constructed in a saloon of the Royal Hotel. Hobart followed in 1833, with occasional seasons in Launceston from 1834, and Adelaide in 1838. Melbourne had a theatre, the Pavilion, from 1841 (the sixth year of our existence) but not a licence to operate it. There were three reasons for this. The first was that it was so badly built that, to quote Garryowen, 'Whenever the wind was high it would rock like an old collier at sea'.[4] The second was that the authorities believed—quite correctly—that any performances given there were likely to be of a scandalous and indecent nature. The third was the lack of anyone competent to manage it or perform in it.

Eventually such competent persons did arrive: the Buckingham family, the Arabins, Thomas Boyd, Conrad and Harriet Knowles, Sampson and Cordelia Cameron and Francis Nesbitt—all well-known names in the history of Australian theatre.[5] But even then it was always a marginal affair. Buckingham's first performances, commencing in February 1842, were given with the assistance of amateurs. Subsequent managers struggled, in the face of appalling behaviour from audiences and deluges of rain through the roof, to keep the place solvent, usually without much success. In April 1844, Knowles had a strike on his hands, following which his actors, having failed to impress the police magistrate with the gravity of their complaint, set up for themselves in competition. Worn out by the cares of management, Knowles died only a month later. Things improved when the Pavilion was superseded in April 1845 by the Queen's theatre, which did not rock in the wind, with a company headed by Sampson Cameron and Francis Nesbitt, and joined for a short but brilliant period by the Coppins and G. H. Rogers; but secure prosperity only came with the blessed arrival of the lucky diggers and gold-boom immigrants in the early 1850s. It should be noted that the theatres were at this time the principal centres for musical performance. They all maintained bands, and programmes would include songs, hornpipes, ballets and entr'acte music during and between the farces and melodramas. The hazards of musical performance included 'the habitual intoxication of an actress, who upon one occasion tumbled head over heels into the orchestra'.[6]

I spoke of this as the phase of the strolling players, and the players I had in mind were the ones whose names I have just mentioned: the Buckinghams, the Arabins, the Knowleses, the Coppins and the Camerons. They were not strolling players in the mediaeval sense. They were all experienced professionals whose natural medium was the proscenium-arch theatre equipped with wing-and-shutter scenery. But they were constitutionally unable to remain in one place. All had worked—singly, in couples or in larger groups—in most of the regular playhouses of the Australian continent. But all had shown themselves (though I think it was chiefly the men who were to blame) as helpless victims of optimism—quarrelling over the terms of their engagements with the Sydney managers, moving on to the new theatrical centres to set up as stars or managers themselves, and then, often as not, having to suffer the same kind of disaffection from their own supporting actors. Get them all together in one city—whether it be Sydney, Adelaide, Hobart, Launceston or Melbourne—and one would see the stock-repertoire plays performed with a real depth of talent. Yet the very act of bringing them together in one city tended to provoke clashes of temperament, divisions of companies, and mutually destructive competition. The beginnings of the professional stage in Melbourne were therefore similar to the beginnings of theatre in the other Australian cities, with much the same performers throwing much the same tantrums.[7] But let them at least receive the credit for creating an enthusiastic following for the legitimate stage, which could be built on by their more persistent successors at the Queen's, Morton King and Charles Young. And if performing conditions at the Pavilion and Queen's were anything like what Garryowen describes and Charles Thatcher illustrates, their task can not have been an easy one.[8]

The Stock Companies

The effects of the gold boom on Melbourne are indicated in a particularly vivid way by the explosive growth of theatre. Whereas in 1853 there was only one moderately sized theatre operating, the Queen's, a decade later there were three very large theatres—by which I mean theatres on the scale of Drury Lane and Covent Garden. These were the Royal (built in 1855), the Princess (which had begun life as Astley's Amphitheatre in 1854) and the Haymarket (1862)—besides the smaller Pantheon in Richmond, the Lyceum in Lonsdale Street and the various halls and music halls.[9] By 1863, Melbourne was also enjoying regular seasons of grand opera from William Lyster's company (sometimes more nights per year of opera than we receive today) and could boast visits by some of the most prominent stars of the English-speaking stage—Laura Keene, Edwin Booth, Mary Provost, Lola Montez, Gustavus Brooke, Avonia Jones, Joseph Jefferson, Barry Sullivan, Charles Dillon and Charles and Ellen Kean, soon to be followed by Celine Celeste, Walter Montgomery, and, in 1870, Charles Mathews Jr. Of these it is Montez, the least talented, who found her way unto Australian folk mythology through publicly horsewhipping the editor of the *Ballarat Times*. Her main vehicle was an autobiographical drama about her adventures in Bavaria. This was followed, Smith notes, by 'the spider dance, executed by herself, from which a good deal of impropriety was expected, but it was so decorous and so drearily dull that everybody was disappointed'. So Lola was a tease—or was it, as Michael Cannon claims, that there were versions and versions of the spider dance?[10] I should also mention here the two most important of the numerous Chinese opera companies which toured the goldfields playing to predominantly Chinese audiences—Lee Gee's and Leong Chan Kwong's—and the very popular troupes of Japanese jugglers, magicians and contortionists who performed in the European theatres.[11]

The change in scale was accompanied by a decided improvement in the comfort of theatres and the behaviour of patrons. George Coppin, in an address to the audience at the Theatre Royal in May 1861, contrasted the 'beauty and elegance' he saw around him with the 'cabbage-tree hats, short pipes, and nobbler glasses' of the old Queen's, and Brooke's Shakespearean productions with the 'blue-fire and thunder dramas' which had dominated the boards only six years earlier.[12] He was not exaggerating in the slightest: theatrical affairs had undergone an astonishing revolution.

The English and American actors I have mentioned belonged to the class of performers who have been described as the 'travelling stars of the railway age', though as the railways did not run quite as far as Australia, and most inter-capital travel was still by sea, we should more correctly call them the travelling stars of the steamship age. Many were old friends of their new audiences, and it was a particularly keen pleasure for immigrant theatre-goers to re-encounter admired artists, such as G. V. Brooke and the Keans, whom they had never expected to see again. J. E. Neild, the splendid and splenetic critic of the day, had first felt the power of Brooke's acting when that brilliant but unstable tragedian was establishing himself as a provincial star in Ireland, the north and the midlands. At that period, Neild recalled, 'there were perfect storms of applause when he came on stage each evening' and he came to feel 'a kind of worship for Brooke'. Later he had been present at Brooke's London debut at the Olympic and 'shed tears of delight at finding my old favorite so supported by a fastidious metropolitan audience'. In 1855 Neild was to encounter Brooke once again with 'the additional pleasure of perceiving that the germs of that bright excellence which had shone with such a lustre in what had become the old time, had expanded into a beautiful growth'.[13] However, there were also to be disappointments, as with Charles and Ellen Kean who had not been kindly treated by time in the years since their admirers among the gold-boom immigrants had last seen them.

Actors like Brooke and Barry Sullivan had found very early in their careers that they could make more money by touring the English provinces, Ireland and North America, appearing in starring seasons with the resident stock companies, than they could have done by managing their own theatres in London. This was the same discovery the Keans were to make: for them the world tour which led them to Australia in 1863–64 was an unwished but necessary precondition for a secure retirement. Railways and steamships made the travel a great deal less painful and this circulation of stars led in turn to changes in the structure of the profession. Stars were essential now to fill the big new theatres. A frequent pattern was for the star personally to lease one of these theatres for a long season, as Brooke and Sullivan both did at the Royal, though the Keans at the Haymarket were managed by George Coppin. Brooke was bankrupted by his managerial activities, while Sullivan amassed a considerable fortune. Coppin teetered regularly between one extreme and the other. Seeing it had taken the stars a long while to get here, they would often stay in Australia for a year or more and would normally give at least two long seasons in Melbourne. Brooke, Sullivan and Jefferson all spent several years in Australia giving performances which became the stuff of legend, and which were recorded in loving detail by the excellent critics of the time, especially Neild and James Smith.

The foundation of this system was the stock companies. As each new lessee took over a major theatre, he or she would engage a stock company from the pool of actors associated with it. The main function of this stock company was to support the travelling stars, so its members would not as a rule be performers of what was called 'leading business' but specialists in the various supporting lines, which at this period of stage history were highly codified. So one might specialise in being a first low comedian, or a second old man or old lady or in 'heavy business'. These performers were expected to know all of the parts pertaining to their line in the current stock plays well enough to perform them at 24 hours notice. The schedule of performances was organised on the assumpton that theatre-goers were to be encouraged to attend as frequently as possible. This meant that a very large repertoire of plays was rotated often on a nightly basis. Thus, in the week of 18 to

24 May 1861, the last of G. V. Brooke's farewell season, the company at the Royal played *Dreams of Delusion* with *The Irish Post* on Saturday, *Coriolanus* on Monday, *The Lady of Lyons* on Tuesday, *The Irish Ambassador* and *The Irish Attorney* on Wednesday, *Virginius* and *To Oblige Benson* on Thursday, and *The Cataract of the Ganges* and a burlesque of *The Corsican Brothers* on Friday. In the preceding week they had performed *Love's Sacrifice*, *The Model Husband*, *The Honeymoon*, *The Serious Family*, *The Corsican Brothers*, *The Comedy of Errors*, *A Lesson to Wives*, *The Hunchback* and *The Chimney Corner*. Under this system, the only shows likely to be played on six or more successive nights would be the *chef-d'oeuvres* of the visiting star and the annual pantomime, which was performed solely by the stock company and, not being intended for revival, would be kept on for as long as it would run. But even the stars, as a rule, would prefer to work through a large number of roles in quick succession, hoping by that means to bring theatre-goers back night after night. Performances would normally include at least two plays—a tragedy, melodrama or three-act comedy followed by a farce—with other entertainments interpolated in the intervals. This was a taxing system and did not encourage immaculate standards of performance; but it did give the working actor a wide range of experience and allowed audiences to develop loyalties towards particular members of the stock company, loyalties which found practical expression in the benefit nights that were brought on towards the end of every starring season. This system of performance survived in Melbourne until the late 1870s, after which it capitulated very rapidly to the long run.

The encouragement given to nightly attendance during the heyday of the stock companies gained impetus from the fact that theatres were never merely places to see shows, but entertainment centres in the widest sense catering to a predominantly male population. All were physically linked with hotels and supplied with generous bar space. Some incorporated restaurants. All were notorious haunts of the *demi-monde*, with the proviso that prostitutes were expected to confine their presence to the stalls, the vestibules and a designated bar in each establishment.[14] There is a particularly vivid recreation of the social atmosphere of the theatres in a letter from Marcus Clarke to Cyril Hopkins of January 1865.[15] It should be noted that lights were not dimmed during performance time and conversations not always stilled. As late as 1870, infants in arms were still admitted to some theatres with consequences that are easy to imagine.

Grand opera was also conducted on a stock-company basis. Australia had possessed a scratch opera company since 1842 when Madame Carandini, Theodosia Yates-Stirling and the Howson brothers began to perform scaled-down versions of stock operas under Mrs Clarke's direction at the Theatre Royal, Hobart. Melbourne's first really substantial season was given with the much-travelled prima donna

Anna Bishop in 1856, and seems to have been an artistic success though, as has happened since, it went considerably over budget. The operas performed were *Norma, La Sonnambula, Martha, Der Freischütz, Lucrezia Borgia* and *L'Elisir d'Amore.* In March 1861 William Saurin Lyster arrived from San Francisco with the famous company headed by Lucy Escott and Henry Squires which was to become in all but name the first Australian Opera.[16] Lyster relied on rapid rotation of a repertoire which, by the time the company broke up in 1868, contained 42 works. New works would be brought in towards the end of a season for runs of around a week, before taking their places as repertoire pieces for future seasons. The most popular operas performed by the 1861–68 company, with numbers of performances given in brackets, were as follows: *Les Huguenots* (90), *Maritana* (83), *Lucrezia Borgia* (78), *Il Trovatore* (78), *Faust* (77), *Martha* (69), *La Sonnambula* (56). *The Bohemian Girl* (54), *L'Africaine* (51), and *Lucia di Lammermoor* (50).[17] The exceptional nineteen-night opening run of *Les Huguenots*, an opera presenting enormous difficulties in both staging and for its singers, was rightly seen as a kind of metropolitan coming of age.

Lyster's soloists varied in ability from the brilliant to the inept. His choruses were often under-rehearsed. His orchestras were highly professional but rarely contained more than ten strings, ten woodwind-cum-brass and a percussionist. The precise composition of the woodwind and brass depended entirely on what good players happened to be available in a particular city at a particular time, and the musical directors had to do a great deal of rescoring. *Les Huguenots* was performed from parts prepared by Julius Siede from a piano score and his memories of performances he had heard in Europe. (A similar method was used in 1877 by Alfredo Zelman to produce Lyster's version of *Lohengrin*, with the difference that in this case Zelman had probably never heard Wagner's orchestration. Audiences seem not to have minded.) Opera was played in the same large theatres as normal drama at only slightly higher prices and drew much the same audiences, though with a fuller and more sparkling attendance in the circle. Operatic music was also a staple of band concerts and the music halls, and in Lyster's hands operatic performances were genuinely for all the classes.

Perhaps the most striking thing about Melbourne theatre during the stock-company phase is the vastness of the repertoire offered by a relatively small number of theatres. A frequency list, prepared by John Spring, of all plays advertised in the *Argus* between January 1860 and December 1869 reveals that a total of 1223 plays received 12356 performances, giving the astonishingly low average of only one performance per play per year.[18] The most popular play, *Hamlet*, was given 95 performances over the decade. The next most frequently performed works were Boucicault's *The Octoroon* (87), and *The Colleen Bawn* (73),

Aladdin, Or the Wonderful Scamp (73), Tom Taylor's *Our American Cousin* (69), Boucicault's *The Flying Scud* (65), Selby's *The Bonnie Fishwife* (64), Lytton's *The Lady of Lyons* (62), *Richard III* (60), Akhurst's locally written extravaganza, *Paris the Prince and Helen the Fair* (60), *Rip Van Winkle*, a compilation by Jefferson from two earlier plays (58), and *Othello* (58). The popularity of the Boucicault plays, *Our American Cousin* and *Rip Van Winkle*, was initially due to Jefferson, that of *Othello* to Brooke and that of *Hamlet* to Walter Montgomery; but it should be stressed that in most cases these figures were built up from short separated seasons rather than from lengthy runs. In order to enable more detailed analysis of the repertory, Dr Spring also assembled the data for a computer record of all performances in the Melbourne theatres between 1850 and 1869, which can be consulted through the English department at Monash University and which includes details of genre, performance locale, principal performer, and some authors. Outside Melbourne, Ballarat, Bendigo and, for a time, Geelong, were all active theatrical towns, maintaining their own stock companies to support week- or fortnight-long seasons from the travelling stars. Most of the larger goldfields and pastoral towns also possessed adaptable halls that could be used by touring players and some were briefly the homes of resident stock companies.[19]

Intercolonial management

I come now to the beginnings of intercolonial management and to the topic of Melbourne's place in the development of national chains. These beginnings were primarily the work of William Saurin Lyster. The stock companies I have been discussing were each attached to a particular large theatre, and to this extent it is really theatres, rather than companies, which are the dominant units of Australian stage history in the 1850s and 1860s. Lyster, as the entrepreneur of an opera troupe, was in the anomalous position of managing a travelling stock company which moved regularly from theatre to theatre and from city to city. His problem was to assure access for himself to the few large and well-equipped theatres that could present grand opera. It was also desirable to lease these theatres for the duration of his seasons so as not to have to pay another manager for services he could perform himself. In 1863 he took a three-year lease of the Prince of Wales theatre in Sydney, sub-letting it when he was absent with his company in Melbourne and elsewhere. From 1870 he had similar arrangements in Melbourne, first at the Princess's and then at the Opera House in Bourke Street which was purchased in 1873 by a company of which he was managing director.

By this time he had expanded his activities to embrace both Italian grand opera, performed by native singers, and a separate English company performing works by Balfe, Wallace and Benedict and

English adaptations of French *opéra bouffe*. For much of the decade he was able to keep one company on tour while the other occupied his Melbourne theatre. Profits on the English company's Offenbach productions helped pay for the much more expensive Italians and such selfless sacrificings of capital as his 1877 *Lohengrin* with the imported soprano Antonietta Link. During the decade he also presented the drama companies of Adelaide Ristori, Joseph Emmett, Lytton Sothern Jr. and Arthur Garner, concert and variety artists, and a troupe of British Blondes. By the time of his death in 1880, he stood at the head of a substantial touring organisation using theatres in Sydney, Adelaide and Melbourne and also sending companies to New Zealand. His grand opera troupes continued to be treated as travelling stock companies in that only the first run of a new opera would be kept on for more than a few nights, and at other times repertoire pieces would be rotated on a nightly or bi-nightly basis—again on the assumption that many operagoers would attend a large proportion of the nights of any given season. With his comic opera and drama companies he experimented with longer runs, a particular triumph being the 65 nights of Joseph Emmett in *Fritz our Cousin German* at the Opera House in 1876. However, he made no attempt to gain permanent control of a chain of theatres, contenting himself with temporary arrangements for his out-of-Melbourne activities. This was not a serious problem as even in the 'sixties there was an over-supply of theatres in the main cities.

The chains

The further opportunities for consolidating a national chain that Lyster had failed or not particularly wished to grasp were taken up in the 1880s by his nephew and successor, George Musgrove. By this time the generation of gold-boom immigrants with their civilised but rather anachronistic tastes was being replaced as the dominant element in theatre audiences by their native-born children, whose preferences were for Offenbach rather than Verdi and for Boucicault rather than Shakespeare. Their advent was signalled in the mid-1870s by a rash of complaints about the bad behaviour of gangs of teenage boys in the gallery.[20] But the theatre audience was also growing in overall size and Musgrove could perceive that it was no longer necessary to woo audiences back night after night by constant changes of programme. The pantomimes, which were always the major investment of the large theatres, were by now often running for a month or more, and runs of over 50 nights, for a single show had been achieved by the Williamsons in *Struck Oil* and Emmett in *Fritz*. The time had come to gamble on mounting a show that every theatre-goer in Melbourne would want to see. In 1880 Musgrove did just this, recruiting an entire company of English imports for a production of Offenbach's *La Fille du Tambour Major*, running it at the Opera House for what turned out to be the first

100-night season of the Australian theatre, and then touring it to the other capitals. Apart from the fact that the intercolonial *Tambour Major* company added a couple of other attractions, Musgrove had virtually invented that great recipe for making (or losing) money that is still being applied by Wilton Morley, the touring production. Increasingly, a single heavily financed show would be put together in Melbourne or Sydney and sent on its travels around the other major centres, and then, perhaps, out to the country towns and the 'smalls'.

Under this new system, which quickly consolidated itself during the 1880s and 1890s, the stock-company methods soon disappeared. Working actors no longer needed to be ready to perform 40 or more parts at a day's notice, but might well perform in no more than two or three productions a year in long runs through a series of cities. Even grand opera, though less frequent after Lyster's death in 1880 and the advent of Gilbert and Sullivan, was now given with less rapid alternation of programmes, culminating in a 24-night season of *Faust* at the Princess's in 1898 with Nellie Stewart. (The death of the Mephistopheles of this production, Federici, on the opening night, gave rise to Australia's best known theatrical ghost story.) Since the logistics of the operation required permanent control over theatres in all the main centres and the elimination of any competition that might threaten the success of these highly capitalised ventures, it was not long before Musgrove had joined with J. C. Williamson and Arthur Garner to found the original 'Firm'. This proved to be the ruin of two good actors and one exceptionally talented manager, though Musgrove recovered some of his old flair when he broke free of Williamson to cash in on his proprietorial interest in Nellie Stewart. Once the juggernaut of a national chain with permanent investments in bricks and mortar had been brought into existence, there was no way of stopping it rolling. Challengers such as Meynell and Gunn and later the Taits knew from the start that their ultimate aim was not to beat it but to join it.

In its early years, the Williamson, Garner and Musgrove enterprise was seriously undercapitalised. Claude McKay tells of an occasion when the survival of the organisation depended on a successful first night for a pantomime, and of another when emergency capital had to be borrowed from two bookmakers.[21] This meant that in Melbourne in particular they remained committed to the largest possible audiences at the lowest possible prices. Shakespeare and grand opera disappeared from the bills (though amends for this were to be made after 1901) and the emphasis was placed on starring seasons with imported leads alternating with home-manufactured Gilbert and Sullivan. As early as 1877, Emily Soldene had complained about the grubby condition of the Australian theatres and expressed surprise at the low admission prices.[22] Dion Boucicault, whom we have already encountered as the most popular writer for the theatre of the 1860s, made an immensely successful tour starring in his own plays in 1885. He got on very badly with the Firm, who did their best to squeeze every penny they could out of him. He described the Melbourne Royal as a 'large, dusty, primitive building, with poor accommodation for the audience, and still more wretched arrangements for the actors'. He was highly critical of disorder and mess backstage, but praised the painting department which was still under the control of the much-admired scenic artist John Hennings. He was told by the Melbourne managers: 'You must not regard our audiences as if they were a West End public; they range between Peckham Rye and Whitechapel. They want strong effects, not fine acting; they want sensation not style', but Boucicault disagreed with this judgement, claiming that Melbourne was 'a fine theatrical city badly catered for'. Arriving in Sydney he noted with relief that 'the rowdy element so conspicuous in the Victorian capital is not prominent here'. There may have been demographic reasons for this difference arising from the so-called 'kink' in the Victorian birthrate.[23]

The real source of Boucicault's dissatisfaction with Melbourne and of everybody's dissatisfaction with the gallery boys was that the huge, high-Victorian theatre of all the classes represented by the original Royal was now obsolete. Yet the Firm was not mature enough to provide the variety of more specialised venues expected by a progressive urban society. Thus Janet Achurch, touring in 1889 with a repertoire that included Ibsen's *A Doll's House*, was still expected to perform before the sympathetic but somewhat baffled *habitués* of the Royal was now obsolete. Yet the Firm was not mature enough to the rebuilding of the Princess's, the building of a new large theatre, the Alexandra, now known as Her Majesty's, which became the home of Alfred Dampier's sensational melodramas and Friday Shakespeare, and the development of the smaller Bijou as a specialist theatre for middle-class light comedy, the new problem dramas of Pinero and Henry Arthur Jones, and occasional seasons of serious opera. Supplementing these, the Opera House shed its pretensions to Wagnerian grandeur to become the headquarters of the other successful chain, Harry Rickard's variety empire, eventually being reborn as the Tivoli.

The theatre scene of the 'nineties, despite the coming of bad times, was once again a lively and varied one: the era of Nellie Stewart, Robert Brough and Dion Boucicault Jr, George Titherage and Phil Day in *The Silver King*, George Rignold in *The Lights of London*, and Grace Palotta and the Gaiety Company ladies—even if we had to share all these distinguished artists season and season about with Sydney. Sydney could even claim a priority in theatrical matters over Melbourne during the 'nineties due to the anomaly that new scenery, costumes and theatrical properties could be imported free of duty into New South Wales but not into Victoria. This meant that it was normally more advantageous to create a new production in Sydney and then move on to Melbourne, by which time the *matériel* would be used and not subject to duty. This problem fortunately ceased at Federation, which also saw the beginning of what was undoubtedly the richest and most varied age of live theatre in Melbourne, with opera and Shakespeare restored to their proper prominence, Williamson and Musgrove both, independently, in full flight, the beginnings of the little theatre movement, and the Cole, Anderson and Bailey managements sustaining a robust tradition of national Australian melodrama.[24] But that is another age and another story.

Music

The most important aspect of public music-making has already been considered in our discussions of opera. My concern now will be to look as comprehensively as possible at musical performance, principally of the period 1860-80, but with the caution that the price for comprehensiveness is superficiality, and that most of my remarks can be little more than pointers to areas of activity which in many cases still await their historian. Furthermore, whereas it was possible to treat theatre coherently as a business, this is impossible with music which is more fruitfully approached as a social activity.

Where instrumental performance is concerned, I must once again stress the dependence of musicians on the theatres and the importance of the theatre bands to Melbourne's public concert life. The opera orchestras assembled by Lyster and his predecessors were basically enlarged theatre bands. That their playing was highly appreciated is shown by the reviews of Neild and James Smith, which often contrast the competence of what was emerging from the pit with the imperfections of what was being represented on stage. Neild once went so far as to wish that all operas were enlarged overtures.[25] Lyster's high opinion of his band is shown by his decision in May 1862 to suspend stage performances and work out the remainder of his lease of the Royal with a series of 27 'Grand Monster Concerts' in which the band played a leading part. Works performed included the flautist Julius Siede's *Faust* overture and *Carnevale di Venezia* variations with solos for flute, clarinet, contrabass, cornet, trombone, petit tambour and piccolo. From time to time, chiefly as a support to benefits or testimonials, virtually all the leading professionals would be united, with a stiffening of amateurs, into an orchestra of symphonic size. At the opening of the Town Hall on 9 August 1870, the orchestra numbered 75. A testimonial concert in the same building on 26 August 1871 to mark the tenth year of Lyster's activity as an entrepreneur in Australia offered an orchestra of 35 present or ex-members of the opera band and 50 amateurs, supported by a choir of 250 voices. Works performed included Siede's *Festival Overture* and a scene from Verdi's *Ernani*. On 1 October 1880 an orchestra of 100, including two harpists, was assembled for the performance of Léon Caron's *Victoria*, composed in honour of the Exhibition of that year and revived for the 1985 celebrations. For the greatest of all Melbourne Exhibitions, that of 1888, the English conductor Frederick Cowen, with fifteen principals, was brought out to lead a 73-man orchestra in a six-month series of 270 concerts. Works performed by this long-remembered ensemble included Beethoven's Symphony No. 9 with a choir of 708. Their 191 purely instrumental concerts were heard by an aggregate audience of 366 607 and the 26 'Grand Choral Concerts' by 57 225.[26] An attempt to retain the orchestra on a permanent basis was unsuccessful, but a foundation had been created for later work by Marshall Hall and Alberto Zelman.

These large-scale commemorative festivals were also a golden opportunity for the locally resident composer. At the opening concert of the Intercolonial Exhibition on 24 October 1866, the programme included celebratory marches by Joseph Summers and Charles Horsley, an overture by S. H. Marsh, Cesare Cutolo's *Triumphal March and Chorus* to a lyric by J. E. Neild, and Horsley's *The South-sea Sisters*, to words by another Melbourne literary light, Richard Hengist Horne. The most warmly received section of Horsley's work was a chorus representing Aboriginal music, to the following words:

No. 6—*Chorus*
From creek of Worooboomi-boo!
And sheep-run Woolagoola-goo!
Come Dibble-Fellow dancing in fog!
All over mount Wooloola-yah!
And earth-holes of Worondi-wah!
Till he vanish in the yellow Wog-wog!
Old Chief of Woolonara-nah!
From the Great River banks, far-far!
Hasten here with spear and boomerang—
Then to snowy Woologoomerang—
For White Fellow comes to make war!

Horne claimed to have derived this travesty from corroboree rhythms of the Goulburn River tribes.[27]

Apart from such monumental gatherings of the talents, symphonic music was also to be heard at the concerts of the amateur choral societies, particularly those of the Philharmonic, founded in 1853, and the two male-voice liedertafels, the Metropolitan and the Melbourne.[28] Oratorio—meaning as a rule the *Messiah* or *Elijah*—was the staple of the Philharmonic, and music by German composers of the liedertafels; but each was prepared to experiment with more challenging scores. The Symphony No. 9 had been performed by the Philharmonic under David Lee as early as 1872. The first Australian performance of the *St Matthew Passion* was given by the same society in 1875 under Joseph Summers. The Philharmonic's vocal soloists included Melbourne's leading professionals and many distinguished visitors, but orchestras were always predominantly amateur. George Peake, conductor from

1889 to 1911, recorded that while some amateurs were excellent, 'others belonged to the Ripieno class, who were scarcely safe, even under the cover of a full orchestra'. Annoyance was also expressed at 'the professional and the quasi-professional who never takes the instrument out of the case from concert to concert until the final rehearsal is announced'. One wonders what 'professional' can be meant to imply in this context. Writing of an earlier occupant of his post, Joseph Summers, Peake explained that 'Under stress of excitement, he apparently failed to perceive the faults or blemishes of any performance of which he was Conductor. His imagination seemed to supply the missing qualities of perfection, and probably saved him from much bitter disappointment.'[29] Yet at least the music was being heard, audiences remained loyal in their support, and the singers must have enjoyed themselves enormously. There are, after all, few musical pleasures equal to that of participating in a lustily sung Handel chorus.

Recitals in nineteenth-century Melbourne differed from recitals today in that they were usually given by groups of performers rather than a single soloist with accompanist. Touring celebrities such as Catherina Hayes and Anna Bishop in the 1850s, Ilma di Murska in the 'seventies, Carlotta Patti and Charles Santley in the 'eighties and Albani in the 'nineties, although they might also appear in opera or oratorio, preferred the more profitable practice of concert-giving with one or two attendant singers, a pianist and an instrumental soloist. Visiting sopranos would often travel with a flautist, a practice that survived until the days of Melba and John Lemmone. Julius Siede, who as instrumentalist, opera conductor, composer, and musical director of the Melbourne Liedertafel, made an immense contribution to Melbourne's musical development; he had originally arrived in Australia as attendant flautist to Anna Bishop, having previously occupied the same post in America for Jenny Lind. Instrumental virtuosi who particularly impressed colonial music lovers during the half-century 1850–1900 were the violinists Miska Hauser, Horace Poussard, Jenny Claus, Camilla Urso, August Wilhelmj, Edouard Reményi and Wilhelmine Neruda (who toured with her pianist husband Sir Charles Hallé) and the pianists Arabella Goddard, Henry Ketten and Max Vogrich. Hauser, having dazzled Melburnians of the late 1850s with his playing, proceeded to amaze them even further with the tall stories he subsequently published about his Australian experiences. Wilhelmj was the first to present wholly classical programmes, his predecessors having taken care to include crowd-pleasing display pieces and variations on favourite themes. Hauser's show-stopper was an imitative piece called 'Bird on the tree' in which he made copious use of harmonics. Virtuosi who chose to settle permanently in Melbourne, such as the violinists Strebinger and Simonsen and the pianist Cesare Cutolo, found it necessary to follow Siede's example by becoming musical jacks-of-all-trades. Martin Simonsen, whose wife Fannie was one of Lyster's best sopranos, later managed and conducted his own opera companies. Cutolo was forced to work for a time in a high-class music hall called the Varieties. His death on 19 January 1867 in a shipboard accident was mourned at a testimonial concert, which included a revival of his *Triumphal March and Chorus* of 1866. Strebinger had the bad fortune to lose a fine Cremona violin when he was forced to abandon it in a married lady's bedroom on the unexpected return of her husband.[30]

Locally resident talent was more shining in the vocal than in the instrumental area. Maria Carandini and her two daughters, Fanny and Rosina, as well as the Howson family, after being driven from the operatic stage by Lyster's companies, were active for many years as concert artists. The Number One and the Number Two *Books of Words* for 'Madame Carandini's Popular Entertainments', were prepared for a concert party consisting of herself, the tenor Walter Sherwin, and the two Misses Carandini, who were also accomplished pianists. Arias from operas by Balfe, Wallace, Donizetti and Verdi mingle with songs by Wallace, Arditi, Loder, Linley and Benedict, the inevitable 'Home sweet home' and 'Comin' through the rye', and concerted vocal pieces by Stephen Glover. The only number than may have been written locally is a 'buffo duet' by Sydney Nelson.[31] Although the books are undated, the tastes are distinctly of the 1860s. In the following decades, Melbourne's concert life was dominated by the English-born tenor Armes Beaumont, a Lyster discovery, whose sight was seriously impaired in a shooting accident in 1867. Although Beaumont subsequently sang for a few months in San Francisco, his disability effectively forestalled what might easily have been a major international career. Those who heard him, even towards the close of his life, regarded him as the equal of any other tenor heard in Melbourne. The consistency of his work is shown by his probably still unbroken record of 67 appearances as a soloist with the Philharmonic. Other promising local talents—Lucy Chambers, Amy Sherwin, Francis Saville, Helen Armstrong, Lalla Miranda, Ada Crossley, and Amy Castles (still an under-regarded figure), along with the violinist John Kruse, and the pianists Florence Richardson (whose career soon turned from a musical to a literary direction) and Percy Grainger—hastened overseas as soon as was conveniently possible and were only seen again on short return visits or as a prelude to retirement. The phenomenal success enjoyed by Mrs Armstrong, also known as Melba, was initially a puzzle to her contemporaries. Brewer, recording a Sydney appearance of 1885, recalled that 'the purity of her voice was at once recognised, but there was certainly no indication of the marvellous in it', adding that 'her wonderful success in opera, in so short a time, rivalling Patti and Albani, is incomprehensible to Australians'.[32] This might be taken as evidence that Australians had been hearing some pretty good singing; however, one needs to remember that in 1885 Melba had no operatic experience and had still to encounter the formidable Madame Marchesi. Still, the number of successful international careers launched from Victoria at this period is a testimony to the quality of local teaching. Before leaving for Paris, Melba studied with Mary Ellen Christian, a visiting English contralto, and Pietro Cecchi, a tenor who had appeared briefly for Lyster.

Beyond the well-publicised sphere of the trained concert artist lies the less well documented performing world of the music halls and dance salons. Dance music—quadrilles, waltzes, galops, mazurkas, schottisches, polkas, varsovianas, jigs and reels—could only at this period be supplied by living musicians with violin, flageolet, concertina or cello in hand, and was probably the largest single source of professional employment. Richard Twopenny found dancing 'more frequently indulged in' than in Britain because of the 'more frank relations between the sexes'. 'Even the servants are accustomed to go to balls', he informed his no doubt flabbergasted English readership, adding reassuringly that this need not be regarded as a bad thing provided 'Biddy' did not attend so many balls 'as to interfere with her capacity for doing her work'.[33] Illustrations of some of Melbourne's grander nineteenth-century balls (probably not attended by Biddy) will be found in Nell Challingsworth's *Dancing down the Years*.[34]

The music halls varied in their specialisms and clientele, but the largest and most successful, like their London models, the Oxford, Canterbury and Alhambra, were concerned to present good music of all kinds, including the operatic. The Varieties in Bourke Street employed musicians as distinguished as Cesare Cutolo and the miraculous multi-instrumentalist, Richard Wildblood Kohler, who in more sober moments could be heard playing the French horn in Lyster's orchestra. A 'middy' celebrating his first night on land in 1862 was delighted on entering the Apollo music hall attached to the Haymarket theatre to be greeted by 'a selection from the never tiresome "Il Trovatore" '.[35] Other halls had less elevated pretensions and might settle for a Cornish clog dancer, a lady vocalist singing 'I'm leaving thee in sorrow, Annie' and similar ditties, or the inevitable blackface minstrels.[36] Later in the century, while the minstrel show element remained constant, grand opera was edged out by its flighty Parisian stepdaughter, *opéra bouffe*, and the comic vocalist began to head the bills. By the 'nineties, Melbourne had a full-time vaudeville theatre in Harry Richard's Opera House, later the Tivoli, and the halls became redundant.

Outside the doors of the theatres and concert rooms lay the streets and parks, performing venue for organ-grinders, *siffleurs*, bands— whether German, amateur or regimental—buskers with battered violins or keyed bugles, and perambulatory hawkers who still kept up the old English tradition of the musical street cry. Band music, then as now, was cultivated with great seriousness and at a high level of accomplishment. Even Lyster was not above calling on the musicians of the

Fourteenth Regiment or the Collingwood Volunteer Band to stiffen the chorus of some especially grand production or to accompany the entry of the soldiery in *Faust*. Visitors to the 1888 Exhibition were serenaded by eight bands in rotation.

The organ-grinder had a very different reputation. 'Many a man, in a tolerably happy frame of mind', we are informed by the *Herald* of 27 February 1864 (page 4), 'has been struck sad and miserable by the sound of a doleful tune, ground on one of those melancholy instruments; and has gone home straightway, and either knocked down his wife or given himself up deliberately to colonial ale'.

On saints' days and other national occasions, Melbourne was saluted with the music of her tribes: the fiddles and fifes of the Irish, the pipes and drums of the Scots, the massed vocal harmony of the Welsh and the strutting marches and lilting ländler of the Germans and Austrians. Beyond the metropolis, the numerous Chinese theatre companies of the 'fifties and 'sixties all had their four- and five-man orchestras which, when not impeded by the protests of European neighbours, would continue to assail their sonorous percussion into the early hours of the morning while puffing placidly on their opium pipes.[37] In some regions of the bush, as late as the 1860s, one might still encounter sad remnants of the corroboree presented as an entertainment for curious Europeans.[38]

Sundays belonged to the churches. In many households Sabbath observance forbade any use of instruments or any vocal music apart from hymns. But there were bells to fill the air, and organs, including the excellent ones built locally by George Fincham, to fill the many new churches. A 25 per cent tariff on imported organs and pipes arranged on Fincham's behalf in 1879 by Peter Lalor as Commissioner of Customs did much to advance his business, but did not please his competitors who still had to import their pipes.[39] The Church of England and Roman Catholic cathedrals made efforts to establish a regular sung liturgy on the model of their mother congregations and a number of parish churches provided stipends for soloists. St Peter's Eastern Hill had eight salaried singers in the early 1860s, including Armes Beaumont. Annie Dawbin, who worshipped there largely on account of the music, was particularly delighted with the singing of the mezzo-soprano Octavia Hamilton, star of several opera performances in the 1850s, who had also performed for Lyster. Miss Hamilton, however, was a lady of scandalous life and in January 1864 an attempt was made by the churchwardens to remove her and her current lover, a wine merchant and fellow chorister, T. H. Davis, by telling them that their salaries must be reduced. After a week's silence, one or the other party must have relented and they both resumed their places. From 1866, however, the paid soloists were dispensed with and music provided by a surpliced choir of men and boys—a Puseyite outrage which must have profoundly grieved the evangelically inclined Bishop of Melbourne, Charles Perry.[40] Neither system would, of course, have been tolerated at the Wesleyan Chapel in Brunswick Street, Fitzroy, under its choirmistress Mrs Spensley, where Beaumont had begun his career as a boy alto.

It should be stressed that among Protestants the devotional value of non-participatory church music was still a matter of debate. In the early days of the colony, some non-conformist churches restricted music to the congregational singing of hymns and metrical psalms led by a precentor and actively resisted the introduction of organs. Bishop Perry considered that parish worship should only employ music in which the congregation could join. In 1857, visiting St Stephen's, Richmond, he was horrified to hear the service intoned and an anthem sung. Laying aside his prepared sermon, he preached instead on the subject of intoning, no doubt employing the excellent arguments advanced on a similar occasion by Obadiah Slope.[41] St Stephen's, however, continued to develop its musical traditions with the help of the brilliant young organist Philip Plaisted and in 1865, while Plaisted was overseas, secured the services of C. E. Horsley, a pupil of Moscheles and Mendelssohn and probably the most gifted composer to work in Victoria during our period.[42] In 1862 dissension of a similar kind broke out at the musically active St Andrew's Brighton when 'the doors of the organ loft were forcibly closed against the choir' by a new vicar installed by Perry for that purpose. On subsequent Sundays they insisted on intoning the responses in their usual way from their seats in the congregation.[43] By the 1890s church music was triumphant throughout all the major denominations, but the wherewithal for its maintenance was severely reduced, a fact that led to hard times for George Fincham and his fellow organ-builders.

So far our music has all been public music. But in nineteenth-century Victoria, when mechanical reproduction was limited to various expensive derivatives of the barrel organ, most musical performance took place within the domestic circle for the private pleasure of the performers or a small audience of sympathetic friends and relatives. *Punch* cartoons and satirical fiction have left us with a mental stereotype of ludicrous gatherings where full-throated baritones raised their voices in unsteady harmony with those of full-bosomed contraltos; where the teenage daughter would be placed, scrubbed and scowling, at the keyboard to render her ruthlessly drilled version of 'The Battle of Prague', before yielding place to the maiden aunt's grand fantasia on themes from *The Lily of Killarney*; or where, late in the evening, a bewhiskered and suitably brandified uncle might attempt a Gilbert and Sullivan patter song without quite getting the words right. Richard Twopenny, a veteran of many such occasions, was convinced that 'there is no part of the world where you hear so much bad music, professional and amateur' as Australia, though he also conceded that 'there are few parts where you hear so much music';[44] and some amateurs, at least, regarded their performing seriously. When John Pierson Rowe took his family on the grand tour to Europe and the British Isles in 1874, one of his aims was to permit his elder daughters, both gifted with excellent voices, to study with the best teachers. Neither, however, would ever have been permitted to sing professionally. After an audition with Randegger, one was told that there would be no point in his teaching her as she already knew 'quite sufficient for a drawing room', and it was in the drawing room, or that extension of the drawing room, the parish or amateur concert, that they were to exercise their expensively cultivated talents.[45]

Everywhere people made music. Twopenny, gazing through the windows of workingmen's cottages, saw 'the old folk after their day's labour gathered round the piano in the sitting-room to hear their daughters play', and reflected, rather cynically, that at least it would help keep the girls out of mischief.[46] In clubs and hotels, other workingmen sang the old songs of their English, Irish or Scottish forebears and helped create the folksongs of their new homeland. The drover sang interminable ballads to his cattle: it made them less restive. The camp-fire was cheered by the harmonica or concertina. At cosmopolitan (even then) St Kilda in the 1860s, Richard Hengist Horne would subject visitors to an obligatory recital of Spanish or Mexican songs, accompanying himself on a guitar hung with blue ribbons.[47] In rural Hawthorn, George Gordon McCrae woke his children every morning by serenading them on ocarinas of his own manufacture.[48] In Pentridge in 1865, a prisoner named Stewart, feigning madness, was allowed to build himself a fiddle 'from which he extracted the most hideous sounds, to the horror of his hearers'.[49] The interest of these last three examples is that the music seems to characterise not only the player but the place where it was played. In a wider sense, the music that was heard and performed by colonial Victorians tells us about their cities and their colony as well as about themselves. This is, I hope, an argument for researching and performing this music, irrespective of whether it is Australian in sentiment or origin.

Notes

1   F. C. Brewer *The Drama and Music in New South Wales*, Sydney, 1892; the volume was part of the New South Wales contribution to the World's Columbian Exposition, Chicago: 1893
2   James Smith *The Cyclopedia of Victoria*, Melbourne, 1905, III, 1–39, drawing on earlier reminiscences listed in Lurline Stuart, James Smith: His Influence on the Development of Literary Culture in Colonial Melbourne, PhD thesis, Monash University, 1983, pp. 300–1. Alexander Sutherland's 'Music and the Drama' in *Victoria and its Metropolis, Past and Present*, Melbourne, 1888, I, pp. 506–19, is full of inaccuracies. Among more recent narrative histories of the Australian stage, the most valuable is

John West's *Theatre in Australia*, Sydney: Cassell, 1978. The most important biographies are Alec Bagot *Coppin the Great*, Melbourne: Melbourne University Press, 1965, Ian Dicker *J.C.W.: A Short Biography of James Cassius Williamson*, Sydney: Elizabeth Tudor Press, 1974, and Eric Irvin *Gentleman George—King of Melodrama: The Theatrical Life and Timers of George Darrell 1841–1921*, Brisbane: University of Queensland Press, 1980.

3 See Elizabeth Webby 'Summary of Theatrical Events, 1788–1853' in *The Australian Stage: a Documentary History*, ed. Harold Love, New South Wales University Press, Sydney: 1984, p. 7.
4 *ibid.* p. 31
5 For their careers see Webby, *ibid.* pp. 1–8
6 Smith *Cyclopedia* III. 1
7 For examples, see Webby in *The Australian Stage*, passim
8 See *ibid.* pp. 31–2, 294; Smith (*Cyclopedia* III, 4) notes that 'the stage manager of the Queen's Theatre in 1847 seems to have suffered from dipsomania'.
9 For theatre buildings, see Ross Thorne *Theatre Buildings in Australia to 1905*, 2 vols, Sydney: University of Sydney, 1971
10 Smith *Cyclopedia* III, 6; Cannon notes that 'as interpreted by Lola it was capable of infinite degrees of eroticism to suit the nature of the audience'. While searching for the imaginary tarantula in her petticoats, 'she was often assisted by shouts from men in the audience: "There he goes!" "Look higher up!" and so on'. (*Lola Montes; the Tragic Story of a 'Liberated Woman'*, Melbourne: Heritage 1973, p. 49)
11 For the Chinese companies, see Harold Love 'Chinese Theatre on the Victorian Goldfields' *Australasian Drama Studies* 3 (1984–5), pp. 45–86
12 *The Australian Stage* p. 79
13 *My Note Book* 18 April 1857, p. 128
14 For the theatre vestibules and 'saddling paddocks', see Julian Thomas *The Vagabond Papers*, First Series, Melbourne, 1877, pp. 198–205
15 Incorporated in Hopkins's uncompleted biography of Clarke, Mitchell Library MSS A1971; for a similar but less detailed account by an anonymous writer, see *The Australian Stage* pp. 82–3
16 For the various Lyster companies, see Harold Love *The Golden Age of Australian Opera: W. S. Lyster and his Companies 1861–1880*, Sydney: Currency Press, 1981
17 For season and repertoire statistics, see Harold Love 'W. S. Lyster's 1861–68 Opera Company: Seasons and Repertoire' *Australasian Drama Studies* 2 (1983–4), pp. 113–24. Eric Irvin 'Our Operatic Beginnings' *This Australia* 3 (1983–4), pp. 54–8 gives statistics for the period 1846–1914 which indicate that the most popular operas and operettas performed in Melbourne and Sydney were *Maritana* (460 performances), *Faust* (423), *H.M.S. Pinafore* (418), *The Bohemian Girl* (320) and *Il Trovatore* (301).
18 J. R. Spring *A Frequency List of Dramatic Performances Advertised in the Melbourne 'Argus' between 1860 and 1869*, Melbourne: Monash University Department of English, 1977
19 For the country circuits as they settled down later in the century, see *The Australian Stage* pp. 110–11. Something of the flavour of goldfields theatre is conveyed by a letter of Avonia Jones reprinted in *The Australian Stage*

Drama and music in colonial Melbourne 199

pp. 78-9 and in two pamphlets by Raymond A. Bradfield: *They Trod the Boards*, Castlemaine, 1977, and *Lola Montez in Castlemaine*, Castlemaine: the author n.d. During the late 1850s and early 1860s, *Bell's Life in Victoria* provided a weekly digest of theatrical news from country newspapers.
20 Cf. *The Australian Stage* p. 97
21 Claude McKay *This is the Life: the Autobiography of a Newspaperman*, Sydney: Angus & Robertson, 1961, p. 80
22 Emily Soldene *My Theatrical and Musical Recollections*, London, 1897, p. 206
23 *The Australian Stage* pp. 102-6. The age distribution of the population of Melbourne was distorted by the huge influx of young adult migrants during the 1850s and a subsequent baby boom.
24 For local dramatists of the period see Eric Irvin *Australian Melodrama*, Sydney: Hale & Iremonger, 1981; Margaret Williams *Australia on the Popular Stage*, Melbourne, 1983, and Paul Richardson 'Theatrical Treatment of Local Realities' in *The Australian Stage* pp. 67-74.
25 Love *Golden Age* p. 98
26 *Official Record of the Centennial International Exhibition*, Melbourne, 1890, pp. 21-6, 259-71. Statistics are drawn from the tables on pp. 270-1 which are not in agreement with the totals on p. 263.
27 See *The South-sea Sisters, a Lyric Masque*, Melbourne, 1866, p. 70; also published in French and German versions.
28 For the Philharmonic, see W. A. Carne *A Century of Harmony*, Melbourne, 1954. The other societies are discussed in Therese Radic, Aspects of Organized Amateur Music in Melbourne, 1836-1890, M. Mus, thesis, Melbourne University, 1969, and Some Historical Aspects of Musical Associations in Melbourne 1889-1915, PhD thesis, Melbourne University, 1977.
29 Quoted in Carne *A Century of Harmony* pp. 247-8, from Peake's *Historical Souvenir* (1912?)
30 Annie Maria Dawbin (also Baxter) manuscript diaries, Dixson Library, State Library of NSW, MSQ 183/8, p. 10
31 Copies in author's collection
32 Brewer *The Orama and Music* p. 84
33 Richard Twopenny *Town Life in Australia*, London, 1883, p. 220
34 Nell Challingsworth *Dancing down the Years; the Romantic Century in Australia*, Melbourne: Craftsman Press, 1978
35 *The Australian Stage* pp. 82-3
36 Cf. 'The Music Halls of Melbourne' *Herald* 8 Jan. 1864, p. 2
37 See Love 'Chinese Theatre'
38 *The Australian Stage* pp. 86-7
39 See E. N. Matthews *Colonial Organs and Organ Builders*, Melbourne, 1969, p. 17
40 Dawbin MSQ 183/8, p. 76; ibid. p. 116
41 Matthews *Colonial Organs* p. 73 The subsequent controversy is summarised in *My Note Book* 1 Aug. 1857, p. 256. See also A. de Q. Robin *Charles Perry. Bishop of Melbourne*, Perth: University of Western Australia Press, 1967, pp. 136-7.
42 Matthews *Colonial Organs* pp. 75, 77

43 *Church Gazette* 16 April 1862, p. 26
44 Twopenny *Town Life* pp. 217–18
45 See Teresa Pagliaro, An Australian Family Abroad, the Rowe Letters, 1873–4, MA thesis, Monash University, 1981, p. 320. A younger sister, Nellie, did in fact become a professional singer and music teacher, but this was after the collapse of the family fortunes.
46 Twopenny *Town Life* p. 218. Humphrey McQueen in *A New Brittania*, rev. ed., Melbourne: Penguin, 1976, pp. 117–19 suggests a political interpretation of the popularity of the piano, noting that 'A working class that could afford such luxuries wanted nothing to do with revolution'.
47 Ann Blainey *The Farthing Poet*, London: Longman, 1968, p. 239
48 Hugh McCrae *My Father and my Father's Friends*, Sydney, 1935, p. 66
49 Henry A. White *Crime and Criminals; or, Reminiscences of the Penal Department in Victoria*, Ballarat, 1890, p. 191

Index

Aboriginal culture, 1, 58; dispossession of inhabitants, 58; effect on literature, 85, 88; environmental knowledge, 59; environmental management, 59; territorial areas, 58
abstract art, 127
Annear, Harold Desbrowe, 150–1, 152, 161, 167, 172; dadoes and beams, use of, 168; homestead style, 169; House, The Eyrie, Eaglemont, 1903, 150; L-plan open areas, 171
Architectural and Engineering Association, 146
architecture, Australian, 144; 'American Romanesque', 153; architects, 146; architectural reformers, 146–7; Art Nouveau, 151; Australian bungalow, 154; churches, 170; craft movements, 146; effect of WW11, 163
English Renaissance, 152–3; fashion, 146; Federation architecture, 145, 148, 152, 160; glass-walled architecture, 164; Gothic Revival, 145; inclusive, 160–1; links between States, 152; Melbourne metropolis, 153–4; new 'mainstream', 151–2; progressive 1930s, 159; schools, 172; suburban, 164, 169; taut, animated structure, 167; 'the new Internationale', 164; unified architecture, 146, 152; universality of form, 163
Argus, 17
art galleries, commercial, 125–6
artistic view of Melbourne, 'bird's eye view', 19–21; conventional picturesque view, 16; cycloramas, 21; engravers, 19, 23;
'Heidelberg School', 19, 26; landscapes, 19; lithographic reproduction, 19; nocturnal scenes, 18, 26; panoramas, 19, 21; pastoral landscapes, 16, 18; photography, 19, 23, streets, of, 25; scenic versions of maps, 13; streetscapes, 16, 18; topographical studies, 14, 18
artists, camps, 116–18; depression, effect of, 120; Heidelberg School, 112, 115, 118–19; Melbourne, 15–17; modern, 112; Sydney, 16; tents, 117–18
Ashton, Julian, 24
Australian Academy of Art, 120
Australian Conservation Foundation 1983, 82; Victorian membership, Fig. 4.5, 81–2
Australian Economic Review, 50
Australian Sketcher, 19
Australian style architecture, 154
Australian tariff, enquiry into effects of, 44

bank crash, 1893, 4
Barrett, James William (1862–1945), activities of, 69–72; conservation and town planning, 69
bayside beaches, 114
Becker, Ludwig, artistic studies, 16–18
Bourke Street School, artists, 119
Boyd, Arthur Merric, artist, 29, 111, 115, 117, 119, 120, 122–3; 'Nude Black Dog and Tent by a Black Pool', 1961, 117
Boyd, Martin, writings on architecture, 155
Boyd, Merric, artist, 115, 121–2, 124
Brack, John, artist, 126–7
Burgess, Gregory, 'Hackford House',

201

Taralgon, 1981–2, 165, 169
Burke and Wills expedition, paintings, 130–1
bushfires, paintings of, 131
Buvelot, Louis, 110, 112–14; 'Wannon Falls', 1868, 111–12

Carnival of Language, 95–6
cinematography, commencement, 28
climate, 1
colonial artists, 110
Condor, Charles, artist, 113–14, 118; paintings of, 114–15, 117
conservationists, 60, 69
Cooke, A.C., artist, 20, 24
Copland, Douglas Berry, economist, 37; background of, 41; 'best plan' of, 45; business community, identity with, 43; consultant, as, 44; economic adviser, 44, 46; farming, links with, 42; Giblin, relationship with, 46; lecturer, as, 42, 46; positions held after WW11, 46; School of Commerce, appointment to, 41–7; 'second best' plan, 45; trade cycle research, 44; travel, 44
Crown land, 64; development, 65; Otways, 65; South Gippsland hills, 65
cultural activities, 9
Cyclopedia of Victoria, 19

dairy industry, 4, farming, 63, 65; technological advances, 63
Dandenong Ranges, 110, 115, 119
depression, 1890s, 27, 40; 1930s, downturn in world trade cycle, 45
deregulation, 38
Development and Migration Commission, 44
Downing, Richard Ivan, economist, 37, 47; background of, 47; Downing Fellowships, 49; editor, 48; economic adviser, 47; economic survey, 48; full employment policy, 48; Keynesian doctrines, 47; research assistant, 47; Richie Chair, 47, 48
drama, American actors, 182; beginnings of, 179; Chinese Opera companies, 182; English actors, 182; function of, 183; Grand Opera, 184–5; intercolonial management, 186; national chains, 187; pantomime, 187, effect on Stock companies, 188, venues, 188–9; repertoire of, 185; schedule of, 183–4; Stock companies, 181–6, effect of new system on, 188
Dudok, Willem Marinus, architecture in

Holland, 159–60

econometric modelling, 51
economic analysis and economic policy-making, distinctions between, 43
Economic Record, 48, surveys of, 48
economists, impact on public policy, 38; organisation of, 45; nineteenth century, 37
Edmond, Maggies, and Peter Corrigan, Chapel of St. Joseph, Strabane Avenue, Box Hill, 1976–8, 170; Primary School, Resurrection Parish Centre, Keysborough, 1974–9, 171
entertainment, melodrama, 102–4; modern drama, 105–6; motion pictures, 106–7; musicals, 104; pantomime, 104–5; popular music, 108; vaudeville, 98–102; waxworks, 107
environment, history of, 57, European settlement contribution, 59
environment and planning, 57; 1834–80, 57–62; 1880–1939, 62–70; 1940–84, 72–82
Environment Protection Policy, 1970s, 76
environmental studies, 44
Eureka rebellion, 2
educational facilities, lack of, 7

factories, establishment of, 4, 6
'fair blank sheet', 58–9
farming, 58
Federal Government, establishment of, 4
Federation, 5
Federation house, 148, 152, 160
Ferntree Gully, national park, 110
Field Naturalists Club of Victoria, 71; excursion venues, Fig. 4.1, 70
Fisherman's Bend, 72
Fitzgibbon, Edmund (1825–1929), Melbourne's Town Clerk, 1854–90, 71
forest plantations, 63
Full Employment in Australia, 48
Furphy, Joseph (Tom Collins), author, 90, 95

gas street lights, introduction, 17
Geelong Advertiser, 56
General Theories of Employment, Interest and Money, 47
Giblin, Lyndhurst Falkiner, economist, 46 economic research, 46; relationship with Copland, 46
Gill, S. T., artistic studies, 14–15
Gippsland, squatting district, 59; subdivision, 65

Index

gold, discovery of, 2; mining, 60; rush, 14
Great Depression, 1930s, 6–7
Griffin, Walter Burley, Capitol Cinema, 1921–4, Swanston St., 157–8; urban architecture, 155–6; works of, 158

HMS Calcutta, 1
Hearn, W. E., economist, 39; Legislative Assembly, entry to, 39; Melbourne University, 39
Hickey, Dale, 'Pie', 1947, 130
Heidelberg Historical Society, 118
Henderson, Ronald Frank, economist, 37; background of, 50; investigation of poverty, 49, 52
Hodgkinson, Clement (1819–93), land reservation policy, 63
homestead architecture, 146–7, 149, 154, 160, 169
horse drawn cabs, 25
House, Marshall St. Ivanhoe, 1956, 168
Housing Commission, establishment, 1938, 7
Hudson, Phillip and J. H. Wardrop, Shrine of Remembrance, St. Kilda Road, 1922–34, 156

Illustrated Australian News, 1873, 21
immigration, 5, 8–9; European contribution, 10
industrialisation, surge of, 8
Institute of Applied Economic Research, 49, 50–2
intercolonial, customs houses, 4; travel and trade, 4
International Exhibitions, 1880, 3, 21; 1888, 3
interstate free trade, 5
Ironmonger, Duncan, econometric modelling, 51

Jevons, W. Stanly, economist, 40

Keyne, Keynesian doctrines, 47; theoretical solutions to unemployment, 47

Land Conservation Council, 76
land development schemes, 44
land use, control over, 73
landscape, 109, 112; modern, 119
leasehold tenures, 64, subdivisions, 64
Life and Adventures of William Buckley (1852) 85–6
literature, Aboriginal culture, 85; beginnings of, 86; colonial years, 88; drama, 92; dramatists, 92–3; first novels, 86; histories, 93; influence of sport on, 87; novels, 89; plays, 89, 92; radicalism, 95; rural experience, 88; squatters, memoirs of, 88; women in, 93–4
livestock, effect on environment, 60
Loan Council, committee, 46; creation of, 44
Lundt, J. W., photographer, 19

McCubbin, Fred, artist, 13, 114, 116, 118; Mt. Macedon, 114; paintings of, 23, 27, 28, 115
Malle country, 64, settlements, 64, 68
Man and Nature, 63
Marshall, Alfred, economist, 40
Mead, Elwood (1858–1936), director of SRWSC, 65–7
meat pie, 131–2
Melba, Dame Nellie, 193–4
Melbourne, artistic view of, 14; Bourke Street, 24; changing picture of, 12–13; Collins Street, 24; development of, 2–3, 5; depression, 1890, 27; economic development, 1960, 29; first settlers, 13; 'garden city' image, 31; height limit on buildings, 28; land boom, 18, 23; planning of urban regions, 1880s, 68; population growth, 18; shipping activity, 23; site, selection of, 13
skyline, 29–30; topography of, 13, 14
Melbourne and Metropolitan Board of Works 1890, 68; administration of, 68–9; chairman, 71; Metropolitan plans of, 78–80, Fig. 4.4, 79; water supply and sewerage, 68
Melbourne Cup (1890), 3
Meldrum, Max, 119; artist, 120
melodrama, 102; Addie Marsden, 102–3; companies, 102–3; Nellie Stewart, 103
Metropolitan Board of Works, 5
mining, environmental destruction, 60–1
modern drama, 105–6
Mornington Peninsula, paintings of, 114
motion pictures, 106–7
Mueller, Ferdinand von, (1825–93), forestry practice, 63; Government botanist, 63
music, Aboriginal, 191, 195; bands, 190, 194–5; buskers, 194; churches, 195–6; composer, 191; conductors, 192; dance music, 194; opera orchestras, 190–1; organ grinders, 194–5; instrumentalists, 192; music halls, 194; Philharmonic, 191; private pleasure, for, 196–7; professional musicians, 192; recitals, 192; symphonic, 191; violinists, 192–3; vocalists, 193

204   Victoria's Heritage

musicals, 104

National Gallery of Victoria, 5, 110, 112–14, 128; architecture, 166
National Gallery School, 115, 119
National Parks Association, 77–8
National Parks and related reserves in post-war Victoria, Fig. 4.3, 77
New South Wales, separation from, 2
Nielson, John Shaw, poet, 91–2
Nolan, Sidney, 117; paintings of, 120–1, 123, 131

Olympic Games, Melbourne, 1956, 9
outdoor recreation, 69

pantomime, 104–5
Perceval, John, 'Merric Boyd', 1946, 121–2, 124
pests and weeds, introduction of, 59–60
photography, aerial, 28; development of, 23, 25; telephoto lens, 27, 29
Picturesque Atlas of Australasia, 19, 23
pioneer pastoralists, 58
planned irrigation settlements, 65; problems, 66
political economy, 38–9; downgrading of study, 40; English economists, 40; free trade, 40, 44; laissez-faire, 39–40; neo-classical school, 40
popular music, 108
population growth, 2, 3, 5; effect of immigration on, 8–9; move to Western Australia, 4
Port Phillip Gazette, 14
Port Phillip region, naturalists, 69
Portland Bay, squatting district, 59
public policy, 37–8

quantitative studies in economics, 44

regional planning, 1940, 73, Central Planning Authority, 75; environmental education, 82; environmental impact statements, 76; metropolitan plans, Fig. 4.4, 79; progress of, 75; regional committees, 75; regional surveys, 76; selected structures, Fig. 4.2, 74
Richardson, Henry Handel, author, 91
Richie Chair, 46, 47
Rise and Growth of Australian Architecture, 1891, 146
Roberts, Tom, artist, 25, 112–14, 118–19; 'Bourke Street', 25; 'Evening Train to Hawthorn', 27; paintings of, 115; 'The Artists Camp', 1888, 115–16
Romberg, Frederick, Hilstan flats, 1945–51, 163; Newburn flats, 1939–41; Stanhill flats, Queens Road, 1943–51, 162
Rowe, George, artist, 21–2

sculpture, recognition of, 125; wood sculpture, 125
Selection Acts, 61
Senbergs, Jan, 129; 'Liardet's Beach', 1980, 130
Shrine of Remembrance, St. Kilda Road, 1922–34, 156
Smith, Adam, philosopher, 38
social reform, 40
Soil Conservation Board, 1940, 73
soldier settlers, 67–8
South Yarra Post Office, 1894, architecture of, 147
Spencer, Walter Baldwin (1860–1929), Professor of Biology, 71
sport, growth of, 9
squatting, 57–9; districts, 59
State Rivers and Water Supply Commission (SRWSC), 65–7
Streeton, Arthur, artist, 26, 113, 118; paintings of, 115; 'Princes Bridge: Between the Lights' (1888), 26
Strutt, William, history painter, 129
suburban growth, 9
Such is Life, 1903, 90
Sydney Harbour, 16

Tariff Board, 44
tariff protection, 39, 41
Tariff Report, 45
technology, 38; changes, 43
television, introduction of, 1956, 9
tents, artists' temporary settlement, 117–18
'The Australian Ugliness', 126, 163, 165
The Fortunes of Richard Mahoney, 91
The Public Lands of Australia Felix (1970), 64
Toorak, Irving Estate houses, 147; Quamby flats, 1941, 160
trade unions, 41–3
'Travencore', John Cupples house, 1899–1900, 148–9
Tucker, Albert, 121; 'Portrait of John and Sunday Reed', 1982, 124

unemployment, 2
Ussher, Beverley, 148–9, 152; Henry Kemp, 'Travencore', John Cupples house, 148

vaudeville, Bourke Street, first theatre, 98; Charles Norman, 100–1; George

Wallace, 99–100; Harry Rickards, 99; houses, 98; Jim Gerald, 99, 101; minstrel shows, 98–9; New Opera House, 99–100; Opera House, 99; Roy Rene (Mo), 99–102
Vernon report, 51
Victoria and its Metropolis, 19, 23
Victorian Arts Centre, architecture of, 166
Victorian National Parks Association, 70
Von Guérard, Eugene, paintings, 108; travels of, 109–10; Waterfall, Strath Creek, 1862, 110, 113

Water Act, 1909, 66
water resources, management, 60–1
waxwork, 107
Wealth of Nations, 38

whaling and sealing era, 57
wheat farmers, 3
Wilson's Promontory reserve, creation and extension of, 70–1; paintings, 114
Wimmera, squatting district, 59
women, literary success of, 93–4
Workers Educational Association (WEA), 42–3
World War 1, 1914–18, 5; economic problems, 41; effect of, 6; post-war economy, 6
World War 11, 7–8, 67; building, effect on, 163

Yan Yean water supply, 2
Yarra River, 13–14, 21, 28